Public Policies
and Political Development
in Canada

RONALD MANZER

UNIVERSITY OF TORONTO PRESS

Toronto Buffalo London

© University of Toronto Press 1985
Toronto Buffalo London
Printed in Canada
Reprinted 1987
ISBN 0-8020-2564-1 (cloth)
ISBN 0-8020-6559-7 (paper)

Canadian Cataloguing in Publication Data

Manzer, Ronald A., 1937-
Public policies and political development in Canada

Bibliography: p.
Includes index.
ISBN 0-8020-2564-1 (bound) 0-8020-6559-7 (pbk.)

1. Policy Sciences. 2. Canada – Politics and
government. 3. Canada – Economic policy.
4. Canada – Social policy. I. Title.

JL75.M35 1985   320.971   c85-098020-8

Contents

Illustrations

Tables

Figure

Acknowledgments

Ten years ago, in *Canada: A Socio-political Report,* I sketched a simple framework for analysing the possibilities for human development in a political community and presented within this framework some of the empirical evidence then available and relevant for assessing the satisfaction of human needs within the Canadian polity.[1] Originally, I intended also to present appropriate evidence about the development of public policies in Canada, but neither the length of the book nor my research time permitted it. This study attempts to complete the task.

Students in my courses on Canadian public policy have listened to lectures and read earlier versions of my arguments, and I am grateful for their patience, encouragement, and criticism over the years. Peter Aucoin, William Christian, Paul Pross, Richard Simeon, and Michael Whittington made helpful comments on my paper, 'Public Policies in Canada: A Developmental Perspective,' given at the 1975 annual meeting of the Canadian Political Science Association. J.E. Hodgetts, Harvey Malmberg, H.P. Moffatt, and Eric Ricker contributed to the development of my paper, 'Public School Policies in Canada: A Developmental Perspective' (an early version of chapter 6 of this book), which was presented at a conference of the Atlantic Education Association in April 1976 and published in *Education and Development in Atlantic Canada* edited by Eric Ricker.[2] David Bell read several chapters of my first draft, made useful suggestions for revision, and encouraged me to think the work was worth publishing. The final version was greatly helped by the comments of three anonymous reviewers for the University of Toronto Press and one for the Social Science Federation of Canada, by Virgil Duff's skilful guidance as editor at the Press, and by the superb copy-editing of Kathy Johnson.

The first draft was typed by Vesna Marjanovic. Joan Barnes, Audrey Glasbergen, Barbara Holst, and Carol Nicholls shared the typing of the later drafts. I am grateful to all of them.

This study of Canadian public policy is a testament of my continuing debt to five teachers: William Y. Smith, who taught me economics at the University of New Brunswick and who first interested me in problems of Canadian public policy; J. Stefan Dupré, now my colleague at the University of Toronto, who taught me Canadian politics at Harvard University with a lively concern for public policies; Samuel H. Beer, whose approach to studies of political culture shaped my concept of public philosophy and reinforced my belief in its importance as a primary explanation of public policy; Christian Bay of the University of Toronto, whose work led me to focus on the connection between human needs and political goods and to recognize the necessity to orient empirical political studies by normative concepts; and C.B. Macpherson, also my colleague at the University of Toronto, who taught me the enduring, fundamental importance of the relationship between political ideas and political economy and whose theoretical work has deeply affected my attempts to construct a model of the Canadian public philosophy. Each of them has contributed vital resources for the particular approach I have taken to studying Canadian public policy. None, of course, is responsible for my failures to get their teaching straight.

This book has been published with the help of a grant from the Social Science Federation of Canada, using funds provided by the Social Sciences and Humanities Research Council of Canada, and a grant from the Publications Fund of the University of Toronto Press.

My family has shared the tedium of writing this book without perhaps experiencing much of the satisfaction. Patricia and Jennifer have expressed a gentle scepticism about my academic masochism and have, happily, insisted on my maintaining a more balanced perspective. Kathryn has been my greatest supporter during the writing and rewriting, and she deserves to have it finished. I am thankful for her help, her patience and impatience, and her love.

PUBLIC POLICIES
AND POLITICAL DEVELOPMENT
IN CANADA

1

Political Goods and
Public Philosophy

From the comparative perspective of Canadian history and the experience
of other political communities, the people who live in Canada today enjoy
very high standards of material prosperity, physical security, and human
rights.[1] Conventional measures of socio-political development – such as
average income, rates of mortality and morbidity, incidence of political and
criminal violence, equality of opportunity for education, and protection of
civil liberties – indicate a relatively high and historically increasing level of
well-being. Only a few other political communities can claim to provide for
the basic needs of their citizens at a level comparable to that attained in
Canada.

None the less, Canada's high average standard of living disguises serious
and persistent maldistributions. For example, a hard core of 15 per cent,
perhaps more, of the population endures material poverty in the midst of
affluence. Racial and sexual inequalities deny sizable numbers of Canadians secure enjoyment of their dignity and self-respect. An upper-status
group possessing position, expertise, and wealth is firmly in control of
economic and political power, lessening the potential for an authentically
democratic polity.

In addition to serious inadequacies in the present distribution of political
goods, Canadians face disquieting prospects for more severe shortfalls in
the satisfaction of their basic needs. In one issue-area after another public
policies seem to have reached an impasse. More than a decade of policy-
making effort to cure weak economic growth, high unemployment, and
persistent inflation has produced no convincing remedies for a stubborn
'stagflation.' Considerable scientific evidence and a popular awareness of
the adverse impact of the industrial system on the natural environment
have so far resulted only in weak and vacillating corrective regulation. A

social order founded on bargaining among power élites verges on immobility when dominant organized socio-economic interests fail to agree, and veers toward injustice when agreement is obtained at the expense of weak, unorganized segments of society. The integrity of the Canadian political community is threatened by the internal strains of two linguistic–cultural communities and four or five economic regions and by the very mixed blessings of an American penetration that reinforces internal divisions and complicates their accommodation. Policies for cultural development and humanistic education that aim at the higher values of individual self-realization consistently are the last to be supported and the first to be eviscerated in disputes over collective priorities.

In the past, Canadians have benefited from the richness of their physical resources and the general benignity of their external relationships, which have facilitated the growth of their well-being. On the whole, they also have been fortunate in the political choices they have made. A complex array of federal, provincial, and local public policies has been instrumental in achieving high levels of need satisfaction.

In the future, the challenge of remedying maldistributions of primary political goods and overcoming impasses in making essential public policies will continue to demand imaginative and sometimes difficult political choices. Making good choices will require a better core of policy knowledge, far-reaching institutional reform, and a new commitment to the principles of liberal democracy.

The challenge of public policy and political development in Canada is one involving policy knowledge and political institutions. Genuine puzzlement about the theoretical assumptions on which to base public policy inhibits the development of policies in such diverse issue-areas as economic stabilization, corrections, and public education. Grave doubts about the responsiveness and effectiveness of federal, provincial, and local political institutions cast a pall on our tentative attempts to create fresh formulations for old policy designs.

Underlying the questions of relevant policy knowledge and effective political institutions is a more basic question about the validity of contemporary political ideas and values. Ultimately, the challenge of public policy and political development in Canada is one of political principles and public purposes.

Public Purpose

The usual justification for government in general and for public policies in particular is the satisfaction of human needs.[2] In their eventual outcomes, specific programs or particular actions to implement policies usually fall far short of their initial promise to serve human needs, and often they are deliberately perverted to satisfy the wants of a few rather than the needs of many. None the less, if we are to understand and evaluate the development of public policies we must have a concept of public purpose that can relate the satisfaction of human needs to the functions of good government.

The construction of a list of human needs is necessarily somewhat arbitrary, but for purposes of policy analysis the fivefold classification of basic needs suggested by Abraham Maslow is a useful schema.[3] First, physiological needs are the requirements for physical survival and the relief of pain. People must have clean air to breathe and adequate food, drink, sleep, and shelter. Second, safety needs are needs for order, predictability, and dependability of the environment. People vary greatly in their capacities to cope with disorder or unpredictability in their personal lives and social relationships, but there are evident limits to go beyond which results in neurosis or psychosis. Third, people have basic needs for love, affection, and a sense of belongingness. The belongingness needs represent the deep, persistent desire of people to get together, to be together, and stay together.[4] Fourth, people need esteem and respect from other people, and they need self-esteem and self-respect. 'Satisfaction of the self-esteem need leads to feelings of self-confidence, worth, strength, capability, and adequacy, of being useful and necessary in the world. But thwarting of these needs produces feelings of inferiority, of weakness, and of helplessness.'[5] Fifth, self-development needs are the needs people have to actualize their full potential as human beings, not simply to survive in safety, with friends, respected, but to achieve to the fullest extent possible what they are capable of becoming.[6]

According to Maslow, these five sets of needs are hierarchically ordered, with higher degrees of 'gratification health' being achieved as higher levels of needs are satisfied. If all needs are unsatisfied, physiological needs will predominate. When physiological needs are satisfied, a concern for predictability and dependability of the environment grows. Then, as physiological and safety needs are satisfied, needs for belongingness, esteem, and self-development successively become predominant.

Maslow is ambiguous about the points at which individual priorities change from one set of needs to another. Basic needs will obviously persist, and subtle transformations express the increasing complexity of expanding desires. Sexual desire grows into love, and love requited demands mutual respect and freedom for self-development. Food and drink prepared with skill and taken with friends become a means of self-expression and affection. In spite of this ambiguity, the higher the level of needs satisfied, the healthier and closer to realizing their human potential people will be. A person who is safe, loved, and respected, for example, will be healthier and closer to full human development than a person who is safe but rejected and unloved.

Each set of basic human needs may be satisfied by planned or spontaneous individual private action, collective private action, or collective public action. A person may act alone to obtain food and shelter, or small groups of people may combine their activities in voluntary co-operative effort to produce goods and services that cannot be produced by one person working alone. For many components of basic human needs, public policies that guide collective public action may be an effective approach to their satisfaction.

Each of the five sets of basic human need has a corresponding conception of political good.[7] They are 'good' because they represent conditions known to be agreeable, beneficial, commendable, right, or proper for the satisfaction of basic needs. They are 'political' because they can only be realized through public collective action, and consequently they provide jusification for compulsory collectivization.

Welfare as a political good implies, for example, that people should have adequate food and shelter and that they should have access to health services adequate to reduce the incidence of illness and to extend their average length of life to what is attainable with current technology. Welfare as a political good also implies a justification for formulating public policies wherever appropriate to achieve the basic conditions for human survival.

Security is a political good because people need, and governments can act to provide, public order and social stability. Security in a political community means protection of people's lives and property; tolerable rates of change in economic, social, and political relationships; and some guarantee of protection from aggression originating outside the community. When security is provided as a political good, a person's entire needs for consistency and predictability are not thereby satisfied; but public security will provide a basic framework of regulated behaviour and will help to ensure dependable outcomes over a wide range of economic, social, and political relationships.

Fraternity expresses the political conditions for the existence within a large political community of primary autonomous groups in which people can get together, be together, and stay together. To the extent that fraternity is their purpose, public policies will aim to ensure that diversity of groups is accepted, that tolerance prevails, and that primary relationships involving families, friends, neighbourhoods, churches, and workplaces are protected and developed.

Equality is a political good because satisfaction of esteem needs depends on it. Who shall be treated alike for what purposes is a recurring question in politics and policy-making. Differences arise over which social and personal characteristics (such as age, sex, and ethnicity) are relevant in determining equality; over which particular personal, social, economic, and political activities should be considered; and over the best approach to resolving these differences in specific public policies. However, if people properly expect equality of treatment in carrying out certain activities but do not get it, they will feel deprived of esteem and respect and will usually lack self-esteem or self-respect. Their unsatisfied need becomes a justification for public policies that promote equality.

Liberty is a political good because people need a private sphere respected by others, especially the state, in which self-expressive activity may be pursued. As a political good, liberty also recognizes the existence of the right and power of each person to participate in collective decisions. No matter how well other needs may be met, self-development requires the double freedom of independence and participation.

From the standpoint of making and implementing public policies to satisfy basic needs, welfare is a political good for which governments can provide directly. Welfare represents basic needs that commonly are satisfied by improving conditions arising in the natural environment – for example, by larger supplies of food, better quality of shelter, or wider availability of health services. Assuming they are correctly designed, public policies that are intended to promote welfare will accomplish their purposes directly during the stage of implementation as general economic production is expanded, as hospitals are built and doctors are trained, or as food and shelter are supplied to the poor.

Security is a political good for which public policies also can provide directly as long as government action is backed by effective coercion. Security as a political good satisfies basic needs by reducing threats arising from the human environment – for example, by deterring criminal violence, containing political instability, or protecting national sovereignty. Again assuming they are correctly designed, public policies that are intended to increase security will accomplish their purpose directly during the stage of implementation as long as the state can exercise successfully its ultimate coercive power. Thus, for example, larger numbers and better organization of domestic police and more vigorous enforcement of the law can deter criminal behaviour, and international diplomacy and military preparedness can protect the sovereignty of the community in the international system as long as sufficient coercive power exists to apprehend law-breakers and to resist potential external aggressors.

Fraternity, equality, and liberty are political goods for which public policies cannot provide directly. They represent basic needs that cannot be satisfied simply and directly by material changes in environmental conditions. Creating a sense of belongingness, feelings of mutual respect, or a sense of freedom involves changes in personal relationships and attitudes that cannot be achieved by coercion. Public policies aimed at attaining these political goods can try to protect and promote a natural and human environment in which people are able to love and respect one another and realize their full potential; but no policy can guarantee that love, respect, and self-development will actually result. That depends upon the responses of people who in these matters cannot be coerced.

The important differences in the implications of the five political goods for governmental action suggest the utility of simplifying an analysis of the patterns of public policy into a study of three categories of governmental functions. First, the function of creating economic progress includes a range of policies designed to achieve and maintain a high standard of material welfare. Maslow argued that physiological needs are prepotent, and hence it is scarcely surprising that much policy-making is devoted to their satisfaction. Second, the function of maintaining social order involves another range of public policies designed to achieve and maintain a high level of public order and social stability, primarily by regulating the way people behave toward one another. Although resorting to coercion is costly and necessarily limited in its actual deployment, social order can in principle be created and maintained by force. Third, the function of furthering individual development requires public policies designed to create or maintain the conditions for satisfying those aspects of basic needs for belongingness, esteem, and self-development that are obtainable through political action. Public policies directed at encouraging full human development are qualitatively different from those aiming at economic progress or social order. Coercion can produce facilitating conditions for individual development, but neither in principle nor in practice can it directly produce full human development.

The classification of basic needs in terms of political goods and governmental functions provides a useful framework for analysing the purposes and assessing the results of government and public policies, but it will not direct us to any obvious resolutions of political differences or put an end to partisan debate.[8] Welfare, security, fraternity, equality, and liberty are comparative ideas; for a number of reasons disagreements can arise about how much of each should be provided in given circumstances. The question is always open as to how much of each good is necessary in order to satisfy basic physiological, safety, belongingness, esteem, and self-actualization needs. People accord different weight to the enjoyment of different goods, and they have different views of the future. In any political community people will be widely distributed in their levels of 'gratification health,' and these differences will be reflected in their politics and their expectations of governments. People also differ in the extent to which they see collective public action, as opposed to individual private or voluntary co-operative action, as the appropriate way to satisfy basic needs.

How much of each good is needed, which goods should have priority, what relative importance should be given to different functions of government, and what balance should be struck between private and public action to satisfy basic human needs are questions that have no easy, objective answers. They are questions on which people living in a political community will differ, often intensely, whether they simply follow their own self-interest or take seriously their moral responsibilities to others. As a result, in order to understand and evaluate public policies both concepts of public purpose and concepts of political ideology are needed.

Political Ideology

A political ideology 'is a doctrine or set of ideas which purports to provide a comprehensive explanation of political arrangements.'[9] The elements of ideological thinking are concepts of human need and political good. A political ideology explicitly or implicitly expresses some conception of basic human needs and establishes a priority for their satisfaction by collective action. An ideology will explain and justify such basic attributes of a political community as the boundaries of its territory, its requirements for citizenship, how its governmental institutions should be organized, what its government ought to do, the appropriate relationships among important social groups, and the appropriate relationship between political authorities and citizens.

A simple first step in thinking about political ideology can be taken by distinguishing opposing conceptions of the probable nature of social relations in a political community and opposing conceptions of the proper basis of social organization. In thinking about human nature and politics, people may believe that social relations among individuals and groups tend to be predominantly or inherently competitive and conflictual or that they are

TABLE 1.1

A Typology of Political Ideologies with Prescriptions for the Priority of Political Goods

Assumption about the basic unit of social organization	Assumption about the basic nature of social relations	
	Conflict	Co-operation
Individual	Liberalism (liberty)	Anarchism (fraternity)
Collectivity	Conservatism (security)	Socialism (equality)

predominantly co-operative. They may assume that the proper basis for thinking about good political arrangements and public policies is the needs or wants of each individual member of the community; or they may think of people in terms of their memberships in families, clans, churches, or classes and argue that individual needs cannot properly be understood or evaluated apart from the social networks in which they are embedded. If these two distinctions are combined, they produce a simple typology of political ideologies which begins to distinguish opposing political doctrines in the development of western political thought (see table 1.1).

Traditional conservatism assumes that people are inherently conflictual in their relations with each other and that a political community should be understood as an integrated hierarchy of social groups. Security is the primary political good for proponents of this doctrine, and social order is the primary function of government. Human nature is regarded as sinful and warring. Civilization is a fragile organism that can only be maintained by constraining individuals within well-established hierarchies of family, clan, church, and economic class. Political rule belongs by divine right and natural ability to a privileged élite. The members of this élite have the responsibility to guide their community in a way of life determined by them to be the good or proper way. Ordinary citizens have the duty to know their place and faithfully obey their superiors. According to conservative doctrine, public policies must give priority to protecting the social basis of order by strengthening family relationships, defending the prerogatives of the church, and protecting the privileges of the governing class. In economic development and regulation, state interventionism into private markets may be fairly extensive, justified by the demands of building and maintaining the power of the state and concomitantly that of its governing class. In the matter of social welfare, conservative doctrines are again likely to accept state intervention, reflecting the norms of a paternalistic relationship between governors and subjects. In practice, however, religious organizations and perhaps municipal authorities are likely to be seen as the appropriate instruments for discharging public responsibilities for community welfare.

Like conservatism, liberalism assumes that people are conflictual or competitive in their relations with each other; but in contrast with the conservative idea of an organic political community, liberals believe that it should be understood as an instrumental organization of individuals. For liberals, the problem of maintaining social order among self-interested individuals can be resolved by creating appropriate economic and political institutions through which the pursuit of individual self-interest can be channelled toward the collective well-being. Liberty is the primary political good for proponents of this doctrine, and economic progress is the primary function of government. All individuals should have an equal opportunity to compete for material prosperity and individual self-realization, which will result largely from private individual efforts or joint self-interested enterprises. The role of the state in liberal doctrine is to set and enforce the rules of competition, especially those concerning economic competition, and to facilitate private enterprise. This means protection of private property, but it may also mean state intervention to ensure fairness of economic competition. Liberalism distrusts state intervention to promote economic development, but it recognizes the necessity for state subsidy and protection of private capital development and for state investment in economic and social infrastructure in order to create the conditions for profitable private economic enterprise. Liberal doctrine equally resists regulation of private markets, but specific conditions of market breakdown, such as monopoly, are admitted to be justifications for state intervention. In social welfare the emphasis is placed on creating conditions for equality of opportunity, leaving individuals free to compete on more or less equal terms. Of course, liberals differ greatly among themselves on how much state intervention is needed and justified in order to create equality of opportunity.

Unlike conservatives and liberals, socialists believe that people are naturally co-operative in their social relations; or at least they would be co-operative and trusting if the capitalist industrial system did not entail the exploitation of the working class by owners and managers of the means of production. Like conservatism, socialism sees capitalist society as a hierarchy of economic classes. Individuals are understood in terms of class relations that define each person's place and function; but for socialists class is a basis for conflict, not for integration. The primary political good for proponents of this doctrine is equality, and individual development is the primary function of government. These political ideals are unattainable, however, as long as a relatively small class of owners and managers of the means of economic production can use its private economic power in pursuit of its selfish interests to dominate the masses, who have no comparable power. The role of the socialist state is to redistribute economic power, in part by changing private ownership and control of large economic enterprises into public ownership and control that is responsive to democratic political direction, in part by redistributing wealth to equalize economic resources. Widespread state intervention is required to control production and direct investment in the public interest. Public ownership should be extensive, and residual private ownership should be extensively regulated to protect the public interest. As for general social welfare, the socialist doctrine is best expressed by the Marxian ideal: 'from each according to his ability, to each according to his need.'

Anarchism as a political doctrine assumes that people are inherently co-operative in their relations and that society should be understood in terms of individuals associating freely. Anarchism shares with socialism a view that private property and class distinctions must be abolished to make room for the growth of individual differences based on personality and accepted by consent. Governments always serve established interests and thus perpetuate injustice. Since they cannot be used to redistribute or control economic power, they should be abolished. Fraternity seems to be the primary political good for proponents of anarchism. Anarchists aim to establish a stateless society based on small autonomous communities in which social harmony is maintained by voluntary agreements between individuals and material prosperity is achieved by a network of agreements among individuals and groups associating freely on the basis of territorial contiguity and functional specialization. Because it would abolish government, anarchism as an ideology holds little interest for students of public policy. None the less, it is important to understand the anarchist position as one more ideal type toward which ideological thinking might tend. Socialist ideology, for example, envisages an eventual withering-away of the state, and participatory liberal democracy makes assumptions about the potential for social organization in small autonomous communities and democratically organized workplaces that tend toward the anarchist position.

These four models or ideal types of political ideology adopt different positions about fundamental questions of human needs and political goods. Which political goods should take priority? What is the primary function of government? What are the standards for good public policies? The answers given here have been deliberately simplified. In reality, political ideologies are more complex and less consistent, and the substance of their doctrines changes over time. Consequently, making generalizations about the pattern of ideologies or the dominant ideology in a political community, whether at one period in its history or over time, is difficult.

Public Philosophy

A public philosophy implies the existence of a set of political ideas and beliefs that enjoy widespread acceptance in a political community and serve as principles to guide and justify governmental decisions. Samuel H. Beer defined a public philosophy as 'an outlook on public affairs which is accepted within a nation by a wide coalition and which serves to give definition to problems and direction to government policies dealing with them.'[10]

A dominant political ideology would constitute a public philosophy, but a public philosophy does not need to be formed from a single ideological position. It might be created from conflict and compromise among the proponents of opposing doctrinal positions. A public philosophy might also encompass substantial inconsistencies in its different parts, relying on one doctrinal position or another depending upon the public problem under consideration. Such contradictions or inconsistencies may be temporary manifestations of political change. They may also be relatively permanent reflections of a political community in which people see problems differently in different policy areas, or in which the participants who dominate policy-making in one area do not share the same ideology as those who dominate another area.

In a democratic polity a public philosophy is necessary to give legitimate coherence to the struggle for power and to condition politics by asserting fundamental moral concerns. The presence of a public philosophy should not be expected to eliminate political conflict, however, as Beer has pointed out.

Even when a public philosophy prevails within a nation, its assertions will provoke counter-assertions, as the 'liberalism' of the 1930s called forth the 'conservatism' of the 1940s. Yet such conflict too has its coherence: one side says 'yes,' the other 'no,' but both are trying to answer the same question. Very different is the model of conflict in which warring groups, emptied of any vision of the social whole and guided only by the residuum of their private concerns, quarrel over the spoils.[11]

A great many students of Canadian political development have analysed and interpreted the Canadian public philosophy. They fall into three broad categories, each of which gives a different emphasis to the contribution of ideological doctrines.

According to one interpretation, the Canadian public philosophy is a joining of the liberalism that predominates historically in English-speaking Canada with the conservatism that predominates historically in French-speaking Quebec. The main ideological elements of the Canadian political tradition are feudal and liberal fragments of European culture brought to the Canadian colonies by French and British settlers. These fragments have dominated the political beliefs of French and English Canadians ever since.

In advancing this interpretation Kenneth McRae has argued that 'Canada offers almost a classic instance of a two-fragment society.'[12] On the one hand, the character of New France was established at a time when conservative authoritarian doctrine was the prevailing ethos of France, and 'French Canada was the closely controlled projection of a highly centralized regime.'[13] Except for a short-lived challenge from the radical Rouge movement of the mid-nineteenth century, conservative beliefs held a strong grip on French-speaking Quebec until the 1960s. Only then did the quiet revolution effectively challenge the subordination of Quebec to its own conservative tradition and its unequal partnership with English Canada. On the other hand, 'as the central figure of the English-Canadian tradition we encounter once again the American liberal.'[14] The small English-speaking population of the Canadian colonies before the American revolution was fundamentally liberal in outlook. The loyalists who came to Canada were representative of their fellow Americans in social background and social outlook. Loyalty to the monarchy and the empire differentiated the Canadian liberal fragment from its American origins but did not alter its American liberal heritage. Successive waves of European immigrants were absorbed into that liberal heritage, irresistibly drawn by the opportunity to own land and to achieve equal social condition. In summary, like the Canadian political community it defines and justifies, the Canadian public philosophy is a continuing expression of dualism.

A second interpretation of the Canadian public philosophy accepts that political ideologies in Canada can be understood as fragments of European political thought and that liberalism has been the mainstream of political thinking in English-speaking Canada. Canadian liberalism is distinguished from its American counterpart, however, by its having come under the influence first of conservative and later of socialist ideology. According to this view, the loyalists brought to Canada a conservative or tory doctrine that was strongly evident in colonial government of the late eighteenth and early nineteenth centuries. Although the influence of liberalism was evident in the nineteenth-century developments of responsible government and industrialization, conservative beliefs continued to be reflected in paternalistic and protectionist governmental institutions and public policies. When political opposition to liberal economic policies arose at the turn of the century from workers and farmers, the tory influence in Canadian politics provided both justification for anti-liberal, left-wing collectivist values and legitimacy for ideological diversity in English-speaking Canada.

Gad Horowitz, the outstanding proponent of this second interpretation, has described the Canadian public philosophy as an 'antagonist symbiosis' of conservatism, liberalism, and socialism.

The three components of the English-Canadian political culture have not developed in isolation from one another; each has developed in interaction with the others. Our toryism and our socialism have been moderated by liberalism. But by the same token, our liberalism has been rendered 'impure', in American terms, through its contacts with toryism and socialism. If English-Canadian liberalism is less individualistic, less ardently populistic-democratic, more inclined to state intervention in the economy, and more tolerant of 'feudal survivals' such as monarchy, this is due to the uninterrupted influence of toryism upon liberalism, an influence wielded in and through the conflict between the two. If English-Canadian liberalism has tended since the depression to merge at its leftist edge with the democratic socialism of the CCF-NDP, this is due to the influence which socialism has exerted upon liberalism, in and through the conflict between them. The key to understanding the Liberal party in Canada is to see it as a *centre* party, with influential enemies on both right and left.[15]

A third interpretation places conservative beliefs at the core of the Canadian public philosophy. Both the heritage of European settlement and the unique requirements of the Canadian physical and social environment combined to justify reliance on large bureaucratic organizations and to inject a powerful strain of conservative doctrine into Canadian politics and policy-making. Whether they were publicly supported private monopolies such as the Hudson's Bay Company or publicly owned corporations such as Ontario Hydro or the Canadian Broadcasting Corporation, the dominant economic institutions of Canadian capitalism created an ideology of hierarchy, inequality, and élitism. The ideology in turn gave legitimacy to the institutions.

S.D. Clark has observed, for example, that because of the threat of American absorption 'the grip of political authority could not be relaxed within new areas of settlement in Canada as it tended to be south of the border.' Military, police, and church were the basic institutions of law and order in Canada. 'The conservatism of the country as a whole operated as a powerful force in checking innovations.'[16]

According to Reg Whitaker, toryism has played a vital role as the legitimizing ideology of capitalist development. 'The colonial administrators came to Canada armed with a mission to build a conservative, un-American, and undemocratic society in the northern half of the continent.' Although Edmund Burke was rarely quoted directly, 'it was the spirit of his rationalized, hard-nosed philosophy with its fusion of market liberalism and anti-democratic conservatism which served early colonial Canada as a blueprint for the nature of the society to be created.'[17] In the original tory image,

the state offered an instrumentality for facilitating capital accumulation in private hands, and for carrying out the construction of a vitally necessary infrastructure; for providing the Hobbesian coercive framework of public order and enforcement of contract within which capitalist development could alone flourish; and, finally, for communicating the symbols of imperial legitimacy which reinforced the legitimacy of unlimited appropriation in a small number of private hands.[18]

Whitaker concludes that in tory thinking the main instrument of economic progress in Canada was not simply private enterprise but private enterprise at public expense. Over time the state and corporate sectors have become ever more interdependent, and the old tory image of the state remains a powerful operational doctrine.

In a more sympathetic portrayal of Canadian conservatism, Thomas Hockin has argued that Canada 'is a conservative country that has not been afraid to employ the state.'[19] According to Hockin, a conservative belief system can be observed both in the thrust to national integration inspired by Upper Canadian conservatism and in the defence of regional particularism based on Maritime and Lower Canadian conservatism.

The use of state power to foster particularisms (or at least to allow them to persist), and to promote at the same time projects which help to develop ties to hold the nation together, have been characteristic of much Liberal and Conservative party public policy at the Federal level since confederation. These two approaches are conservative in two senses. The liberal faith in the iron discipline of the market (regional, national and international) has not been allowed to dominate Canadian development completely. Nor can these approaches be called quasi-socialist because, in the pursuit of more regional vitality, they did not aim primarily, if at all, to transform the power structure inherent in the particularisms or in schemes of transcontinental cohesion.[20]

Each of these three interpretations of the Canadian public philosophy presents a different combination of ideological elements. In the first interpretation Canadian public philosophy is an ideological dualism of French-Catholic conservatism and English liberal beliefs. In the second it is an antagonist symbiosis of conservatism, liberalism, and socialism. In the third it is an enduring alliance between liberal belief in private property and market capitalism and conservative belief in élitism, inequality, and deference. Liberal doctrines are common to each of these major interpretations of Canadian public philosophy. Unfortunately, none of them gives much attention to the changing substance of Canadian liberal democracy.

According to C.B. Macpherson, the constant characteristic of the liberal tradition from Locke to the present has been acceptance of a capitalist economy and a class-divided society. Within that common assumption three distinct types of liberalism can be identified. First, the seventeenth- and eighteenth-century liberals from John Locke to Edmund Burke fully accepted capitalist market relations, but they were not at all democratic. Second, in the early nineteenth century Jeremy Bentham and James Mill developed a concept of protective liberal democracy that preserved the traditional competitive capitalist market society and reluctantly added a limited democratic franchise as an instrument to protect the governed from oppression by the government. Third, about the middle of the nineteenth century John Stuart Mill advanced an ideal of developmental liberal democracy that had at its core a moral vision of the human potential for improvement. In Mill's theory of liberal democracy, 'the good society is one which permits and encourages everyone to act as exerter, developer, and enjoyer of the exertion and development, of his or her own capacities.'[21] A democratic political system and capitalist market economy would facilitate this human advancement better than any other political economy.[22]

If Macpherson's distinction between protective and developmental liberal democracy is adopted, then five basic doctrinal positions must be aligned and reconciled in order to understand the historical evolution of the Canadian public philosophy (see table 1.2). Traditional conservatism has been clearly manifested in the agrarian Catholic tradition of French-speaking Quebec, but its anti-market orientation also has won allegiance

TABLE 1.2
Five Basic Doctrines of the Canadian Public Philosophy

Assumption about the basic unit of social organization	Assumption about the basic nature of social relations	
	Conflict	Co-operation
Individual	Protective liberal democracy	Developmental liberal democracy
Collectivity	Anti-democratic liberalism (toryism)	Non-Marxist social democracy
	Traditional Catholic conservatism	

from at least a small band of English-speaking intellectuals. Conservative, anti-democratic liberalism, the liberal tradition from Locke to Burke that has been commonly labelled as 'toryism' in Canadian studies, has defended an alliance of capitalist markets and business élitism. Historically, Canadian socialism or social democracy has been British in its ethnic origins and predominantly non-Marxist in its doctrines. Its presence as a significant and legitimate political movement is undeniable, but its direct expression in policy development is more problematic. Finally, protective or equilibrium democracy and ethical, developmental democracy are two contradictory and competing meanings of liberalism that need to be located in the history of the Canadian public policy. 'For "liberal" can mean freedom of the stronger to do down the weaker by following market rules; or it can mean equal effective freedom of all to use and develop their capacities. The latter freedom is inconsistent with the former.'[23]

My purpose in this study of public policies and political development in Canada is not to describe and explain the process of making policy.[24] Rather, it is to describe the substance of policies as they have been made over time and to interpret the political ideas and beliefs that appear to be implicit in them. The historical record covered here sets out what federal and provincial governments have done to promote economic development, relieve poverty, regulate markets, control crime, build school systems, and protect human rights. The policies that comprise this record, I assume, 'can be treated as evidence for what went on in the minds of those who created them.'[25] They can be analysed in terms of standard concepts of political ideology and their patterns can be interpreted as collective responses to enduring questions of human need and political good in the Canadian polity.

My thesis is that the original Canadian public philosophy was a relatively uncomplicated, highly integrated political doctrine forcefully shaping a simple pioneering society. It has evolved through concentrated critical experiences and prolonged incremental adjustments to become a complex, highly fragmented public philosophy. Now it grapples uneasily and inconsistently with the problems of an advanced industrial society, and it has at its core a fundamental contradiction between economic and ethical liberalism.

If Canadians hope to find a way out of current impasses in policy-making, they must reconsider this evolution of their public philosophy as it has been expressed in policy development. Only then can it be properly appraised and reformulated to serve as the foundation for a creative renewal of Canadian public policy.

2

Economic Growth

In order to produce and distribute the economic goods and services that will satisfy basic physiological needs, two fundamental choices have to be made: the best form of collective organization for economic planning and production, and the best way to combine the factors of economic production.

In modern economies four types of economic organization are commonly found. Privately owned business enterprises produce and sell their goods and services in markets; their ability to make profits to cover their costs of production and provide material rewards to their owners is the test of their efficiency. Government enterprises also produce and sell their goods and services in markets. Their planning and production decisions may be modified by political considerations, but their ability to cover most, if not all, of their costs of production from their sales is still the main test of their successful operation. Government departments, in contrast, have no market for their goods and services. Their planning and production decisions are made by reference to political criteria such as the public interest, group pressures, or electoral prospects. Finally, private voluntary associations, like government departments, have no market for their goods and services. Their planning and production decisions are made according to non-profit-oriented, essentially political criteria, such as the interest of the association's members or the group's perception of public needs.

If each type of organization were the only one or at least the largely predominant one in the economy, we would have one of four ideal types of economic systems – free enterprise, command economy, market socialism, or co-operative commonwealth (see table 2.1). In practice Canadians have always operated a 'mixed economy,' but the balance of

TABLE 2.1
Basic Types of Economic Organizations and Economic Systems

System of decision for production and distribution	Ownership and management of producing and distributing organizations	
	Public	Private
Markets	Government enterprises / market socialism	Business enterprises / free enterprise
Politics	Government departments / command economy	Voluntary associations / co-operative commonwealth

organizational types represented in it has changed markedly over time. During the colonial era and the early years of national development, business enterprise was the major type of economic organization. At first individual business enterprises (mostly farms) were predominant, but in the late nineteenth century corporate business enterprises grew rapidly in importance. Voluntary associations such as religious communities and charitable organizations were a small but significant complement in an essentially free-enterprise system. Today government departments and government enterprises are major producers and distributors of goods and services, reducing but not displacing the predominance of business enterprises and eclipsing but certainly not erasing the contribution of voluntary associations. The history of public policy for economic growth is first of all a history of the changing importance of private and public agencies in economic production and distribution.

The development of a mixed economy can mean a changing balance between public and private organization; it can also mean a changing balance between public and private economic planning. Although ownership and management remain private, governmental intervention, either outside the market by regulation or exhortation or within the market by inducement or persuasion, can alter the decisions of private agencies about economic production and distribution without changing the basis of ownership and management or the system of exchange. Governmental intervention of this type has always been used in Canada to affect the operations of business enterprises and voluntary associations, but the steadily increasing degree of public planning for private agencies is an essential characteristic of the emergence in Canada of the modern mixed economy. Thus, the history of public policy for economic progress is not just a history of the changing balance between private and public agencies for production and distribution; it is also a history of increasing reliance on public rather than private economic planning.

According to the classical theories of economic growth, wealth is created by combining three factors of production – land or natural resources, labour, and capital. Recently, economic theorists have tended to identify additional factors of production, in particular managerial skills (reflecting the increasing separation of ownership and management in modern business enterprises) and technological innovation (reflecting the increasing importance of research and development in modern industrial expansion). A theory that explains how these factors of production can be combined to maximize physical output will provide the guidance needed to create public policies for economic development. At least three broadly different strategies of economic development can be detected in the history of Canadian economic policies, and each implies a different role for the state.

Economic Growth by Resource Appropriation

The strategy or principle of appropriation holds that economic growth results from private individual enterprise in settling and developing the land and exploiting its resources. The principle of appropriation derives from a development theory and applies to an economic system in which increases in material welfare result from combining two factors of production, land or natural resources and labour. To some extent capital investment is required for production, but capital is assumed to be a relatively unimportant factor. In the ideal type of appropriative economy units of production are small; there is strong, individualistic competition in pursuit of opportunities for resource exploitation and workers own their own means of production. Public policies aim at creating access to natural resources and encouraging or directing human effort toward their exploitation.

In order to understand the original appropriative strategy we can usefully refer to a classic statement of liberal philosophy that expresses the value assumptions about economic progress that were widely accepted in making policy from the seventeenth to the nineteenth centuries. In his *Second Treatise on Civil Government* (1690) the great theorist of liberalism, John Locke, begins his argument with the assumption that the earth and its fruits originally were given to people for their common use; but before anyone could be sustained by them, they had to be appropriated. This was accomplished by labour, which removed land and its produce from the state of nature and turned them to personal use, thereby enhancing human welfare. In the state of nature there were limitations on appropriation; in civil society those limitations were transcended. Locke eventually provided a justification for unlimited accumulation of capital through the medium of money and the use of wage-labour in a developed commercial economy in which all land had been appropriated. In so doing Locke also justified the unlimited appropriation of land and its produce as a principle of economic progress.

'In the beginning,' Locke wrote of his state of nature, 'all the world was America.' The liberal view that Locke articulated fitted comfortably with the developmental requirements of North America. In a continent perceived by European settlers as a vast common possession, the principle of appropriation provided a strong justification for private individual enterprise in the settlement and development of the land and the exploitation of its resources. The principle also provided a straightforward justification for governmental assistance to facilitate that appropriation. The more difficult the physical problems of economic development (as in Canada), the greater the role accepted for government; but it was always subordinate to private individual and collective enterprise.

Staple Production

The leading instances of appropriation prior to Confederation were fishing, fur-trading, and lumbering. In assessing the influence of appropriation as a concept of development, concentration in the organization of the staple trades must be distinguished from dispersion in the production of the staples traded. Each trade was dominated by monopolistic companies that organized and financed the trade and controlled the commerce between North America and Europe; but each trade also based production on the individualistic enterprise of relatively small groups which wrested the produce of a new continent from a challenging environment: the fishermen from Nova Scotia and Newfoundland who harvested the cod, especially those engaged in the dry fishery; the Indians who trapped and the coureurs de bois who traded with them and transported their pelts out of the hinterland; and the timber gangs who cut and rafted squared timber down the Ottawa or the Saint John for shipment to England.

The fishing industry historically was based on the work of small groups of relatively independent commodity producers. As described by Harold Innis, the requirements for capital and the interests of the merchant class in the fishery were subordinate to problems of individual co-operation and group competition in production.

The fishing industry has been conducted on the Atlantic seaboard of North America for centuries through small units of capital – the ship or small boat. It is essentially dependent on individual initiative and enterprise and was particularly so prior to the introduction of large-scale units of capital in the nineteenth century. Various devices depending chiefly on the size of the unit of equipment were developed to reward the fishermen in proportion to his catch and to stimulate his interest. The dependence on individual initiative was tempered by the necessity of cooperation since it was only rarely that an individual fisherman could command and direct his own capital equipment. The small boat required three to five men, and the ship a crew which was disciplined in relation to its operations. It required, moreover, the support of capital interests whether in providing the ship or the supplies and provisions, but the risks of the industry compelled a wide division of capital interests as a means of insurance. If conducted within narrow geographical limits such as a single port or a small number of ports in a definite region these capital groups had large common interests. The industry was therefore characterized by individual enterprise which was sharply competitive and by types of cooperation ranging from the fishermen of a small boat to the group of merchants in definite regions.[1]

In the fur trade the interior production and trade relied on Montreal merchants for stakes and trading goods, and the merchants exercised strong bargaining power with respect to the prices of delivered furs. When trapping and transporting furs, however, men worked alone or in small groups with relative independence to appropriate their product from the natural environment. In his classic work on the fur trade, Innis showed that the trade with Europe was an organized oligopoly or monopoly, while the fur trade in the interior was dispersed and competitive.

Trade from Quebec and Montreal with canoes up the Ottawa to Michilimackinac, La Baye, and Lake Superior could be financed with relatively small quantities of capital and was consequently competitive. Further extension of trade through Lake Superior by Grand Portage (later Kaministiquia) to Lake Winnipeg, the Saskatchewan, Athabaska, the Mackenzie River, and New Caledonia and the Pacific coast involved heavy overhead costs and an extensive organization of transportation. But the organization was of a type peculiar to the demands of the fur trade. Individual initiative was stressed in the partnership agreements which characterized the North West Company. The trade carried on over extended areas under conditions of limited transportation made close control of individual partners by a central organization impossible.[2]

Melville Watkins has pointed out the extent to which production for the fur trade fitted the traditional native economy, which was based on appropriation.

The prosecution of the fur trade depended, at least initially in each region into which the trade expanded, on the Indian as fur gatherer. As such the Indian was a commodity producer, not a wage-earner, and the fur trade was literally a trade, or a commercial activity, not an industrial activity. The Indian became vulnerable to the exigencies of the trade, but he did not have to make two critical and traumatic adjustments ... Firstly, he did not have to become a wage-earner, and secondly, which is really the opposite side of the coin, he did not have to yield up his ownership of the land. To put the matter differently, neither his labour-time nor his land had to become themselves marketable commodities.[3]

The timber trade developed along similar lines in the first half of the nineteenth century. After 1808, cut off from Baltic supplies and encouraged by the British government, large London timber houses began setting up branches in Quebec and Saint John; and factors employed in these branches bought the timber rafted down river to the ports and arranged for its shipment to England. In contrast, domestic production of timber in the first half of the nineteenth century was essentially appropriative. Timber gangs were small and relatively autonomous without much need for capital. In Ontario, for example, crown ownership of timber lands was combined with a system of ground rents designed to encourage small operators and prevent the wealthy from buying up the land for speculation (1851 legislation set rents at 2s 6d a square mile payable after the timber was sold). After mid-century timber operations became increasingly capitalized, involving many camps and bringing many rafts down river. Before that, however,

it seemed so easy for the pioneer farmer, at the end of his harvest, to go into the woods – the crown lands, defended by regulations on paper only, in reality open to everyone – with his sons and neighbours and 'make' a little timber. The raw material cost him nothing and he probably had a good deal of equipment. A timber-making expedition would seem like not much more than a winter's adventure with the prospect of some ready money into the bargain.[4]

State Support

In each of the main appropriative activities that provided the base for early Canadian economic development, governmental policy was an important factor in opening and protecting access to the resources and in providing and encouraging labour for their appropriation. Foreign and defence policies were directed by a concern to secure territorial control of potential resources, and public investment in canals and railways opened up the northwest for colonization. Favourable rental arrangements and land-settlement policies were combined with active promotion to attract workers to the land. Regulation of appropriation rights was effected directly by public grants, licensing arrangements, and outright alienation of crown land and resources, and indirectly by relying in an era of weak public administration on monopolist private enterprises to manage resources and regulate trade.

The power of government determined who had access to the North Atlantic fishery. From the sixteenth to the eighteenth centuries the requirement for bases adjacent to the fishery was translated into an international competition for control of adjacent territories, a competition that was won by the English and the French. The American Revolution produced a new competitor, improvements in technology reduced the need for adjacent bases, and settlement in the Maritimes resulted in a sizable inshore fishery. Action by the British government to protect the colonial fishery in the nineteenth century therefore shifted to the realm of international diplomacy. The controversy with the Americans over inshore fisheries was particularly acrimonious. 'As far as Nova Scotia and New Brunswick were concerned, the issue was one of establishing control over resources that were rightfully theirs. To make good this claim they relied on the power of the state, in the form of the British government.'[5]

The role of government in the development of the fur trade is well known. Mercantilist policies resulted in a series of monopoly charters during the seventeenth century, but, as with the early fishery, the vital contribution of government was occupation and defence of the routes to fur-trading territories. The fierce competition between the North West Company and the Hudson's Bay Company was stopped in 1821 when the British government brought about a union of the companies under the name and charter of the Hudson's Bay Company. From 1821 to 1870 the company used its quasi-governmental powers to preserve the Northwest Territory as a source of furs and to inhibit agricultural settlement.[6]

The lumber industry, especially the trade in square timber, depended on preferential tariff protection.[7] The desire to obtain a reliable supply of timber for the British navy was aroused during the American Revolution and renewed during the Napoleonic wars. As a consequence, the British government imposed duties on foreign timber (eventually amounting to over 100 per cent), while colonial timber remained duty-free. The duties remained largely intact until 1846, by which time the industry was efficient enough to diversify and survive without governmental protection.

Dominion lands policy from 1870 to 1930 provides another illustration of a government's facilitating economic progress under the principle of appropriation.[8] From 1872 to 1894 a free-homestead policy was subordinated to land grants for railway development. Twenty-five million acres were given to the Canadian Pacific Railway as part of the inducement to build the railway, which was a prerequisite for prairie settlement. The regional 'colonization' railways and the continental Canadian Northern system also were recipients of sizable grants of public lands. Usually these grants were sold to private land-grant companies which in turn sold them to prospective settlers in the United States and Europe. The very successful Saskatchewan Valley Land Company, for example, got its start by purchasing for a nominal price 840,000 acres from the Qu'Appelle, Long Lake and Saskatchewan Railway. The federal Department of the Interior aided the company by selling it another 250,000 acres of homestead lands for one dollar an acre. The land grants acquired by the Canadian Northern system were developed in a similar way by the Saskatchewan Valley and Manitoba Land Company.

By 1908 about half the western lands had been alienated to subsidize the railways, and the Department of the Interior opened the remaining dominion lands to homesteading. The acreage of free homesteads increased in Saskatchewan from 12.5 million in 1905 to 30.7 million in 1930, and the population rose from 257,763 in 1906 to 921,785 in 1931. In Alberta free-homestead acreage increased by 16.4 million acres, and the population rose from 185,195 in 1906 to 731,605 in 1931.[9]

The federal free-homestead policy ended in 1930 when jurisdiction over public lands and natural resources was transferred to the provincial governments of Saskatchewan and Alberta. Settlement had been accomplished, but the record of cancellations provided grim evidence of its human costs. 'The record here not only of dilapidation in farm buildings and machinery but of deadly attrition in human material and morale during the best years of a settler's life and family is beyond calculation. The free homestead looked cheap but in practice it seems to have proved one of the costliest devices of frontier settlement.'[10]

Immigration policy supplemented lands policy by advertising opportunities for settlement in Canada, subsidizing agents to solicit immigrants in Europe and the United States, and imposing few restrictions on prospective immigrants. The rate of emigration exceeded the rate of immigration from the 1860s to the 1890s; but during the decade 1901–11 immigrant arrivals equalled 24.6 per cent of average population, the rate of net migration was 12.9 per cent, and the percentage of those foreign-born in the population increased from 13 per cent in 1901 to 22 per cent in 1911.

Although many immigrants gravitated to growing urban areas, the immigration policy of the federal government aimed to encourage immigrants in agricultural occupations.[11] The government paid agents in major cities of the United States, the United Kingdom, and northwestern Europe to conduct a campaign to increase immigration to Canada. Circulars and newspaper advertisements contained glowing accounts of the opportunities awaiting immigrants, and Canadian products were exhibited at agricultural fairs. Bonuses were paid to steamship agents who steered European immigrants to Canada (one pound for adults and ten shillings for children, and salaried agents in sixteen American cities employed sub-agents who received a commission of $3 a man, $2 a woman, and $1 a child on settlers induced to move to western Canada.[12] The government also sent farmers who had been immigrants to visit Britain and tell the story of their success in Canada.

Governmental restrictions on the entry of immigrants into Canada were relatively few and generally similar to those applied by the United States,[13] but the rate of rejections in Canada was lower than in the United States. In 1908, for example, 0.4 per cent of immigrant arrivals were rejected for entry to Canada compared with 1.4 per cent in the United States. Inspection of immigrants coming to Canada from the United States only began in 1908, and a more restrictive immigration law in 1910 led to more rejections. During the period 1910–18 7.4 per cent of immigrant arrivals were rejected; at the United States border the rate was 15.4 per cent.[14]

During the late nineteenth century appropriation was progressively displaced as the dominating principle of economic policy by the increasing importance of capital accumulation as the basis for economic progress, and purely appropriative activities today contribute only marginally to production in an industrialized economy. The impact of changing technology on the offshore fishery, the triumph of big timber operators over individualist gangs, and the conversion of family farms into agricultural businesses illustrate the change in the character of economic activity that occurred along with the increase in importance of capital relative to land and labour.

Examples of appropriative activity can still be found where individuals own their means of production, work the land, and gain its products; but usually these activities are economically marginal. The people who pursue them live in comparative poverty. Although some reject by choice the higher incomes available in the industrial economy, most do so by necessity because they lack the capital to increase their production or the mobility to change their occupation. In circumstances where appropriation means involuntary poverty the state's role is to rescue such activities from decline by changing their character, making them more capital-intensive and accordingly more 'efficient.' If rescue fails or seems unlikely, then assistance may be offered to transfer workers from appropriative occupations to more productive jobs in the industrial economy; and if the remedial policies do not succeed, the role of the state may be reduced to supplementing low incomes through welfare payments.

Economic Growth by Capital Accumulation

Since the early stages of the industrial revolution a conception of economic progress as a process of accumulating capital has been central to theories of political economy and policies of economic growth. Just as reference to John Locke reveals the ideological currents that guided initial policies for resource appropriation, the strategy of economic development that relies on state support for private accumulation of physical capital can be understood by reference to the classical tradition of liberal political economy from Adam Smith's *The Wealth of Nations* (1776) to John Stuart Mill's *Principles of Political Economy* (1848–52). In these works the classical liberal defence of private property and individual enterprise is combined with a recognition of the potential for wealth creation that results from larger economic organizations, more intensive application of physical capital as a factor of production, and efficiency of competition among entrepreneurs in directing the allocation of economic surplus controlled by the capitalist class.

Capital consists of humanly produced material goods and equipment that are used as inputs in the production process. As the means of production, capital represents a diversion or saving of goods from current consumption for the purpose of increasing future consumption. A more capital-intensive process of production thus takes more time and resources to get started, but properly applied it is eventually much more productive. The higher productivity of capital-intensive processes comes in turn from scientific discoveries and changes in technology and organization which result in continual improvements in producer goods and production processes. These improvements make possible not only increases in net output using the same amounts of labour and raw materials more efficiently but also expansion of gross output using more labour and many more raw materials.

The transformation of an appropriative political economy into one based on capital accumulation has at least three important consequences for the organization of production and distribution. First, ownership and control of capital is progressively concentrated in the hands of a relatively small entrepreneurial class, and workers become dependent on capitalists to supply the means for their productive employment. Second, small individual business enterprise is displaced by large corporate business enterprise and the organizational environment for work is progressively bureaucratized. Third, both the expansion of business enterprise and the dependency of bureaucratized workers necessitate the development of mass markets and the progressive replacement of production for personal consumption by production for mass consumption. The principle of accumulation offers the prospects of greater material prosperity, but its prerequisite is a transformation of economic society.

In Canada the era of appropriative political economy stretched from the sixteenth-century fisheries to the prairie settlement and mineral exploration of the early twentieth century. In the second half of the nineteenth century, however, industrialization began to transform an agricultural and commercial economy, and capital accumulation emerged as the predominant strategy underlying public policies for economic growth. In an accumulative political economy that gave primacy to private property, private planning, and private production, the central problem of economic policy was to ensure that private decisions to save and invest would result in the desired rate of capital formation. Accordingly, the goal of economic policy became the inducement of private investment, either directly by public subsidy or indirectly by public investment. Public subsidy in the form of expenditure, fiscal, and regulatory policies favourable to business enterprises was designed to induce private savers to invest their capital by improving their expectations of profits. Public investment added directly to capital accumulation; but its justification in sectors such as transportation, communication, health, and education also depended on its contribution to creating economic and social conditions favourable to the expansion of industrial society and the growth of private investment.

Public Investment

Until the end of the nineteenth century the major direct investments of Canadian governments appear to have been based more on the principle of appropriation than on the principle of accumulation. The progress of industrialization in Ontario and Quebec from the 1870s to the 1890s should not be underestimated, however;[15] by 1900 there was a decisive shift in the

TABLE 2.2
Distribution of Direct Investment by Governments, 1901–30

Period	Federal, %	Provincial, %	Municipal, %	Total, %*	Total, millions of dollars	Total as percentage of gross construction
1901–5	61.2	4.8	34.0	100.0	94.0	13.8
1906–10	65.5	9.8	24.8	100.1	247.9	17.2
1911–15	51.1	17.8	31.2	100.1	439.7	21.9
1916–20	43.2	22.5	34.3	100.0	292.1	13.7
1921–5	29.7	33.9	36.4	100.0	438.8	19.3
1926–30	35.7	35.9	28.4	100.0	602.0	19.4

*Totals may not add to 100 per cent because of rounding errors.
SOURCE: Kenneth H. Buckley *Capital Formation in Canada, 1896–1930* (Toronto: University of Toronto Press 1955) 54

rationale of most public investment away from appropriation toward accumulation.

Governmental direct investment, as table 2.2 shows, jumped from 13.8 per cent of gross construction in 1901–5 to 21.9 per cent in 1911–15 and remained around 19 per cent throughout the 1920s.[16] Before the First World War the federal government's expenditures on railways and canals accounted for almost nine-tenths of federal investment and one-half of total public investment. After the war, higher provincial and municipal expenditures on roads and streets, building construction, and public utilities compensated for the federal government's inability or unwillingness to continue its pre-war investment policies. Such expenditures gave a vital new dimension to public investment in the socio-economic infrastructure of an emerging urban industrialized society, and provincial governments soon gained an influence in the field of economic development that had been neither envisaged in the British North America Act nor reflected in previous policies.

The years of the two world wars were years of rapid industrialization for Canada. Disruptions in international trade created additional protection for domestic manufactured goods, and governmental expenditures for military purposes financed a rapid expansion of private industrial productive capacity. At the end of the Second World War the Department of Reconstruction and Supply estimated that roughly two-thirds of the special war industry structure could be adapted to peacetime production, and the reconversion was quickly accomplished. As Caves and Holton conclude, 'The nasty truth remains ... that World War I advanced Canada's industrial

TABLE 2.3

Distribution of Expenditures on Gross Capital Formation by Governments, 1926–80

Period	Federal, %	Provincial, %	Local, %	Hospital, %	Total %*	Millions of dollars†
1926–30	31.9	31.4	36.7		100.0	809
1931–5	28.5	40.3	31.2		100.0	621
1936–40	21.7	54.1	24.1		99.9	704
1941–5	27.6	37.4	35.0		100.0	551
1946–50	7.3	47.2	45.4		99.9	1,704
1951–5	17.9	35.6	46.5		100.0	4,036
1956–60	18.8	38.7	42.4		99.9	6,951
1961–5	13.8	35.0	43.6	7.6	100.0	9,953
1966–70	15.6	33.6	43.9	6.9	100.0	15,058
1971–5	16.6	38.1	39.7	5.5	99.9	23,830
1976–80	15.0	36.8	42.7	5.5	100.0	36,193

*Totals may not add to 100 per cent because of rounding.
†Gross capital formation comprises gross fixed capital formation plus value of physical change in inventories.
SOURCES: Statistics Canada *National Income and Expenditure Accounts, Volume I: The Annual Estimates 1926–1974* (Ottawa: Information Canada 1976); *National Income and Expenditure Accounts: The Annual Estimates 1968–1982* ((Ottawa: Minister of Supply and Services 1983)

facilities and skills in ways which would have taken much longer under normal peacetime stimuli. World War II brought the same sort of changes to the Canadian economy as did its grim predecessor.'[17]

After reconstruction, both provincial and local governmental expenditures on capital formation continued to make a relatively greater contribution to capital accumulation than expenditures by the federal government (table 2.3). Table 2.4 shows that total governmental expenditures on capital formation varied from 14 to 20 per cent of gross capital formation for the five-year periods from 1946 to 1980. Governmental expenditures on capital formation increased steadily from under 3 per cent of gross national expenditure in the late 1940s to a peak of 4.6 per cent of gross national expenditure in 1966 before declining below 4 per cent because of expenditure restraints in the 1970s.

Statistics for gross fixed capital formation understate the direct contribution to capital accumulation by the public sector in Canada. The national accounts identify as public investment the capital formation carried out by government departments, publicly administered social insurance and trust funds, and various agencies, boards, and commissions such as Atomic Energy of Canada Limited, the National Research Council, the

TABLE 2.4

Distribution of Gross Fixed Capital Formation by Governments, Private Residential Construction, and Business Enterprises, 1926–80

Period	Govern-ments, %	Resident-ial con-struction, %	Business enter-prises,* %	Total %†	Millions of dollars	Total in-vestment as percentage of GNE at market prices	Government investment as percent-age of GNE at market prices
1926–30	14.7	20.2	65.1	100.0	5,515	19.3	2.8
1931–5	26.1	18.0	55.8	99.9	2,378	11.7	3.1
1936–40	19.7	15.5	64.7	99.9	3,523	12.8	2.5
1941–5	10.0	19.8	70.2	100.0	5,247	9.8	1.0
1946–50	13.5	22.8	63.7	100.0	14,390	18.9	2.5
1951–5	14.7	22.7	62.6	100.0	27,389	21.7	3.2
1956–60	16.4	22.5	61.2	100.1	42,344	24.1	4.0
1961–5	19.6	20.7	59.7	100.0	51,217	21.9	4.3
1966–70	18.3	19.5	62.2	100.0	81,990	22.4	4.1
1971–5	16.3	24.7	59.0	100.0	146,003	23.0	3.7
1976–80	13.0	24.6	62.4	100.0	275,902	23.1	3.0

*Business enterprises includes government business enterprises that are financed on an essentially commercial basis.

†Totals may not add to 100 per cent because of rounding.

SOURCES: See table 2.3.

National Film Board, and provincial health services commissions which are financed on an essentially non-commercial basis. They do not include federal, provincial, and municipal government enterprises, which constitute an increasingly important instrument of economic growth.

The origins of government enterprise can be variously attributed to the failure or chronic instability of important private firms, requirements of defence and national security, demands for state intervention during economic depression or post-war reconstruction, reluctance of private enterprise to undertake large and risky developmental projects, tenets of social democratic ideology, and requirements for interdependent public and private economic activity in an advanced capitalist economy. Over most of the history of Canadian economic development the resort to government enterprises can be explained most often by the practical demands of ensuring essential services, resource development, and economic integration in a vast country that is rich in natural resources, small in population, and dominated by an economically powerful neighbour.[18] The recent expansion in the scope and nature of government enterprises to include steel mills, aircraft companies, financial institutions, and energy corporations reflects mounting pressures, also observable in other capitalist industrial countries, to preserve and renew national and provincial industrial structure and promote internationally competitive enterprises by closer intermingling of private and public economic activity.[19]

Public Subsidy

The direct contribution to capital accumulation by government departments and enterprises is a vital component of Canadian economic development, but the predominant instrument of capital accumulation always has been private business enterprise. Reference to three important policy areas – foreign investment, fiscal policy, and research and development – will serve to illustrate the range and type of governmental subsidy of private capital accumulation. First, the historical openness of the Canadian economy to foreign investment was the result of deliberate governmental policy to increase capital formation. Second, the regressive structure of the national tax system gave a substantial benefit to the high-income class, the class of savers and investors, during the transformation from agriculture to industry between the 1860s and the 1950s. Third, a substantial part of federal expenditures on research and development has taken the form of direct investment, but in the 1970s a policy to buy rather than make R&D resulted in a shift of emphasis to public incentives for private-sector performance.

Canadian economic growth has always depended on a sizable inflow of foreign capital. The owners of foreign capital, predominantly located in Britain and the United States, have been attracted to Canada by the combination of political stability, capitalist values, and profit-making opportunities, a combination that has generated private domestic capital; but federal and provincial governmental policies have also actively promoted foreign investment.

The 'national policy' of high tariff protection for domestic manufacturing industries encouraged the inflow of foreign, especially American, investment.[20] As a regressive tax in the national fiscal system, tariff protection strongly favoured accumulation; but, as a study of business attitudes from 1883 to 1911 concluded, 'the branch-plant creating effect of the tariff was well-known during the period and always hailed as one of protection's greatest achievements.'[21] Foreign investment also has been encouraged by the material inducements offered by municipal governments to entice foreign capitalists to set up plants in their communities, by imposing a manufacturing condition on the export of natural resources to force American corporations to set up branch plants, and by manipulation of the Canada Patent Act to discriminate in favour of domestic manufacturing.[22] Finally, the flow of foreign capital into Canada has been facilitated by the virtual absence of any governmental regulation of foreign investment. The longstanding unwillingness to regulate foreign investment began to be questioned seriously in the 1960s. Amendments to federal and provincial business corporation acts now require a majority of Canadian residents on boards of directors, and a limited review of foreign takeovers of Canadian-owned enterprises was initiated under the Canada Foreign Investment Review Act of 1974. By international standards Canadian regulation of foreign investment remains very hesitant, however, and places only weak restrictions on the inflow of foreign capital.

Tables 2.5 and 2.6 show the sources of budgetary revenue for the federal government from 1970–1 to 1980–1 and the revenue from income, consumption, and property taxes for all governments from 1933–4 to 1979–80. Fiscal policy at all levels of government has consistently favoured capital accumulation by taxing low-income groups proportionately more heavily than high-income groups. During the nineteenth century the main sources of governmental revenue were federal customs duties and municipal property taxes. Even as late as 1913, when total revenue equalled $324 million, 35 per cent was accounted for by customs duties and 28 per cent by local property taxation.[23] Customs duties and property taxes are strongly regressive taxes. The growing reliance from the 1890s to the 1930s on additional sources of revenue – federal excise duties and sales taxes; provincial corporation, sales, and gasoline taxes; and provincial revenues from motor-vehicle licence fees and liquor control – did not change substantially the regressive structure of the tax system.

Not until 1939, when the federal government decided to finance the Second World War primarily by taxing current income rather than by borrowing or inflation, did the federal personal income tax and the corporation excess profits tax begin to bite heavily into high incomes. Revisions to the personal income tax in 1947 and the corporate profits tax in 1949 retained important features of the wartime tax structure which were progressive in their impact on high-income groups, and to this extent the post-war tax system has not been as favourable to high-income groups as it was from 1867 to 1939. Yet the personal income tax continues to give a substantial benefit to investment income (notably through the favourable treatment of capital gains), the corporate profits tax is probably in part

TABLE 2.5
Sources of Federal Government Budgetary Revenue, Selected Fiscal Years, 1870–1 to 1980–1

Fiscal year	Income taxes			Consumption taxes				Non-tax revenue,* %	Total, %†	Total, millions of dollars
	Corporate, %	Individual, %	Total, %	Sales tax, %	Excise duties, %	Customs import duties, %	Total, %			
1870–1	–	–	–	–	21.0	63.2	84.2	15.8	100.0	19
1880–1	–	–	–	–	16.7	60.0	80.0	20.0	100.0	30
1890–1	–	–	–	–	17.9	59.0	76.9	23.1	100.0	39
1900–1	–	–	–	–	18.9	52.8	73.6	26.4	100.0	53
1910–11	–	–	–	–	14.4	61.0	75.4	24.6	100.0	118
1920–1	3.2	7.6	20.1	8.7	8.5	37.3	64.3	15.8	100.2	437
1930–1	12.3	7.5	19.8	5.6	16.2	36.6	63.1	17.0	99.9	358
1940–1	15.1	11.9	31.3	20.6	10.2	15.0	58.1	10.8	100.2	872
1950–1	25.7	20.9	50.0	14.8	7.7	9.5	39.5	10.5	100.0	3,113
1960–1	22.2	31.2	56.2	15.9	5.5	8.0	34.2	9.7	100.1	6,221
1970–1	16.5	43.5	62.5	15.5	3.8	5.5	27.6	9.9	100.0	14,717
1980–1	17.4	42.7	62.0	11.7	2.2	6.8	25.4	12.6	100.0	46,507

*Includes special receipts and credits.

†Totals may not add to 100 per cent because of rounding.

SOURCES: *Historical Statistics of Canada* 2d ed. edited by F.H. Leacy, M.C. Urquhart, and K.A.H. Buckley (Ottawa: Minister of Supply and Services 1983) H1–18; *Public Accounts of Canada 1981* vol. 1 (Ottawa: Minister of Supply and Services 1981) table 4.1

TABLE 2.6

Revenue of All Governments Derived from Income, Consumption, and Property Taxes, 1933–4 to 1979–80

| Fiscal year | Percentage of net/gross* revenue | | | | Total revenue, millions of dollars |
	Individual income tax	Corporate income tax	Consumption taxes	Property and related taxes	
1933–4	5.1	4.2	32.1	31.7	742
1939–40	5.7	8.3	36.7	23.1	1,077
1949–50	16.4	18.7	33.2	9.9	3,790
1959–60	19.8	16.2	31.4	13.2	9,138
1969–70	28.9	13.8	26.1	12.4	26,740
1969–70*	25.9	12.4	22.8	10.0	29,819
1979–80*	27.9	9.5	17.3	8.1	105,641

*The historical series is interrupted by a change in methodology and coverage in 1970. Among other changes, total revenue is calculated on a gross rather than a net basis from 1970 onward. SOURCES: *Historical Statistics of Canada* 2d ed. edited by F.H. Leacy, M.C. Urquhart, and K.A.H. Buckley H52–74, H221–33; Statistics Canada *Consolidated Government Finance 1979* (Ottawa: Minister of Supply and Services 1982) table 1

shifted forward as a tax on consumers through higher prices, and a regressive property tax remains an important source of revenue. The result is a tax system that overall is still regressive for those with very low incomes and apparently no worse than proportional for the middle-income and high-income earners.[24]

The emergence of a mature industrial economy typically leads governments to a more direct concern for promoting scientific discovery and technological innovations, which are the foundation for expanding the productivity of labour by capital investment. In Canada the federal government's direct investment in scientific research has a considerable history in such agencies as the Geological Survey (1842), Experimental Farms of the Department of Agriculture (1886), and the Fisheries Research Board (1912). The establishment of the National Research Council in 1917 marked the beginning of organized public support for industrial research in Canada. At first the NRC operated indirectly by co-ordinating research activities and providing financial support. In 1932 it opened its own laboratories, and during the Second World War the system of NRC laboratories was expanded rapidly. By 1950 the number of personnel in NRC laboratories had grown from 300 in 1939 to over 3,000.[25]

After the war the trend of policy favoured the creation of more specialized agencies and the diversification of governmental support for research and development. The Defence Research Board took over de-

TABLE 2.7

Gross Expenditures on Research and Development by Sectors of Funding, Selected Years, 1963–82 (percentages)

	Sectors of funding						
Years	Federal govern- ment	Provincial govern- ments*	Business enter- prises	Univer- sities	Private non- profit	Foreign	Total†
1963	48.7	4.2	31.4	12.4	1.2	2.1	100.0
1967	47.8	5.6	32.0	11.5	1.0	2.1	100.0
1971	46.7	4.6	31.6	13.3	1.5	2.4	100.1
1975	41.7	5.7	34.3	14.0	1.6	2.6	99.9
1979	35.3	6.6	39.9	12.9	1.9	3.3	99.9
1982	35.1	5.6	44.5	9.6	2.0	3.2	100.0

*'Provincial governments' includes provincial research organizations.
†Totals may not add to 100 per cent because of rounding.
SOURCES: Statistics Canada *Annual Review of Science Statistics 1980* (Ottawa: Minister of Supply and Services 1981) 55; *Annual Review of Science Statistics 1982* (Ottawa: Minister of Supply and Services 1982) 10

fence research from the NRC in 1947, Atomic Energy of Canada was given responsibility for the atomic energy program in 1957, and the Medical Research Council replaced the NRC in 1960 as federal granting agency for research in the health sciences.[26] Federal government departments – particularly Agriculture, Energy, Mines and Resources, Environment, and Industry, Trade and Commerce – expanded their commitments to research and development through extramural grants and contracts and through larger expenditures on intramural research activities. In addition, eight provinces have research councils or foundations that are responsible for assisting firms with technical problems and for aiding the development of provincial natural resources.[27]

As table 2.7 shows, the federal government is the leading source of funds for research and development. As a performer (see table 2.8) the federal government declined in relative importance, as did business, during the 1960s when the rapid expansion of Canadian universities was accompanied by their undertaking a larger share of research activities. At the same time a succession of public studies by the Royal Commission on Government Organization, the Science Council, and the Senate Special Committee on Science Policy urged stronger central co-ordination of federal science policy and greater reliance on extramural, especially industrial, performance of research and development.

Soon after the Ministry of State for Science and Technology was set up in

TABLE 2.8

Gross Expenditures on Research and Development by Sectors of Performance, Selected Years, 1963–82 (percentages)

Years	Sectors of performance					Total	
	Federal govern-ment	Provincial govern-ments*	Business enter-prises	Univer-sities	Private non-profit	Percent-ages†	Millions of dollars
1963	37.8	3.6	39.0	18.6	0.9	99.9	463
1967	33.0	3.0	39.9	24.1	0.7	100.1	854
1971	29.5	2.9	40.1	26.7	0.7	99.9	1,157
1975	28.2	3.6	41.8	25.8	0.7	100.1	1,675
1979	23.6	3.7	47.7	24.2	0.8	100.0	2,669
1982	22.3	3.4	52.6	20.9	0.8	100.0	4,390

*'Provincial governments' includes provincial research organizations.
†Totals may not add to 100 per cent because of rounding.
SOURCES: Statistics Canada *Annual Review of Science Statistics 1980* (Ottawa: Minister of Supply and Services 1981) 54; *Annual Review of Science Statistics 1982* (Ottawa: Minister of Supply and Services 1982) 8

1971, 'buying' rather than 'making' research and development became the focus of its policy efforts. The package of incentives designed to encourage R&D in the private sector included directives to federal departments and agencies to increase substantially their research contracts with private industry, changes in federal governmental procurement policies to favour purchases of products and services involving Canadian research and development, and special tax credits to business enterprises for increases in their scientific expenditures. The incentives seem to have succeeded in increasing the relative contribution of business enterprises to funding and performing research and development, but the policy of buying has not so far affected the total output of R&D. For the years shown in tables 2.7 and 2.8, for example, gross expenditures on research and development in 1963 were 1.0 per cent of gross national product; in 1967, 1.3 per cent; in 1971, 1.2 per cent; in 1975 and 1979, 1.0 per cent; and in 1982, 1.2 per cent.

Economic Growth by Economic Stabilization

During the 1930s the Canadian economy experienced a severe drop in employment and production and a very weak recovery. The problems of the policy-makers during that period cannot be minimized. They faced the failure of their institutions and of their ideas about the inevitability of economic progress through capital accumulation. According to Safarian, 'The actual reaction to the problems of the thirties was compounded partly of the view that policy was helpless in the face of external factors, and partly of the lack of experience of such a collapse, lack of institutions through which policy could be expressed, and problems of governmental allocation of powers and finances by the constitution.'[28] In such circumstances there was no easy remedy. A thoroughgoing reform of national economic institutions depended on a transformation of the accepted paradigm for thinking about the conditions of economic growth. When that change in ideas was eventually accomplished, it resulted in a view of economic growth that made governmental steering the critical factor in the national economic performance.

The goal of stabilization policies is to minimize fluctuations in the level of economic activity that reduce output below its potential given the stock of capital, increase the proportion of unemployed workers beyond the normal rate of frictional unemployment, produce inflationary price increases, or disrupt the balance of external trade. In his classic theoretical work on controlling short-term fluctuations in economic activity, *The General Theory of Employment, Interest and Money* (1936), J.M. Keynes distinguished the demand for producers' goods or capital spending from public and private demand for current consumption. He argued that private investment spending is very sensitive to variations in business expectations and concluded that fluctuations in economic activity resulting from the volatility of private capital spending could be offset by appropriate adjustments in governmental monetary and fiscal instruments. For example, a reduction in interest rates brought about by a central bank's purchasing government securities would encourage capital expenditures by reducing borrowing costs, whereas selling government securities would reduce the money supply, raise interest rates, and discourage investment. Reductions in taxes on corporate profits, more favourable tax treatment for depreciation of capital assets, increases in public investment to offset a decline in private investment, and tax or expenditure subsidies to promote private consumption and improve business expectations are examples of fiscal measures to counteract a decline in aggregate demand. Each of these instruments can be reversed to curb inflationary pressures resulting from excessive demand. In this 'new political economy' the task of government is to 'balance the economy' by appropriate adjustment of monetary and fiscal instruments rather than simply to 'balance the budget,' which formerly was the criterion of good economic management.[29]

Monetary and Fiscal Management

By 1945 the development of Keynesian macro-economic theory, a surge of social idealism that made a return to the high unemployment of the 1930s politically unacceptable, and the experience of financing the war had wrought a deep change in the economic policy-making environment. In its white paper on employment and income, the federal government 'stated unequivocally its adoption of a high and stable level of employment and income, and thereby higher standards of living, as a major aim of Government policy.'[30] As W.A. Mackintosh, the principal author of the white paper, later observed, 'The White Paper did not invent a policy; it simply recognized that the responsibility for employment policy, which the Dominion had rejected in 1937–38, it could not avoid in 1945, and the Government fully recognized this.'[31]

The 1945 white paper made it plain that the goal of full employment could and would be achieved within the framework of a capitalist economy by manipulating private investment and aggregate demand through changes in the supply of money and the balance of the federal government's budget. Anticipating unemployment when the war ended, the white paper announced that 'the Government desires and expects low interest rates after the war. It proposes to pursue a monetary policy which will encourage through low interest rates, the investment of funds in productive capital contributing to employment.' As for fiscal policy, 'the Government will be prepared, in periods when unemployment threatens, to incur the deficits and increases in the national debt resulting from its employment and income policy, whether that policy in the circumstances is best applied through increased expenditures or reduced taxation. In periods of buoyant employment and income, budget plans will call for surpluses. The Government's policy will be to keep the national debt within manageable proportions, and maintain a proper balance in its budget over a period longer than a single year.'[32]

From the late 1940s to the middle 1960s the goals articulated in the 1945 white paper were achieved with reasonable success.[33] Inflation was a serious problem in the late 1940s, particularly in 1948, during the conversion from wartime to peacetime production, and again during the Korean War; and unemployment rose over 4.5 per cent during the recession of 1954–5 and over 7 per cent during the recession of 1958–62. For most of this period, however, Canada's economic performance was very good. Gross national product increased at annual rates of 4 to 7 per cent, reaching 9.4

per cent in 1955; unemployment varied from 3 to 5 per cent of the labour force; and the consumer price index rose about 2 to 3 per cent annually. Reflecting this experience in its first annual report in 1964, the Economic Council of Canada set as targets for stabilization policy during the remainder of the 1960s an average annual increase in total output of 5.5 per cent, a 3 per cent rate of unemployment, and annual price increase of 1.5 to 2 per cent.[34] Given the experience with stabilization policy over the previous two decades these targets were probably reasonable, as the council argued. Unfortunately, they were not met, and there is little hope that they will be.

Beginning in the late 1960s annual rates of growth in national production became more erratic; and, as figure 2.1 shows, the trade-off between unemployment and inflation became much more unfavourable. According to the expectations of Keynesian macro-economic theory, the optimal choice in economic policy-making should be somewhere between rather high inflation and growth combined with low unemployment on the one hand and quite high unemployment combined with low inflation and growth on the other. This policy choice became increasingly unpalatable in the real economy of the 1970s. A tolerable level of unemployment seemed to be impossible to achieve without unacceptably high inflation, and an acceptable rate of inflation appeared to be accompanied by an insupportable level of unemployment.

In such circumstances the policy prescriptions of Keynesian economics appeared both economically irrelevant and politically unfeasible. Raising interest rates to curb inflation would simply make high unemployment worse; increasing an already large government deficit in order to reduce unemployment would only worsen inflation (and by putting upward pressure on interest rates in order to finance the government's debt perhaps make unemployment worse). Not surprisingly, governmental policymakers began to search for an alternative policy instrument that would allow them to implement an expansionary policy to reduce unemployment without worsening inflation.

Income Controls

Announced in the government's white paper of December 1968, *Policies for Price Stability*, the Prices and Incomes Commission was set up to study costs, prices, productivity, and incomes in key sectors and to carry out research on the causes of inflation. The commission approached business groups, trade unions, professional associations, and provincial governments to get their co-operation in creating a comprehensive program of

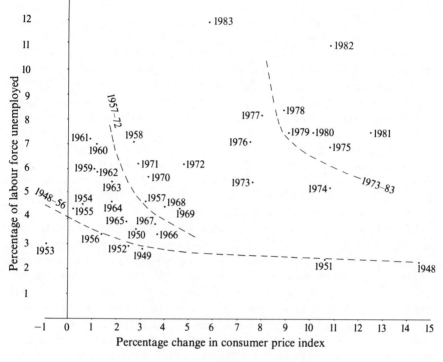

Figure 2.1
Rates of unemployment and inflation, Canada, 1948–83

voluntary income restraint. The commission did succeed in getting a commitment to support a system of price and income reviews from business and professional leaders as well as from the provincial governments; but trade-union leaders refused to co-operate with a voluntary program, contending that a mandatory freeze on prices and incomes was required. When its proposal for adopting a guideline of 6 per cent wage increases was rejected by the unions in 1970, the Prices and Incomes Commission ended its efforts to set up voluntary guidelines. Thereafter its work was limited to surveillance, policy analysis, and research until its mandate expired in 1972.

In 1975, as unemployment rose to 7 per cent, the economy stagnated, and prices continued to rise, the federal government once again tried to get a voluntary agreement with business and labour to limit wage and price increases.[35] When that effort failed and the finance minister had resigned, the government hastily introduced a three-year anti-inflation program that included restraints on public expenditures and employment; initiatives to resolve sectoral problems in energy, housing, and food supplies; restrictions on the growth of the money supply; and mandatory wage and price controls. Declared constitutional as temporary emergency legislation by the Supreme Court of Canada in July 1976, the control measures included guidelines for increases in profits, prices, dividends, wages and salaries, and professional fees. An Anti-Inflation Board was established to make detailed regulations to implement the controls, review actions on wages and prices in relationship to the guidelines, and negotiate compliance where breaches occurred. A separate administrator with legal powers to order compliance with the guidelines (if negotiations failed) and to require repayment of income derived from breaches of the guidelines was appointed, and an Anti-Inflation Appeal Tribunal was authorized to hear appeals from decisions of the administrator.[36]

In June 1982, with production stagnant and inflation and unemployment running at 10 per cent, the federal government introduced another partial controls program that imposed compulsory pay restraints on the federal public sector and purported to set an example for provincial governments and private firms. All wage and salary increases for federal governmental employees were limited to 6 per cent in 1982-3 and 5 per cent in 1983-4, existing contracts were rolled back, and collective agreements were extended for the life of the program. All of the provinces followed the federal government's lead and adopted some form of public-sector wage restraint, except in Manitoba, where the New Democratic Party government completely rejected wage controls. However, the evidence indicates that the majority of firms in the private sector instituted pay restraints as a reaction to world-wide recession and high levels of unemployment rather than because of the example of federal controls.

The long-term economic impact of mandatory wage and price controls between 1975 and 1978 remains a matter of controversy, and their admitted administrative difficulties and high political costs make understandable the government's reluctance to resort again to a comprehensive controls program. Furthermore, as Eugene Swimmer has argued, the federal wage controls program of 1982-4 is best described as 'political grandstanding' that had little to do with declining wage and price increases.[37] So far, apparently, neither voluntary guidelines nor mandatory controls have proved themselves capable of counteracting the failure of conventional stabilization policies to achieve acceptable levels of growth with price stability and full employment.

Political Economy and Economic Ideology

Comparisons of economic consequences and social costs are made between the depression of the 1930s and the deep recession, if not depression, of the 1980s; but the strongest parallel between the two periods is not often articulated. As in the 1930s, in the 1980s Canadians are suffering from a double failure of economic institutions and economic ideas. The real problem in making coherent policies for economic growth is the collapse of consensus in the economic policy-making community about how to explain current stabilization problems and what policy measures are required to resolve them. Briefly, three general positions can be identified in this renewal of ideological conflict within the economic policy community.

First, the neo-conservative monetarist position holds that inflation is explained by excessive increases in the money supply which result from the uncontrolled deficit financing of liberal governments. A sustained policy of strict limits on the money supply, high interest rates, and a sizable reduction in government expenditures is the only way to break persistent inflationary expectations. That these measures will cause high unemployment is dismissed as a regrettable necessity arising from the spendthrift policies of post-war liberal governments.

Second, the socialist or social-democratic post-Keynesian position explains inflation as the inevitable outcome of administered prices and wages struck in bargains between big corporations and big unions with the active collusion of political and bureaucratic élites. A radical redirection and extension of governmental intervention in the economy is necessary to represent popular as opposed to corporate producer interests. The advocates of this position recommend an expansion of public enterprise to ensure greater public accountability in key industrial sectors and the adoption of permanent wage and price controls to curb corporate economic power.

Third, somewhere between the right and left, a beleaguered liberal neo-Keynesian position argues that inflation can be explained by policy mistakes, in particular by a recurring failure, which began in the 1960s, to counter inflationary dangers strongly enough, and by price shocks, in particular the increases in world commodity prices that occurred during 1972–5. According to this view economic stabilization requires continuing fiscal-monetary restraint and perhaps a medium-term incomes policy, preferably one based on the indirect incentives of tax rewards and tax penalties rather than directly administered controls. The standard policy instruments and, more important, the essentially Keynesian economic ideas are assumed to remain valid.

Some resolution of this conflict of economic ideologies is a prerequisite for rediscovering a coherent strategy of economic growth in Canada. Such a resolution has certainly been impeded by the absence so far of any positive evidence that either conservative or socialist programs are economically effective, let alone politically feasible. In the absence of strong evidence for economic policy effectiveness, considerations of political feasibility become paramount, and here Canadian policy-makers operate within a tight pattern of economic political interests and cultural constraints emanating from the historical development of the Canadian political economy.

The first constraint is economic individualism. The colonial political economy of appropriation has been superseded by a political economy that gives primacy to capital accumulation, but the old ideals persist in the Canadian liberal tradition. Interpretations of Canadian political culture that focus on its differences from the liberal tradition in the United States stress the interdependence of large, centralized business enterprises and the power of the state in Canadian national development. According to this view the requirements of Canadian economic progress and social order served to blunt individualism and democracy in favour of a collectivist, conservative conception of state and society. Historically, the norms of Canadian citizenship emphasize a subject rather than participatory competence in government and politics – obedience to recognized authority, preservation of hierarchical organizations, acceptance of social inequalities, deference to power élites.

In economic development this interpretation of the Canadian political tradition focuses on concentration in the organization of trade and commerce; what it neglects is the individualist organization of production in an appropriative political economy. Not bureaucratic values but the individualist values of independent commodity producers constitute the cultural legacy of the appropriative political economy – a strong sense of individual independence; a commitment to work as the source of economic progress and individual achievement; a deep attachment to the land; recognition and respect for the rights of private property; and resistance to the pressures for economic dependence from monopolistic fur traders, timber merchants, railway companies, grain traders, mortgage companies, and private banks.

These ideals of the independent commodity producer may well be illusions in a mature capitalist economy. C.B. Macpherson has argued that 'the independent commodity producer's double relation to the market – that is, his independence of the labour market either as seller or buyer and his dependence on the price system which is ruled as a whole by the rate of profit on the productive employment of wage labour – tends to give him, as a fundamental part of his outlook, an illusion of independence.'[38] Even so, the values persist as real ideals and aspirations that forcefully shape Canadian expectations for economic progress, social order, and individual development. No account of the public philosophy that gives purpose to policy development in Canada can afford to ignore them.

The second constraint is private enterprise. Uneasy questions about the long-term consequences of persistent inflation with unemployment, foreign ownership of the Canadian economy, underinvestment in research and development, and the growing interdependence of private and public economic enterprise have not yet revealed anomalies sufficiently great to shake confidence in the efficacy of private economic planning and production as the foundation for economic progress. Incrementalist legislation to promote private capital investment by establishing state investment and development corporations, to review the investment proposals of new foreign entrants to the Canadian economy, to encourage increased business expenditures on industrial research and development by favourable tax benefits, or even to intervene for three years with mandatory controls on wages and prices reveals no inclination to question the fundamental premises of a strategy for economic development that makes private capital accumulation synonymous with achieving material prosperity and assigns government the function of inducing and maintaining private investment by positive expenditure and regulatory policies.

The bias of the prevailing public philosophy toward private accumulation as the condition for material prosperity serves to justify a privately organized economic collectivism that encompasses vast inequalities of power among economic producers and presupposes dependence of workers on private bureaucracies. Although the economic individualism of independent commodity producers survives widely as an ideal and is occasionally realized, in general the historical tensions between the private collectivism of an accumulative political economy and the private individualism of an appropriative political economy have been resolved in favour of accumulation. In the process, ironically, the arguments for individual economic independence have been bent to serve the needs of private corporations; and individualist economic aspirations have been banished to subordinate competitive markets, increasingly exceptional cases of individual entrepreneurial success, and popular ambitions for home ownership.

The third constraint is social security. The goals of steady growth, full employment, and stable prices in economic policy had their counterparts in public policies for income maintenance and social services. Popular expectations were created for an equitable satisfaction of basic physiological needs, and understanding how these expectations for economic and social justice came to be created and how they have been fitted into the Canadian public philosophy is crucial to understanding the current parameters of public policy in Canada. In the end, the promise of material propensity alone was not enough to purchase the transformation of economic individualism into a political economy of state-supported, private economic collectivism. Promises of social security and individual development also were made, and expectations about their fulfilment add another fundamental to popular economic values and an undeniable limit to élite options for economic policy-making.

3

Income Security

In a liberal political economy founded on the principles of economic individualism and private enterprise, paid work is assumed to be the means to gain an income and provide for basic needs. Inevitably, some individuals fail to support themselves and their families by their earned income. Their failure may be temporary, caused by sickness or unavailability of employment, or it may be permanent, caused by physical disability or old age. It may also result from an inability to find work that pays an income large enough to provide properly for the basic needs of dependents.

Failure to earn an income is disastrous for individual workers and their dependents, but it is also a public problem. Two beliefs interact in the history of Canadian policy development with respect to income security. One is the fear that the poor will undermine public order. Poverty causes begging, thievery, or even rioting, which threaten the security of those who are not poor; public expenditures to alleviate poverty are supported as an alternative or a supplement to public expenditures on police control. The other is the recognition that in certain circumstances the poor have a moral right to material assistance. In liberal political philosophy, individuals are responsible for their own welfare, but they also deserve help when their best efforts fail. In nineteenth-century Canada charity toward the deserving poor arose from the obligation of one good Christian to provide for the welfare of another. In the twentieth century, political democratization carried liberalism beyond Christian charity, establishing principles of common citizenship and economic rights which give a different but equally compelling justification to the moral argument for income redistribution.

However powerful fears of public disorder might sometimes be, it is the moral belief that is critical for understanding the development of poverty policies in Canada. Under the assumptions of a liberal political economy, whether appropriative or accumulative, the individual's work creates a property right that, other things being equal, should be respected and protected by the state. Any program that attempts to reduce poverty by a compulsory redistribution of income from those who work and earn their livings to those who do not work or whose work is insufficient to allow them to earn their livings must include a specific and legitimate criterion that will identify the poor and establish their entitlement to public income support. Because a belief in individual responsibility is a fundamental tenet of the public philosophy, a person's inability to earn a living must be clearly established before public assistance is granted. The poor always must qualify as deserving poor.

Four different criteria for redistribution predominate in Canadian policy development. The criterion of longest standing is the means test: when the income and assets of an individual or family head falls below a certain level, he or she can apply for public assistance. The modern variant is a needs test, in which assessment of individual or family need is substituted for an arbitrary income ceiling. A second criterion is contingency. Unexpected misfortunes such as disability, sickness, and unemployment may deprive an individual or family of income and hence justify, either temporarily or permanently, some form of assistance. Contribution constitutes a third criterion. The previous payment of premiums, either by the beneficiary or specifically on behalf of the beneficiary, create the right to a transfer of income or delivery of social services. A demographic characteristic such as youth or old age serves as the fourth criterion for redistribution where virtually all members of the demographic category are known to require assistance.

One or, more often, two of these four criteria can be found in the design of each of the three main types of redistributive programs that have been developed in Canada. First, relief programs treat poverty by institutional care ('indoor relief') or by transfer payment ('home relief' or 'outdoor relief') based on the application of a means test and either a contingency test (assistance because of disability, blindness, illness, or unemployment) or a demographic characteristic (old age assistance). Second, social insurance programs usually combine the criteria of contribution and contingency as present taxpayers (whether employers, employees, or the general public, but usually including prospective beneficiaries) establish rights to future benefits regardless of income in contingencies such as unemployment, sickness, disability, or death. An important exception is the contributory pensions program, which combines a criterion of prepayment with a demographic characteristic in its design. Third, universal redistributive programs provide transfer payments or social services without a means test or prepayment to any citizen who belongs to the designated demographic category (young, old) or who incurs the designated contingency (illness, physical handicap, unemployment).

Relief, social insurance, and universal redistributive programs are very different approaches to resolving the issue of individual responsibility. Taken together they reveal a progressive trend toward greater state intervention to provide for income security. This widening set of justifications for state intervention responds to deep historical changes in the Canadian political economy. Poverty occurs in specific economic, social, and political contexts. Public policies to reduce poverty reflect élite and popular beliefs about which criteria justify state intervention to redistribute income to the poor; they also depend on the common understanding of what causes poverty and what can be done about it. The history of redistributive programs in Canada shows us the changing criteria for income redistribution and the changing perceptions of poverty as Canadian economic society evolved from its original reliance on appropriation through an emergent accumulative political economy to an advanced industrial society.

Poor Relief by Institutional Care

The appropriative political economy of the early nineteenth century was characterized by a generally low standard of living, substantial production for use rather than for sale, and relatively small production units which often were made even more cohesive by the family ties of their members. Land was assumed to be readily available, and not much capital was required to work it. A living, it was firmly believed, could be made by almost anyone who was able and willing to work.

For those who could not work, the principal material support was expected to come from their immediate families with supplementary assistance from other relatives and sympathetic neighbours. Economic production organized in close-knit fishing villages and farming communities provided the communal structure and flexible employment necessary for families and neighbours to sustain this system of voluntary mutual aid. It also fitted well with the colonial ideal of Christian charity while avoiding unwanted state interference to enforce income redistribution.

The formally organized social welfare provided by charity organizations, religious communities, and local governments was mainly concerned with people who could neither care for themselves nor rely on relatives or friends for support. They were children and old people with no family or friends to support them, or perhaps they were insane or physically disabled persons whose requirements for care exceeded the simple facilities of family homes. Thus, although outdoor or home relief for the poor was available in some districts, the organized welfare sector in the nineteenth century was set up primarily to supply institutional care. Houses of refuge for the unemployable, houses of industry for the unemployed, orphanages, and even jails were used to separate the worst cases of poverty from their society and provide for their subsistence.

Since the Second World War, ironically, as institutions became less important in welfare policies, standards of care have been raised above subsistence levels; but throughout the nineteenth century and well into the twentieth, only the minimum required for survival was provided. This policy was in part a result of the generally low standard of living in the colonies; but it also reflected the prevailing belief, at least among élites, that people were lazy and would if possible avoid the arduousness of working to earn their livings. The tests for receiving organized social welfare had to be so strict that only those desperately in need would opt for it. Canadian practice in this respect followed the reform of the English poor law in 1834. Under it institutional care 'was to be made as bleak and degrading as possible so that a job – any job at any wage – would be attractive by comparison, and there were not even to be exceptions for unemployables since there was always the presumption that they had brought their unfortunate condition upon themselves.'[1]

In Nova Scotia in 1763 and New Brunswick in 1786 the old English poor law was formally adopted which gave responsibility for the institutional care or outdoor relief of paupers to the municipalities. In New Brunswick each municipal council appointed poor-law commissioners who were given responsibility for carrying out the law. In Nova Scotia the Poor Relief Act created poor-relief districts with overseers appointed by the councils to 'furnish relief and support to all indigent persons having a settlement in such poor districts when they are in need thereof.' In both provinces settlement regulations were strict, local assistance was niggardly and haphazard, and poor-law authorities were completely free of provincial supervision. This system was maintained with little change until the Second World War. Consider the case of the county homes of Nova Scotia in the 1940s:

The general reliance upon institutional care rather than home relief is indicated by the fact that in 1942 the city of Halifax granted no home relief, offering only care in the City Home or nothing at all – a nineteenth century poor law practice which has been long since condemned by authoritative opinion. In the county homes there is indiscriminate mixture of various types of needy persons – the aged and the widows ineligible for pensions, the physically handicapped, the chronic invalids, the shiftless adults of low mentality, and even the 'harmless insane.' This cannot but lead to evil results for the inmates and the community at large, as the British Royal Commission on the Poor Laws pointed out so clearly in 1909 when it castigated the 'promiscuity' of the British work houses of that day.[2]

In Quebec governmental involvement in social welfare was also weak; but assistance provided voluntarily by religious orders, however inadequate, probably attained a higher standard than that provided by poor-law authorities in New Brunswick and Nova Scotia. During the French colonial regime, public welfare had been regarded as the preserve of the church; after the conquest the religious orders continued to occupy the field. As in the other colonies institutional care was the main method of caring for the poor. Beginning in the nineteenth century, provincial grants were made to religious orders to maintain hospitals, asylums, and orphanages. These grants increased over time, but there was almost no attempt at governmental regularization or control of public welfare until the 1921 Public Charities Act set up a Bureau of Public Charities to investigate applications for grants, distribute subsidies, and supervise subsidized institutions. The bureau succeeded to some degree in rationalizing governmental support for private charitable institutions, but intervention into institutional operations and standards of care remained beyond its powers until the system was overwhelmed by the depression of the 1930s.

In Ontario the first statute passed by Upper Canada's legislative assembly in 1792 established English civil law in the colony, but it specifically excluded the application of the English poor law. An 1810 statute declared jails to be houses of correction to which might be committed 'all and every disorderly person, and rogues and vagabonds, and incorrigible rogues.'[3] By the time of Confederation, counties, cities, and towns were authorized to establish houses of refuge, make grants to charitable institutions, and grant outdoor relief;[4] but the principle of public responsibility was slow to develop and was not entirely accepted until 1903. In the absence of adequate public provisions for the care of the poor, voluntary religious, fraternal, and patriotic organizations set up and incorporated hospitals, houses of refuge, orphanages, and homes for unmarried mothers and pressed the provincial legislature for grants of assistance. In 1874 the Charity Aid Act regularized provincial subsidies to eligible institutions and asserted governmental authority to inspect institutions and approve management policies. The more generous grants resulted in a rapid expansion of private non-profit hospitals, refuges, and orphanages in the last part of the nineteenth century.[5] The number of county homes also increased in this period – twenty were eligible for the provincial construction grants offered in 1890 – and in 1903 an act was passed to require all counties to establish houses of refuge. Bryden remarks that 'as a result, institutional facilities expanded considerably, and some of the most yawning gaps of the ninetenth century system were partly filled. Actually it was and continued to be a make-shift rather than a system. Many people in need fell through the net, but the relatively well-developed system of jails provided a certain reservoir of accommodation.'[6]

Poor Relief by Income Transfers

As an alternative to institutional segregation of the poor, relief programs can be set up to provide material or financial assistance without removing the recipients from the community. Goods and services are provided or allowances are paid to those who qualify for assistance so that they can maintain themselves in the community. Throughout the nineteenth century, outdoor or home relief from charitable organizations and religious orders, parsimoniously assisted by provincial and municipal grants, was a minor element in comparison with institutional care in providing subsistence living for the poor. The transformation of Canada from a rural agricultural to an urban industrial society led governments to resort to income transfers as one means of coping with the poverty of industrialization.

Industrialization of the Canadian economy changed the nature of the public problem of poverty. Unemployment became a greater threat to income security as workers became more dependent on the owners of capital and were exposed to the vicissitudes of periodic lay-offs. At the same time the eclipse of the appropriative economy, especially family farming, reduced the economy's capacity to absorb surplus labour. The growth of cities as the centres of the accumulative economy also weakened the cohesion of families and neighbours that had sustained the system of voluntary mutual assistance in rural communities. Urban migration to industrial employment opportunities separated people from relatives and friends, and urban living was generally not conducive to making new mutually supportive relationships. These economic changes combined with a sharpening of class conflict and a trend toward political democratization to increase pressure on organized social welfare. As the clients of the organized welfare sector grew in numbers, their needs for assistance became more diversified. The circumstances of poverty that were accepted as establishing eligibility for public welfare assistance became less restricted as beliefs about work and poverty slowly adjusted to the new socio-economic realities, and new instruments of public policy were adopted to give them effect.

The first significant departure in organized social welfare from reliance on institutional segregation did not come until the 1893 Ontario Act for the Prevention of Cruelty to and Better Protection of Childen. This act was a landmark in the development of social welfare in Canada.[7] It established a pattern of protection and assistance which was adopted throughout Canada and which remains substantially unchanged. The act provided penalties for mistreating children, empowered voluntary children's aid societies to apprehend neglected children, required municipalities to finance temporary shelter for such children, and authorized the children's aid societies to manage and supervise childen in temporary shelters. The act was more than simply a program for institutionalization, however, since the children's aid societies were not permitted to keep children indefinitely in their municipally financed shelters. Within a reasonable time the societies had to place children in a family home without public payment or provide for boarding them in private homes at municipal expense. A superintendent was appointed to encourage the formation of children's aid societies throughout the province, inspect shelters and foster homes, and report back to the legislature.

The requirements that institutional care be temporary only and that neglected children be cared for in the community marked a shift in the approach to public assistance for children which was gradually adopted in other provinces. By 1939 there were about ninety children's aid societies in Canada, fifty-three of them in Ontario. Of 41,782 children then reported under public care, 14,607 were in the care of children's aid societies (9,644 in Ontario; 1,744 in Manitoba; and 1,433 in Nova Scotia); 5,330 children were living in public homes for adults and children; and 11,179 were in orphanages. Quebec continued to be most reliant on institutional care, with 3,866 children in homes for adults and children and 6,185 in orphanages.[8]

The first general income transfers for relief of the poor were provincial mothers' allowances. Mothers' allowances were introduced in the state of Illinois in 1911. When Manitoba began to provide mothers' allowances in 1916, four provinces quickly followed with similar programs: Saskatchewan in 1917, Alberta in 1919, and British Columbia and Ontario in 1920.

These programs all provided for a monthly allowance to mothers who had dependent children and who passed tests of means and character.[9] In British Columbia a mother with childen under sixteen whose husband was dead, disabled, or institutionalized could collect $42.50 each month for herself and one child plus $7.50 for each additional child. The British Columbia scale was the most generous of the original programs, but the resulting annual income must still have been well below the existing poverty line.[10]

The 1927 Old Age Pensions Act represented the first significant and continuing intervention by the federal government in the social welfare field.[11] Not only did it anticipate the regime of co-operative federalism that was to attain major proportions in the 1950s and 1960s, it also confirmed income transfers as an accepted approach to poor relief in Canada. Under the act, $20 a month was paid to applicants aged seventy or over whose annual outside income did not exceed $125; the pension was reduced by the amount of any outside income exceeding $125; and a person with income above $365 was ineligible for assistance. The federal government reimbursed a province with an approved scheme for one-half the cost of its pensions. British Columbia was the first province to implement an approved program in 1927, followed by Saskatchewan and Manitoba in 1928 and Ontario and Alberta in 1929. In 1931 the federal government increased its share to three-quarters of the cost of pensions; and Prince Edward Island (1933), Nova Scotia (1934), and Quebec and New Brunswick (1936) were drawn into the program. The same approach was again employed in federal legislation for blind pensions in 1937 – $20 monthly to blind persons over 40 who passed a means test – and all the provincial governments passed the necessary enabling legislation in 1937–8.

Relief by income transfers was the main approach adopted by all three levels of government to alleviate the poverty caused by unemployment in the 1930s. The federal government passed the first national unemployment relief act in 1930, which authorized assistance to the unemployed through provincially administered work projects and direct relief. As with old-age assistance, costs were shared with the provinces, which in turn usually required some municipal financial contribution. In 1934 the federal government replaced its percentage grant with monthly lump-sum payments for direct relief which were adjusted to fit federal estimates of provincial need, and the provinces and municipalities were expected to finance all costs above the basic grant. Four years later a percentage grant was reintroduced which contributed 30 (later 40) per cent of local costs up to a specified monthly ceiling until the grants ended in March 1941. Altogether,

$972 million was expended for unemployment relief between 1930 and 1940, with $394 million, about 40 per cent, coming from the federal government, 40 to 50 per cent paid by the provinces, and 10 to 20 per cent raised by the municipalities, depending on how much burden was placed on them by their provincial government.

Income Protection by Social Insurance

Social insurance was the second policy innovation designed to relieve the poverty of urban industrial society. The introduction of home relief for poor people who were able to meet the stiff tests of means and contingency adapted the principle of relief to the requirements of an accumulative political economy, but social insurance was a new type of income-maintenance program. It depended for its implementation on the private economic bureaucracies and dependent labour force of an economic society now dedicated to raising material prosperity by private capital accumulation. It also introduced the criterion of contribution to replace means as the test for distributing public welfare benefits.

Under social insurance programs, payments for income maintenance are made conditional on previous contributions paid by the beneficiaries and/or by employers and government on behalf of the beneficiaries. Typically, compulsory social insurance to cover the risks of income loss occasioned by industrial injury, disability, sickness, or temporary unemployment and to provide pensions for the beneficiary's retirement and survivors involves creating an insurance fund administered by an independent governmental commission. Contributions are paid into the fund by employees and/or employers and occasionally by government, and benefits are paid out to meet defined contingencies.

A compulsory insurance program 'with all its associations of security, respectability, and virtuous providence'[12] has a special appeal as an approach to alleviating poverty in a capitalist market society. By imposing a new contractual obligation, social insurance programs interfere with the employer-employee relationship, however, and create a new kind of obligation between the state and the insured worker by making the government a party to the contract. Public insurance programs also differ from private insurance plans because 'the ultimate guarantee of any public scheme is the power of the State to levy taxes,' and divergence from strictly actuarial terms is always possible.[13] Governments can give flexibility to pubic insurance schemes by supplementing contributions, protecting benefits against erosion by inflation, and covering the costs of protecting high-risk categories. As a result, whatever the initial conception, adoption of an insurance program does not succeed in removing the issue of income-maintenance provisions from the arena of politics.

The first public insurance programs in Canada covered industrial injuries. A public workers' compensation scheme was introduced in Germany as early as 1884, but in North America the first attempts at legislation in Maryland (1902) and Montana (1909) were declared unconstitutional. The Quebec Workmen's Compensation Act of 1909 was the first valid legislation in North America.[14] However, the Quebec law did not create an independent commission to administer the program; nor did it make insurance compulsory until 1931. It simply established a procedure for claims and a schedule of payments for disabilities and death benefits.

Between 1910 and 1915, thirty American states passed laws providing for compulsory insurance; and the New York statute was upheld in the Supreme Court in 1917. The 1914 Ontario Workmen's Compensation Act followed from this American campaign. It established a fund built up from levies on industrial employers, set up an independent public board to administer the fund, provided benefits for personal injury or death arising out of employment, and deprived workers of the right to institute civil suits against employers. The Ontario system in turn became the model for the rest of Canada, and by 1920 most provinces had established programs imposing collective liability on employers for work-related deaths and injuries and requiring them to pay for a system of public insurance.[15] Since these first compensation programs were established, coverage has been extended to include more contingencies, such as certain industrial diseases, and more categories of workers; but the basic model and its organizing principle have remained unchanged.

The timing of Canadian legislative action for unemployment insurance also was inspired by an American example; but, where the New Deal legislation set up a joint federal–state scheme with the proceeds of a national payroll tax paid to federally approved state insurance programs, the Canadian Employment and Social Insurance Act of 1935 generally followed the British act of 1911 by providing for a national unemployment insurance commission to administer a fund based on contributions by employees, employers, and the federal government. The main difference between the British and the Canadian plans was the Canadian provision for earnings-related rather than flat-rate benefits. The 1935 act was declared unconstitutional in 1937; but following the Rowell–Sirois Commission's recommendation to make unemployment insurance part of the federal jurisdiction, in 1940 the King government obtained the necessary constitutional amendment for legislation that was substantially the same as the 1935 act.

Coverage under the unemployment insurance plan in 1940 was limited to a narrow class of urban industrial wage-earners. It has been periodically expanded since then, and conditions for eligibility have become much less restrictive. The Unemployment Insurance Act of 1971, the first comprehensive revision of the system since its inception, increased coverage from 80 per cent to 96 per cent of the labour force. The act improved sickness benefits, introduced maternity benefits, reduced qualifying periods, and raised financial benefits to equal two-thirds of the contributor's wage, The federal government also committed itself to pay for the costs of benefits that result from a national unemployment rate over 4 per cent.

The loss of the Liberal government's majority in 1972 was widely blamed in party circles on the high cost of unemployment insurance.[16] As pressure for cutbacks in governmental spending increased, surveys of public opinion showed strong support for tightening up the unemployment insurance system. Amendments passed in 1975, 1977, and 1978 featured stiffer accessibility requirements and less generous benefits; for example, the benefit rate was cut in 1978 from two-thirds to three-fifths of weekly insurable earnings. Indeed, the experience of unemployment insurance in the 1970s illustrates the way in which political decisions aimed at economic stabilization and backed by payments out of current general tax revenue tend to undermine the original concept of a self-supporting public insurance fund; and it is a good example, too, of the misunderstandings that usually accompany such a development.

Income Security in the Welfare State

The experience of economic depression in the 1930s and the acknowledgment of a wider conception of social rights during the Second World War inspired a campaign for 'social security' in all of the industrialized democratic countries. In the welfare state the range of governmental intervention in social policy-making was decisively extended by new measures to moderate or supersede the free play of market forces in the interests of serving the social welfare of all citizens.[17] In particular, the principle of social security in the modern welfare state has meant the deliberate use of public authority to modify the market in three directions: to guarantee individuals and families a minimum income; to enable them to meet certain contingencies such as sickness, old age, and unemployment; and to ensure that all citizens have access to essential social services without regard to status or class.[18] These goals spring from a relatively more lenient view of individual responsibility for earning a living and a relatively more generous view of the state's obligation for those who fail.

The economic argument for implementing a welfare state owed much to Keynesian employment theory. Income-maintenance policies were not only compassionate, they were efficient as 'automatic stabilizers' for preserving consumer demand and countering cyclical fluctuations in production. The economic defence of the welfare state also accepted that economic growth in industrial societies inevitably gives rise to disabilities and insecurities. A society that wants rising standards of living must be ready to compensate those citizens who have borne a relatively heavy burden of the social costs of economic progress.

The emphasis today on 'welfare' and the 'benefits of welfare' often tends to obscure the fundamental fact that for many consumers the services are not essentially benefits or increments at all; they represent partial compensation for disservices, for social costs and social insecurities which are the product of a rapidly changing industrial–urban society. They are part of the price we pay to some people for bearing part of the cost of other people's progress.[19]

The political justification for the welfare state discarded existing class definitions of income maintenance and made income security a right of citizenship. Public relief programs defined a class of paupers who were stigmatized as being outside normal society and grudgingly given a subsistence living. Public insurance concentrated on the income insecurities of the working class and resorted to compulsory contributions to cover the risks of industrial employment. The modern conception of social security rests on the belief that people are entitled to receive certain welfare benefits not because they are destitute and not because they have made contributions entitling them to benefits, but simply because they are citizens of the community and as such are entitled to an adequate standard of welfare. The objective is well expressed in article 25 of the 1948 Universal Declaration of Human Rights: 'Everyone has the right to a standard of living adequate for the health and well-being of himself and his family, including food, clothing, housing, medical care and necessary social services, and the right to security in the event of unemployment, sickness, disability, widowhood, old age or other lack of livelihood in circumstances beyond his control.'

The economic and political justifications for the welfare state shift priorities in applying criteria for the distribution of benefits. Although means and contribution do not disappear as tests, in the welfare state a principle of universality is expressed directly in policies that serve to maintain income by providing transfer payments or social services to all citizens without regard to their current means or their prior contributions. The dominating criterion is a contingency, expressed directly in the definition of need or indirectly in the identification of groups whose members generally are in need of organized welfare.

The theory of the welfare state was not developed by Canadians. The theorists most influential in shaping Canadian policies were British – Keynes with his economic theory and William Beveridge with his 1942 report on social security in Britain. Together they created a framework of policy ideas and instruments within which political and bureaucratic planners could work out a detailed set of policies and programs to meet the goals of full employment and social security in Canada.

Just as the federal government's white paper on income and employment articulated the new set of purposes and instruments for economic policy-making, so the federal government's proposals to the Dominion-Provincial Conference of 1945 (the 'Green Book' proposals) outlined the new set of state commitments and program instruments envisaged in social policy-making. The 'Green Book' in turn owed much to a report prepared by Leonard Marsh in 1943 for the federal government's Advisory Committee on Reconstruction.[20]

Marsh's *Report on Social Security for Canada* and the federal government's formal proposals to the 1945 conference differed in their details, but they were agreed in their commitment to social security and the main direction of policy development. Social welfare programs should be extended to fill the gaps in existing relief and insurance programs by providing comprehensive coverage of the major risks to income security caused by death, disability, sickness, retirement, and unemployment. New welfare programs should be introduced using the principle of universality to provide comprehensive coverage for essential health care and income supplementation for families with dependent children. All welfare programs should be redesigned to minimize reliance on the selective criteria of means and contributions, to concentrate on satisfying the basic needs of all citizens, and to reduce as much as possible the stigma historically attached to receiving welfare.

The failure of the 1945 federal–provincial conference to reach agreement on transferring provincial income tax powers to the federal government eventually caused the federal government to withdraw its social security proposals, but they did not disappear from the post-war politics of the welfare state. Instead, the reconstruction planning of 1943–5 provided a detailed agenda for two decades of social welfare policy development covering extension and integration of social assistance, social insurance, and universal redistributive programs.

Social Assistance

Since the Second World War relief programs have occupied a modest place in welfare planning, but they still play an important role in income support. The 1951 Old Age Assistance Act and the Blind Persons Act renewed with more generous terms the original acts of 1927 and 1937. In 1954 a Disabled Persons Act gave similar assistance to the totally and permanently disabled who were eighteen or older and eligible under a means test for assistance. The Unemployment Assistance Act of 1956 provided for a federal contribution of up to 50 per cent of the unemployment relief payments made by provinces that participated in the program. Conditions for benefits or eligibility would be determined by the provincial governments. Two amendments to the 1956 act passed by the Diefenbaker government in 1958 permitted provincial governments to make claims for federal sharing in provincial allowances paid to certain categories of people who were unemployed and unemployable, and thus extended federal funding of unemployment assistance into support for a modest measure of general public assistance. In 1966 the Canada Assistance Plan brought together within a single federal–provincial shared-cost scheme separate programs of relief for the elderly, blind, disabled, or temporarily unemployed; and it extended federal sharing to include one-half the cost of assistance to needy mothers and widows and certain welfare services not previously covered.[21]

Tables 3.1 and 3.2 show the allocation of governmental transfer payments among major income security programs and the relative growth of governmental expenditures for transfer payments from 1926 to 1982. Since 1965 15 to 18 per cent of public expenditures under federal and provincial income security programs were paid out for direct relief, old-age, and blind persons' allowances and allowances for mothers and disabled persons. In addition, 14 to 17 per cent of federal expenditures on old-age security payments in the late 1960s and 24 to 29 per cent since 1971–2 were distributed according to an income test under the Guaranteed Income Supplement introduced in 1966 and the Spouse's Allowance (added in 1975). As a result, in recent years 22 to 25 per cent of income-security transfer payments have been based on an income or needs test. Given a strong revival of advocacy in the welfare-policy community for basing public assistance on income tests, this percentage may be expected to rise in the future.

TABLE 3.1

Percentage Distribution of Governmental Transfer Payments to Persons through Major Income Security Programs, 1926–82

	Federal government				Provincial governments					Local governments: direct relief	Totals	
Period	Family and youth allowances	Unemployment insurance benefits	Old-age security fund payments	Canada Pension Plan	Direct relief	Old-age and blind persons' allowances	Mothers' and disabled persons' allowances	Workers' compensation benefits	Quebec Pension Plan		Percentages*	Millions of dollars
1926-9					1.5	7.7	26.2	64.6			100.0	65
1930-4					48.1	18.2	6.0	14.1		13.6	100.0	418
1935-9					48.5	24.2	5.8	10.3		11.3	100.1	691
1940-4		0.9			13.6	48.5	10.2	24.3		2.6	100.1	470
1945-9	55.8	9.7			1.8	20.6	3.1	8.3		0.8	100.1	2,107
1950-4	38.4	16.0	23.1		1.7	10.4	2.6	5.9		1.9	100.0	4,334
1955-9	29.5	22.5	31.4		1.2	4.7	3.5	5.1		2.1	100.0	7,307
1960-4	25.7	20.6	34.4		2.0	4.7	3.9	5.1		3.6	100.0	10,286
1965-9	20.6	12.8	42.7	0.3	8.8	2.4	2.9	5.7	0.1	3.7	100.0	14,833
1970-4	13.2	23.1	38.1	3.1	11.7	0.9	0.6	4.6	1.1	3.6	100.0	32,853
1975-9	13.2	25.3	32.1	6.8	10.6	2.1	0.5	5.1	2.4	1.9	100.0	74,908
1980-2	8.1	23.9	33.3	9.6	11.0	2.4	0.6	6.0	3.4	1.8	100.1	73,721

*Totals may not add to 100 per cent because of rounding.

SOURCES: Statistics Canada National Income and Expenditure Accounts: The Annual Estimates 1926–1974 (Ottawa: Information Canada 1976) vol. 1, table 50; National Income and Expenditure Accounts: The Annual Estimates 1968–1982 (Ottawa: Minister of Supply and Services 1983) table 50

TABLE 3.2

Relative Growth of Governmental Expenditures for Transfer Payments to Persons through Major Income Security Programs, 1926–82

Period	Federal expenditures on income security transfer payments as percentage of federal governmental expenditures*	Total governmental expenditures on income-security transfer payments as percentage of total governmental expenditures	Total governmental expenditures on income-security transfer payments as percentage of GNP at market prices
1926–9	0.3	2.1	0.3
1930–4	10.8	8.3	1.9
1935–9	14.3	12.1	2.8
1940–4	1.1	2.4	0.1
1945–9	12.4	10.9	3.0
1950–4	19.5	14.9	3.7
1955–9	23.7	16.5	4.4
1960–4	25.2	14.5	4.7
1965–9	23.6	12.1	4.4
1970–4	27.7	13.4	5.9
1975–9	29.7	14.3	7.0
1980–2	28.7	14.2	7.4

*Federal expenditures include transfers to persons and transfers to provinces to aid provincial and local income-security transfers to persons.
SOURCES: Statistics Canada *National Income and Expenditure Accounts: The Annual Estimates 1926–1974* (Ottawa: Information Canada 1976) vol. 1, tables 1, 43, 50, 53; *National Income and Expenditure Accounts: The Annual Estimates 1968–1982* (Ottawa: Minister of Supply and Services 1983) table 1, 43, 50, 53

Social Insurance

Compared with Germany (1889), Australia (1908), Great Britain (1925), or even the United States (1935), Canada was very late in introducing a program of contributory public pensions. A contributory plan was rejected in the 1920s debate about old-age pensions because of its administrative difficulties in a federal setting.[22] In his 1943 report to the Advisory Committee on Reconstruction, Leonard Marsh pointed out that the trend in industrial countries was away from non-contributory assistance toward contributory pensions, and he recommended such a plan for Canada.[23] The government also appeared to expect a recommendation for a contributory scheme from the 1950 parliamentary joint committee on pensions rather than the universal pension actually proposed. After the passage of the non-contributory scheme in 1951, contributory pensions emerged again as an issue in the 1957 election campaign when John Diefenbaker, the Conservative leader, advocated the u.s. social security system as a model for Canadian policy-making; and by the 1962 and 1963 elections the federal Conservative, Liberal, and New Democratic parties were all committed to the principle of a contributory, earnings-related pension scheme.[24] The Liberal government carried out its campaign promise, and the complementary Canada and Quebec Pension Plans, passed in 1965, now cover about 92 per cent of the labour force with earnings-related pensions for retirement or disability and death benefits for survivors.

Public insurance to cover health services has been a political issue in Canada at least since 1919, when a British Columbia royal commission recommended setting up a provincial program.[25] British Columbia, Alberta, and Saskatchewan all passed statutes creating provincial health insurance programs between 1935 and 1944, but they were either not proclaimed or not implemented. A very strong movement to include national health insurance in the plans for post-war reconstruction culminated in 1945 in a federal 'Green Book' proposal to contribute to the provinces 60 per cent of the costs of provincial insurance coverage of general-practitioner and hospitalization services. That proposal died when the provinces rejected the prerequisite tax agreement at the 1945 Dominion-Provincial Conference.

In the early 1940s voluntary hospital insurance schemes were organized in Manitoba, Ontario, Quebec, British Columbia, and the Maritimes. The failure to get a national health plan led the Saskatchewan government in 1946 to set up a provincial hospital insurance program modelled on the Blue Cross plans operating in other provinces. In 1948 British Columbia, where only 15 per cent of the population were enrolled in Blue Cross, passed a Hospital Insurance Act with benefits similar to those in Saskatchewan. Alberta's hospital insurance program, passed in 1949, gave provincial subsidies to plans administered and financed by municipalities. Finally, at the 1955 federal–provincial conference, the federal government proposed a program of conditional grants for provincial hospital insurance plans. The details were worked out at a series of meetings over the next year, and the federal Hospital Insurance and Diagnostic Services Act was passed in 1957. By 1961 public hospital insurance plans had been set up in all the provinces.

As for medical services, the Saskatchewan government established a comprehensive public insurance scheme in 1961, and Alberta in 1963 and British Columbia and Ontario in 1965 provided for public regulation and subsidization of voluntary insurance. Following another 1965 Liberal campaign promise, a positive recommendation from the Royal Commission on Health Services, and protracted negotiations with provincial governments, in 1966 the Pearson government received parliamentary approval for federal funding of one-half the costs of approved provincial medical-care programs. By 1971 all of the provinces had established approved plans; and except for those in Alberta, British Columbia, and Ontario, which have retained some form of direct contributory provision, they are financed out of general provincial revenues.

Canada's health insurance system is one of the best examples of the realization of the social security ideals of comprehensiveness and universality first articulated in the mid-1940s. Unfortunately, as Malcolm Brown has pointed out, the system may prove to be unstable.[26] Especially under the depressed economic conditions of the 1970s and 1980s, making health care a public responsibility has intensified the issue of costs. Governments have responded by trying to impose economies, which in turn threaten the quality of programs. Established Program Financing exacerbated this problem after 1977 by creating greater discretion and stronger incentives for hospital user charges and private billing by physicians outside the public plan.[27] To counter these apparent threats to the effectiveness of national health insurance, the Canada Health Act was passed unanimously by the House of Commons in April 1984. The act attempts to force provincial governments to curb hospital user charges and extra billing by doctors. Henceforth, provinces that permit user charges or extra billing will lose one dollar of federal health grants for every dollar paid by patients as a result of user charges or extra billing.

Universal Transfers

The first family-allowance programs in Belgium (1930) and France (1932) were organized as public insurance funds into which employers paid contributions according to the number of their employees and out of which benefits were paid to each employee according to the number of his children. Their purpose was to supplement the earnings of industrial workers, converting an individual wage into a family wage.[28] William Beveridge proposed family allowances as an essential part of his plan for social security in Britain, but he recommended financing the allowances out of general revenue. Leonard Marsh included a similar recommendation in his report on social security in Canada. The 1944 Family Allowances Act provided for monthly payments financed out of general revenue ranging from $5 for children under six to $8 for children aged thirteen to sixteen (substantially more modest than Marsh's proposal for a scale of $5 to $12.50 with an average of $7.50 a month). In 1961 Quebec introduced school allowances for young people aged sixteen and seventeen, and these were added to the federal program in 1964.

Following a proposal in the 1970 white paper on income security, the Family Income Security Plan proposed to allocate family allowances according to family size and income with an upper income limit of $10,000 (later amended to $18,000) on eligibility. Although FISP was strongly criticized, there was apparently an all-party agreement to pass it; but the plan died on the order paper in July 1972 when the government failed to get unanimous consent to continue debate. Dependent on the support of the New Democratic Party after the federal election of October 1972, the Liberal minority government dropped its direct attack on the principle of universality. The amendment to the family allowance program passed in 1973 increased benefits from $7.21 to $20 a child and retained the principle of universality in the payment of benefits; but it introduced an indirect income test by making family allowance benefits taxable as part of personal income.[29]

The inclusion of a universal transfer in the design of the Old Age Security Act, 1951, was the result of a recommendation by a Joint Committee of the Senate and House of Commons which was set up during the 1950 session of Parliament.[30] The original legislation provided for a payment of $40 a month to persons aged seventy and over. The amount of the pension has been increased by legislative action a number of times, usually as part of the governing party's electoral promises, and most recently in 1973 when it was raised to $100 a month. Since 1968 pensions have been additionally and automatically adjusted upward to correspond with inflation of the pension index; by April 1984, for example, the basic monthly pension was $266.28. As part of the mid-1960s pension reforms the age of eligibility also was lowered from seventy to sixty-five.

Family allowances and universal pensions ensure that universal transfers are a sizable part of current income-security transfer payments, but their high cost and the concomitant rise in taxes make governments unwilling to take this approach to income maintenance in new programs. Universal redistributive programs are most unlikely to regain the favour they enjoyed in the original planning for Canada's social security system. Instead, the prospect is a gradual erosion of their place in the system and perhaps even a major reform in favour of income-tested transfer programs.

Income Security as Guaranteed Income

By the middle of the 1960s the plan for the implementation of the welfare state that had been devised between 1943 and 1945 was essentially fulfilled. Two decades of incremental reform included the introduction of family allowances and old-age pensions as universal transfers; the reform of public-assistance programs for old, blind, disabled, and unemployed persons; an extension of the coverage of unemployment insurance; and the introduction of hospital insurance. In 1965 and 1966 the belated introduction of a national contributory pension plan, final achievement of a federal–provincial program of medical insurance, and integration of categorical public relief programs signalled the end of a policy-making era. Except for the 1971 reforms to national unemployment insurance that effectively extended its coverage to the entire labour force, the goals that had been set in the middle 1940s were at last achieved. Yet even as the fundamentals of the plan were finally being put in place, vital assumptions on which social security had rested were being severely challenged; and the resulting uncertainty among policy-makers in the social welfare community about the proper direction of policy development is analogous to the ideological divisions in the economic policy community.

Social welfare policy-making during the post-war period rested on two assumptions: a steady growth of material prosperity and a progressive diminution of the problem of poverty in an increasingly affluent society. The rising standard of living of the majority served to strengthen the justification for redistributing part of their larger income to those who were still poor. The diminishing size of the poverty group ensured that compulsory state redistribution could be designed to be both relatively painless for the donors and without stigma for the beneficiaries.

The assumption about the diminution of poverty in advanced industrial societies was the first to be challenged. In his study of the affluent society published in 1958, J.K. Galbraith argued that post-war material prosperity was combining private affluence with public squalor as a result of underspending in the public sector. Galbraith devoted a chapter to the survival of 'grim, degrading, and ineluctable' poverty in the United States, which he attributed to 'the failure to maintain social balance.'[31] In 1962, Michael Harrington provided a more complete analysis of 'the other America,' 'an underdeveloped nation, a culture of poverty' that was culturally, economically, politically, and physically separated from affluent America. This other America was not suffering the privation of Asian peasants or African tribesmen, but 'the mechanism of the misery is similar. They are beyond history, beyond progress, sunk in a paralyzing, maiming routine.'[32]

This new perspective on poverty in the midst of affluence produced a major redefinition of the problem of poverty in Canada. In its fifth annual review in 1968, the Economic Council of Canada argued that 'poverty in Canada is real. Its numbers are not in the thousands, but millions. There is more of it than our society can tolerate, more than our economy can afford, and far more than existing measures and efforts can cope with. Its persistence, at times when the bulk of Canadians enjoy one of the highest standards of living in the world, is a disgrace.'[33] The council defined poverty in relative terms: families and individuals who spent 70 per cent or more of their income on basic necessities (the Canadian average is 50 per cent) were considered to be living in poverty; by that standard, almost 29 per cent of Canadians were living in poverty in 1961.

According to official calculations, poverty in Canada declined to 17 per cent in 1969,[34] but in its 1972 report the Special Senate Committee on Poverty contended that this estimate understated the real extent of poverty in Canada. By allowing for large families and making adjustments for a rising standard of living, the senate committee estimated that about 25 per cent of Canadians were living in poverty in 1969. It concluded that 'the welfare system is increasingly unable to deal with the needs of its clients. It has failed to achieve its humanitarian goals. It deprives its recipients of dignity and provides no incentive or rewards for those who wish to escape from poverty. It has become punitive and demeaning. It is a mess – a social wasteland and an economic morass.'[35]

Liberal planning for social security in the 1940s assumed the existence of an effective policy of economic stabilization. If stabilization policies succeeded in moderating cyclical fluctuations in economic production and employment, then the problem of achieving income security through a system of universal transfers, social insurance, and public assistance would become manageable. In the general theory of the welfare state, Lord Beveridge assumed Lord Keynes. In Canadian planning for the welfare state, the proposals advanced by the federal government in its 1945 'Green Book' assumed the implementation of its white paper on employment and income.

The welfare state's assumption of full employment and the steady growth of material prosperity collapsed in the 1970s. Persistent inflation and high unemployment increased both the demand for organized welfare and its costs. A much larger clientele and soaring costs raised the visibility of welfare programs at the same time that occupational interest groups concentrated on self-interested protection of their members' real incomes and relative statuses against the ravages of inflation. Holding the line on increases in governmental social expenditures and taxes appeared as a popular way of shifting some of the burden of the economic recession.

The rediscovery of poverty in the 1960s implied a need for much higher public expenditures on income security and social services. The immediate policy response was to shift away from universal grants and social insurance back to income tests for the beneficiaries of social welfare programs. In order to protect the universal, comprehensive ethos of social security, the revival of income-tested programs in the 1960s and 1970s was incorporated in proposals for a guaranteed annual income or a negative income tax. In the recommendations of the Special Senate Committee on Poverty, for example, a set of basic allowances was established for individuals and families of varying sizes. For each dollar of earned income the basic entitlement would be reduced by some fixed percentage sufficiently below 100 per cent to preserve a strong work incentive for those who were employable. Thus, if the basic allowance for a family of four was set at $3,500 and the reduction rate at 70 per cent, an income supplement of $2,800 ($3,500 − (0.70 × $1,000) = $2,800) would be paid to a family with an earned income of $1,000, making a total family income of $3,800. The supplement would be reduced to $1,400 for a family having an earned income of $3,000, making that family's total income $4,400; and it would disappear entirely for families earning $5,000 or more. Such a scheme could be designed as a guaranteed annual income plan administered by a social welfare department or as a tax rebate system administered through the department of revenue.[36]

The Senate Committee on Poverty proposed that a single guaranteed annual income should replace the major existing income-maintenance programs. In their review of social security between 1973 and 1975, federal and provincial ministers of welfare, without extensive debate or discussion, rejected such a solution as impractical.[37] Instead the ministers proposed a two-tier system that would provide a relatively high income support for people unable to work or for whom employment could not be found and a lower income supplement for families with low earned incomes. For example, at the higher tier of income support a family of four would be eligible for a basic allowance of $4,800 with a reduction rate of 75 per cent on earned income. At the lower tier a family of four would be eligible for a basic allowance of $1,700, and a one-third reduction rate would be applied to earned income. A test of 'employment availability' would be used to determine eligibility for the higher tier of income support.

This scheme, which would have cost $2 billion, failed to win approval of cabinet, which by 1975 was deeply concerned about expenditure restraints. A revised plan costing about $240 million was approved by cabinet in 1976. Ontario rejected even that cost, however; and other provincial governments, presumably also concerned about limiting their social expenditures, were less than enthusiastic in their support. The social security review process ended without major reform of existing income-maintenance programs.[38]

The magnitude and persistence of poverty in Canada was thoroughly documented in the late 1960s and early 1970s. Proposals for policy reform were made which attempted to break out of the social security paradigm created in the social welfare community in the middle 1940s. Seen in the context of the history of social welfare policy-making, the 1970s proposals failed not only because of their costs but also because they presupposed changes in public policies that were inconsistent with the accepted liberal tradition.

The proposal for a guaranteed annual income did not fit easily into a liberal public philosophy that recognized an ethic of work and individual responsibility for economic welfare. A.W. Johnson has argued that the ministers of welfare saw this aspect of the Canadian public philosophy very clearly during their social security review (and budget ministers, no doubt, would be even more clear-sighted).

It was recognized, at least so it seems to me, that most Canadians believe people should save for the contingencies of life, including retirement, not be guaranteed an income by others. This was reflected in the fact that social insurance is commonly accepted as the first line of defence for retirement, and against temporary income losses. The benefits are seen as a 'right' – are relatively stigma-free, in other words; the apparently regressive payroll tax as a partial mode of financing is seen as savings, and the structuring of benefits on the basis of past income rather than on the basis of current need – with redistributive elements thrown in, of course – is accepted as normal. Social insurance, in short, is based upon a generally accepted community value – the 'work and save' philosophy, if you will – and Ministers were not about to eliminate the plans involved in the name of efficiency or simplicity.[39]

Beginning thus with individual responsibility, the liberal tradition in social welfare policy-making continues to insist on explicit justifications for providing the benefits of public assistance. Significantly, only the original programs for old people and families with children have won acceptance as a basis for universal transfer payments. As the character of the political economy and perceptions of poverty changed, the criteria for justifying benefits were extended from strictly defined means to include contributions and a variety of contingencies. The application of the tests became more generous as new conditions of poverty were recognized and accepted as legitimate grounds for income redistribution policies. In particular, the emergence of urban industrial society in the 1890s and the depression of the 1930s caused deep changes in popular and élite perceptions of the nature of poverty and the requirements for remedial public policy; and the social idealism that pervaded planning for post-war reconstruction in the 1940s envisaged a much greater application of policy and scale of benefits. Yet none of these developments of policy changed the fundamental requirement of public welfare in a liberal society: the beneficiaries must be demonstrated to be 'deserving' of public charity. A simple desire to redistribute income to achieve greater economic equality could never be accepted as a legitimate basis for program design.

The limits of welfare policy reform ultimately must be understood in terms of liberalism's ideal of political equality and its belief in economic inequality. The social security plan of the 1940s can be seen in retrospect as one aspect of the final achievement of liberal political democracy. Full recognition of individual political rights had to include a right to public welfare, not unconditional but justified by strictly defined contingencies, which would ensure the individual's continuing ability to function as a citizen of the community. This belief in political equality in no way affected the liberal belief in material inequalities as economically natural and ethically just.

In the liberal view social security should ensure that all members of the community have their basic physiological needs satisfied and can function as full citizens, but social security cannot and should not aim to restructure economic society in the direction of equality of condition. Given varying individual efforts in the pursuit of individual rewards, unequal outcomes are inevitable; and collective material prosperity depends on defending this inequality. Public welfare assistance can never be allowed to undermine the competitive inequality that is the condition for the growth of material prosperity. Liberal charity is always limited by its theory of economic progress.

4

Economic Regulation

Economic exchange in a liberal political economy operates through private markets. Producers offer goods and services for sale at prices that are expected to cover their costs of production and give them a profit. Consumers spend their limited incomes to buy the goods and services they most prefer. As producers try to maximize their profits and consumers try to maximize their satisfaction, progressive adjustments in the prices at which producers are willing to sell and consumers to buy should result in a balance between supply and demand for each product and service.

The economic argument for relying on private markets to organize economic exchange emphasizes their superior efficiency in allocating scarce factors of production. In his classic statement in *The Wealth of Nations*, Adam Smith showed that economic welfare was enhanced by planning production in response to expressions of preference resulting from self-interested exchanges between individual consumers and producers.[1] Smith's attack on the plethora of regulations that governed the eighteenth-century British economy was inspired by his belief that wealth and welfare for all classes would be increased by relying on the expressed preferences of consumers in markets rather than on governmental intervention to direct the allocation of scarce resources.

In the late nineteenth and early twentieth centuries, particularly in the work of Alfred Marshall and Léon Walras, the efficient distribution of productive resources among alternative uses became the core of modern liberal economics.[2] In this analysis the prices of factor inputs and production outputs are determined by the scarcity of each of the factors, consumer preferences for each of the products, and the technology that combines factors to produce outputs. In a perfectly competitive market firms can maximize their profits by expanding production to the point where the marginal cost of producing an additional unit just equals the revenue from selling it. When supply equals demand in all product markets, all firms will be in this equilibrium position, and total consumer utility will be maximized. There will be no more transfers of factor inputs among alternative uses unless there is some change in preferences, costs, or technology. In the real world such changes occur constantly, but according to the liberal argument private markets provide the best co-ordinating mechanism for making the necessary adjustments on a continuous basis.

The political argument for relying on private markets to organize economic exchange emphasizes their superior potential for achieving individual freedom of choice in economic decision-making. In contrast with governmental policies under which at least some individuals will be forced to participate, in markets all individuals buy or do not buy goods and services or sell or do not sell land, labour, and capital, depending on their own preferences.

According to the liberal argument in the tradition of Locke, Smith, the Mills, Spencer, and Dicey, in the market system one responds – for example, takes a particular job – only if the proffered benefits are attractive, hence only if one chooses to do so. In any authority system one is required to work where assigned and obey any other command regardless of benefit. As some people see it, no more needs to be said to prove men freer in markets than in authority systems.[3]

The virtues of a system of private markets can be realized only if at least four conditions are met. First, competition is essential for markets to work effectively. Both efficiency and liberty in market systems depend on the existence of many buyers and sellers. No buyer or seller is able arbitrarily to manipulate prices in the market, and everyone is able to escape coercion by any one buyer or seller by turning to another. Second, if producers and consumers are to make rational choices, they must have full information about the benefits and costs of their choices. Consumers must know their preferences and the qualities of the goods and services available for purchase. Producers must know the preferences of consumers and the alternative uses to which the factors of land, labour, and capital might be put. Third, all interests potentially affected by a transaction must be included in the market. The operation of markets can generate harmful or beneficial effects for individuals who are not directly involved in the transactions. Unless the market can be extended so that these effects are taken into account, the existence of uncounted costs or uncounted benefits will result in involuntary costs or unexpected windfalls for third parties. In either case the market allocation of resources will not be efficient, and the existence of involuntary costs is clearly not compatible with freedom of economic choice for all. Fourth, the costs of adjustment to changes in the market must be relatively small and approximately equal in their distribution. A market system assumes that factors of production can be transferred fairly easily from one use to another as technology, preferences, and costs change. The instabilities and insecurities of exchange in markets become much less tolerable as prospective costs of adjustment rise for all or become concentrated on a few participants in the market. In such circumstances fear destroys the desire for freedom in economic decision-making.

The liberal theory of political economy assumes that these four conditions of competition, information, inclusiveness, and adjustments are usually met and that the benefits of private markets are much greater than their costs. Where a condition is not met, however, a case exists for governmental intervention to improve efficiency or to protect economic freedom. Public regulations may be designed to protect and promote competition by restructuring the distribution of economic power among the main participants in a private market. Alternatively, public regulations may be designed to replace market decisions by political or administrative decisions that better satisfy the conditions for economic justice.

Economic Regulation to Restructure Economic Power

The efficiency of private markets in allocating scarce economic resources and their effectiveness in protecting individual economic freedom depends on the existence of competition, the availability of information, the inclusion of affected interests, and tolerable adjustment costs. Where one or a few participants in the market possesses greater economic power, they may be able to coerce other buyers or sellers in the market by setting prices more or less arbitrarily, to manipulate outcomes by controlling the flow of information to participants, to exclude affected outsiders from participation in bargaining, or to use their power to protect themselves against the costs of market adjustments.

The transformation of an agricultural into an industrial political economy at the end of the nineteenth century produced a significant realignment of economic power. New forms of business organization, the big corporation and the trade association, emerged to reduce the disequilibria of rapid economic growth for businessmen and to control the distribution of its material benefits and costs according to their interests.[4] Workers and farmers found their bargaining power in markets growing weaker against these new forms of business organization. Workers began to organize trade unions to create a collective bargaining power over their wages and conditions of employment. Farmers expressed their discontent through a succession of social movements, protest demonstrations, and political parties before their bargaining position was fully institutionalized with the formation of national and provincial farmers' associations and marketing boards.

The disruptions that accompanied industrialization thus gave rise to a succession of social movements and political organizations to protest its consequences and redistribute its burdens. The political reaction to these populist demands for state intervention to restructure economic power and restore fair competition produced three types of corrective policies. First, demands for state intervention to preserve competition in markets were met in part by including criminal-law prohibitions on restrictive trade practices. Second, state assistance was extended to members of weak or unorganized interest groups to increase their bargaining resources and enable them to create more competitive organizations. Devices such as legal protection for the right to organize, compulsory membership, and enforcement of group recognition for bargaining purposes were commonly adopted to strengthen disadvantaged groups for market competition. Third, public regulations attempted to limit monopoly power by institutionalizing fair collective bargaining in private markets. Rules for bargaining were prescribed by law and regulation, and public agencies in the form of departments, tribunals, courts, or commissions assumed responsibility to referee the competition and where necessary judge its outcome.

Business Competition

The classic case of state intervention to preserve competitive private markets is found in the legal prohibition of restrictive trade practices. The English common law had evolved a doctrine of unreasonable restraint of trade; but the growth of industrial concentration by mergers, especially in the United States but also in Canada, in such industries as cement, asbestos, steel, textiles, tobacco, brewing, milling, and paper, aroused political concerns about the need to regulate industrial organization in order to maintain competition. To provide at least symbolic reassurance the common-law offence was redefined as a 'conspiracy in restraint of trade' and incorporated into statute law in 1889. Neither that legislation, which made it illegal to restrict 'unduly' production or distribution, nor the Combines Investigation Act (1910), which prohibited monopolies and mergers 'to the detriment or against the interest of the public,' had much effect in slowing the Canadian businessman's flight from competition.[5] Only eight combines cases were prosecuted from 1889 to 1910; five convictions resulted. There was one more unsuccessful prosecution before amendments were made to the law in 1923; between 1923 and 1950, fifteen prosecutions resulted in twelve convictions, an average of less than one each year.[6]

Post-war combines investigations and prosecutions were facilitated by legislative amendments in 1951 and 1960. The 1951 amendments set up a Restrictive Trade Practices Commission to evaluate the findings of investigations carried out by the Department of Justice Combines Investigation Branch and to make recommendations to the minister for or against prosecution. The minister's decision to prosecute would lead in turn to a trial either in a provincial court or in the Exchequer Court (now the Federal Court) of Canada. Under the 1960 amendments it became an indictable offence liable to two years' imprisonment to limit unduly entry into any line of goods production, to prevent or lessen unduly competition in the production or sale of goods or insurance, or to restrain or injure trade or commerce in relation to any article. The 1960 amendments explicitly prohibited mergers or monopolies that would lessen competition against the public interest, and reinforced the 1951 amendment preventing manufacturers and wholesalers from fixing retail prices and markups so long as retailers were providing customary levels of service, not using goods for loss-leader selling, and not advertising goods in a misleading way.

Revision of the anti-combines law has been a continuing item on the federal government's legislative agenda since the early 1970s when it was recognized that stronger prohibitions against restrictive trade practices would facilitate basic structural adjustments in an ailing economy. Following an interim report on competition policy by the Economic Council of Canada, the minister of consumer and corporate affairs introduced a bill in 1971 which essentially adopted most of the council's recommendations and even went beyond some of them. Protests from the business community caused the government to withdraw the original bill and split it into two parts. The first part, which dealt with marketing practices and misleading advertising and extended the act to include services, was introduced in 1973 and passed in 1975. The second part of the revision was designed to remove mergers from criminal law and make them subject to review by a competition board, a body of seven permanent and five associate members that would supersede the Restrictive Trade Practices Commission. Apart from some changes empowering the competition board to review certain types of monopolistic practices, the criminal sanctions against monopolies and monopolistic practices remained in force; and the role of the director of investigation and research in the Combines Investigation Branch continued essentially unchanged under the new title of competition policy advocate.

Part two was introduced in March 1977, and once again business interests voiced strong criticisms at hearings of the House of Commons Standing Committee on Finance, Trade and Economic Affairs. Part two was modified, reintroduced in November 1977, and finally dropped by the Liberal government.[7]

Combines investigations and prosecutions have increased markedly in recent years compared with the low rate that existed before the Second World War. W.T. Stanbury, for example, found that 104 of the 157 combines prosecutions (excluding those involving misleading advertising) from 1889 to 1975–6 occurred between 1960–1 and 1975–6, and 61 of them occurred between 1970–1 and 1975–6.[8] The courts have been more willing to condemn price-fixing agreements, resale price maintenance, and misleading advertising; and, spurred by the advocacy of the Consumers' Association of Canada, the government has been more active in seeking convictions in areas where the public seems to be aware of infractions.

Even with this increased activity, however, the effect of Canadian anti-combines legislation is more symbolic than substantial. Implementation continues to be hampered because the staff and budget of the Combines Investigation Branch (now called the Bureau of Competition Policy) are small, ministers are unwilling to prosecute, courts are reluctant to convict prominent businessmen on criminal charges, and fines levied upon conviction are modest. Business interests have been unrelenting in their opposition to revision in the legislation. Add to that opposition the low priority given by the government to its merger amendments, and the likelihood of significant change in policy becomes very much in doubt. Neither the increased pressure of the Consumers' Association nor the transfer of combines investigation to the new Department of Consumer and Corporate Affairs in 1967 has been sufficient to change very much the balance of interests in this policy subsystem where large corporations and trade associations continue to predominate and where the impact of the law is correspondingly weak and ineffective.

Labour Relations

Labour unrest and industrial conflict in Canada have occurred in three waves.[9] The first began around 1900 and reached its peak with the Winnipeg General Strike of 1919. Conflict lessened during the 1920s and early 1930s, increased in the late 1930s, and reached a second peak in 1946. After lessening again in the late 1940s and remaining relatively low throughout the 1950s, a third wave of industrial conflict occurred in the 1960s and 1970s.

Before the 1940s violence and illegality in Canadian industrial relations were out of all proportion to the numbers of strikes and strikers because of basic inequities in both the common and the statute law.

Both were strongly tilted in favour of employers and were unduly restrictive and punitive towards workers attempting to unionize, bargain collectively and strike to gain their objectives. Understandably, then, the prevailing legal and legislative bias engendered, in the ranks of organized labour, a deep sense of injustice, contempt for the law, and a penchant for illegal and violent action.[10]

Because the common-law doctrine prohibiting restraints of trade was applied to workers' associations, from the 1870s to the 1940s one of the major objectives of workers who were seeking to strengthen their bargaining position was to remove the restrictions placed by the criminal law on their rights to organize unions and express their grievances.[11] Following a printers' strike in Ontario that led to the imprisonment of twenty-four union members on charges of a criminal conspiracy in restraint of trade, the Macdonald government in 1872 passed the Trade Union Act and the Criminal Law Amendment Act, modelled on British legislation of the previous year. This legislation provided protection from conspiracy charges for the members of trade unions registered under the act, but it prohibited workers from using any methods that would have the effect of coercing an employer in order to settle a dispute. Since few unions were registered under the act, most workers continued to be liable to conspiracy charges; and legally picketing an employer during a dispute was virtually impossible.

Amendments to the criminal law in 1876 enacted a long list of prohibitions against workers in their disputes with employers, including resorting to violence, intimidation, persistent or disorderly following, deprivations, and watching and besetting; but peaceful picketing, 'attendance or approach to communicate information,' was excluded from the meaning of watching and besetting. By another amendment in 1877 breach of a contract for service, an offence that had been used by employers to help break strikes, was no longer a crime for workers in registered trade unions.

When the criminal law was codified in 1892, most of the 1872 legislation was incorporated, and the previous limitation to workers in registered trade unions was dropped. The 1876 amendment that allowed peaceful picketing was omitted, however, and as a result picketing continued to be legally restricted until the protection was reinserted in 1934. Finally, in 1939 the Criminal Code was amended to make it an indictable offence for an employer to refuse to hire or to try to dismiss an employee because the worker was a member of a trade union or was trying to organize one. The use of intimidation by means of threats of loss of work or wages to discourage workers from joining unions was also made a criminal offence.

Around the turn of the century, most businessmen accepted that workers had the right to form collective organizations to try to bargain with employers; but employers were assumed to have equal rights to refuse to recognize them, to dismiss workers who went on strike, and to break up unions by hiring strike-breakers.[12] The power wielded by business groups, the priority attached to capital accumulation, and the dominance of laissez-faire ideology can be seen not only in the legal constraints placed on workers' freedoms of association and expression, but also in the persistent reluctance of federal and provincial governments to impose obligations on employers to recognize trade unions and bargain with them. Eventually, the growing membership of workers' organizations began to exert enough political and economic pressure to force governments to institutionalize employer–employee collective bargaining under the regulation of labour relations boards.

The earliest provincial legislation on collective bargaining, such as the Ontario Trades Arbitration Act (1873), the British Columbia and Ontario Trade Disputes Acts (1894), and the Quebec Trades Disputes Act (1901), provided for conciliation boards to be set up with the joint agreement of employers and employees; but employers consistently refused to agree to conciliation because it implied recognition of the unions. In 1907 the federal Industrial Disputes Investigation Act did provide for conciliation at the request of either party, which forced employers to join conciliation proceedings and prevented work stoppages by strike or lock-out until after conciliation. This act was used fairly extensively – 619 applications were made under it and 441 boards established – until 1925, when it was declared beyond the jurisdiction of the federal government. The act was then amended to cover labour relations within the federal jurisdiction only, and over the next few years each province except Prince Edward Island adopted a version of it.

During the 1930s ideas about the desirability of governmental intervention to protect workers' rights changed significantly. Following the example of the National Labour Relations Act in the United States, the provinces finally began to respond to union demands for legislation that would require employers to recognize trade unions and accept collective bargaining. For example, legislation passed in Nova Scotia, Alberta, Saskatchewan, and British Columbia provided for fines or imprisonment for employers refusing to bargain. The usefulness of this legislation was sharply reduced, however, by the absence of any machinery except the courts to enforce its requirements.

At the beginning of the Second World War the federal government used its emergency powers to make the Industrial Disputes Investigation Act applicable to all war industries, but not until 1944 was an order-in-council issued that established the Wartime Labour Relations Board and required employers to recognize and bargain with duly certified unions. In 1948 the Industrial Relations and Disputes Investigation Act extended this wartime policy to the post-war federal jurisdiction, and the provinces passed substantially similar legislation to cover labour relations in their own jurisdictions.

The institutionalization of collective bargaining probably accounts for the low level of illegality and violence in labour relations during the 1950s. The federal and provincial labour relations agencies and procedures proved less successful in moderating the upsurge of strikes in the 1960s and 1970s. The higher rate of industrial conflict is partly explained by such factors as the rapid extension of the labour relations system in the late 1960s and early 1970s to cover employment in the public sector and the highly politicized situation of organized labour in Quebec. However, the main cause of recent conflict appears to be a rate and scope of economic, political, and social change that generated maladjustments and conflicts in industrial relations beyond the control of any legal structure or collective bargaining system, 'no matter how wise, fair, and equitable' it might be.[13]

Marketing Boards

Farmers have long attempted to achieve favourable public policies with regard to their sectoral interests such as land, credit, insurance, marketing, taxes, tariffs, and transportation. In 1910 eight hundred farmers marched on Ottawa to demand lower tariffs and demonstrate support for a reciprocity agreement with the United States. The agrarian platform developed by the Canadian Council of Agriculture between 1916 and 1918 called for sharp reductions in tariffs and freight rates, public ownership of utilities and natural resources, progressive income taxes, proportional representation, and direct democracy. The Progressive Party elected sixty-four farmers to the Canadian House of Commons in 1921, and United Farmers parties governed Alberta (1921–35) and Ontario (1919–23). A national pressure group was not established until the Canadian Chamber of Agriculture, later the Canadian Federation of Agriculture, was formed in 1935.[14] At about the same time compulsory marketing arrangements were established to regulate production, prices, and distribution of agricultural commodities.

The depression of the 1930s wreaked its most severe hardships on the agricultural sector. Farmers' efforts to organize and operate marketing co-operatives in order to counter falling prices and control over-production brought only limited success. Accordingly, the Bennett government in 1934 passed the Natural Products Marketing Act, which proposed to establish a Dominion Marketing Board with extensive powers to regulate marketing in Canadian agricultural commodities. One of the eight federal statutes submitted to the courts by the King government elected in 1935, it was declared outside the federal constitutional jurisdiction by the Supreme Court of Canada in 1936 and by the Judicial Committee of the Privy Council in 1937. Similar legislation passed by the government of British Columbia in 1936 was upheld by the courts however; and the other provinces then followed British Columbia's lead, from Ontario and New Brunswick in 1937 to Quebec in 1956.[15]

Over one hundred commodity boards have been authorized by provincial governments to market grains, hogs, milk, fruit, potatoes and other vegetables, tobacco, poultry, eggs, soybeans, honey, and maple products; sales under marketing boards now account for about three-fifths of farm cash income in Canada. In Ontario, for example, the five-member Farm Products Marketing Board appointed by the government is responsible for administering the Farm Products Marketing Act and co-ordinating the activities of twenty-one commodity boards; and the Milk Commission, established under the 1954 Milk Act, acts as an appeal tribunal and licence-review board and supervises the marketing plans developed by the milk and cream producers' marketing boards, to which the bulk of the commission's marketing powers have been delegated. In addition to provincial legislation, the 1949 Agricultural Products Marketing Act empowers the federal government to delegate marketing powers over interprovincial and export trade in agricultural commodities to provincial marketing boards. About three-quarters of the provincial boards have been granted such authority.

The federal government itself operates one national marketing board that deals directly with producers, and four other marketing boards have been set up to deal with provincial agencies. The Canadian Wheat Board, which annually sets minimum guaranteed prices and quantities for purchase from producers, was established in 1935 to purchase prairie wheat, oats, and barley and sell them in the interprovincial and international markets.[16] The Canadian Dairy Commission (1966) has a mandate to stabilize the dairy industry by producers' subsidies and marketing plans. The commission and the Ontario and Quebec marketing boards agreed on a system of quotas for market-sharing in milk and cream in 1971; and similar agreements with other provincial boards (except for Newfoundland's) were concluded over the following two years. The federal government's Farm Products Marketing Agencies Act (1972) provides for the creation of national marketing boards, with the agreement of commodity producers and provincial boards, when agricultural commodities cannot be marketed effectively under the jurisdiction of provincial boards. The Canadian Egg Marketing Agency (1973), the Canadian Turkey Marketing Agency (1974), and the National Chicken Marketing Agency (1979) operate in conjunction with provincial egg, turkey, and chicken marketing boards rather than dealing directly with producers. Whether there will be similar national agencies for other agricultural commodities such as beef and cattle will depend on the requirements of commodity producers for supply management and on the effectiveness of consumers' associations as a countervailing pressure against agriculture departments and producer groups.[17]

An evaluation of marketing boards made by W.H. Drummond in 1960 is still a valid assessment of the attempt by farmers to gain price and income advantages by substituting collective for individual bargaining.

Prior to the organization of the boards large numbers of small scale producers had to bargain individually with processing firms which were becoming very large and few in number. Moreover, in many cases producers had to depend on selling the larger part of their output to the processors since costs of transporting to larger consuming centres placed early limits on the proportion that could be marketed in the fresh form. In addition the highly perishable nature of many of the commodities made it difficult to postpone sale in the hope of securing a better price. Under these circumstances it is not surprising that producers felt themselves in a relatively weak bargaining position and firmly believed that their selling prices reflected this weakness. Other things being equal, it would seem that the bargaining power of producers must have been strengthened considerably by using negotiating committees. For one thing, adoption of the collective bargaining method meant that processors could no longer play one producer off against another. In the second place one would expect that the bargaining capacity of the producer members of negotiating commodities would be somewhat greater than that of the average individual producer. Producer members of a committee would ordinarily be selected, at least in part, on the basis of their general marketing experience and knowledge and their recognized skill as bargainers. There is little doubt also that producer members of committees have been able to add appreciably to their supply of market information. Collection of statistical data relative to their particular products has undoubtedly placed them in a better position to estimate the significance of price determining factors ... all in all the mere fact that negotiating boards have made for greater equality of bargaining power between the two parties has probably meant some improvement in producer prices.[18]

In its recent review of economic regulation the Economic Council of Canada also concluded that agricultural marketing boards, such as the hog boards, fruit and vegetable boards, and the Canadian Wheat Board, have been successful in establishing countervailing power for farmers and generally have operated in the public interest. The council expressed serious reservations, however, about the new supply-management boards for eggs, chickens, turkeys, tobacco, and milk. These boards have exclusive powers to determine prices and to set production quotas for individual producers. Especially when their powers are supported by import controls, such boards are essentially cartels that contribute to high prices and restricted outputs and fail to achieve a reasonable balance between the interests of producers and consumers.[19]

Economic Regulation to Replace Market Decisions

Market failure often cannot be corrected by restructuring economic power. In industries where economies of scale permit only one or at best a few large firms to operate efficiently, enforcing competition will be difficult and costly. A public policy to promote the organization of countervailing powers will be ineffective in markets where adversely affected interests are not sufficiently intense or concentrated to be organizable. A typical case involves consumers, for whom the costs of organizing their bargaining power against monopolistic or oligopolistic producers greatly exceed their prospective returns in better products and services. Even where competition is effective, consumers may not have the knowledge required to make competent choices. Market competition alone is unlikely to make available sufficient information on the nature and extent of hazardous products; and even if the necessary information were produced, consumers probably would lack the technical expertise to interpret it. Finally, effective market competition can promote efficient resource allocation and individual economic freedom, but its operation may be inimical to the achievement of other social values. In particular, the physical security, political autonomy, or cultural identity of a community may be threatened by the results of market decisions that maximize individual utilities at the expense of collective well-being.

When markets fail and restructuring economic power is not a viable remedy, public regulation that replaces market decisions is an alternative approach. Democratic politics creates a group of political leaders who are responsive to powerful economic interests but who also appeal widely to popular electoral constituencies. Consumers who cannot be organized or who are not competent to protect their own interests in markets may be able to use their influence as voters to secure the displacement or modification of market decisions by political and administrative decisions. Political decisions may also be used to override market decisions that threaten community values (or, more accurately, the values of those who have political power in the community).

An appeal to majoritarian preferences and democratic politics is not normally a sufficient justification to replace market decisions in liberal democracies. The values of economic efficiency and individual liberty continue to have priority, and the political or administrative decisions that replace the market are expected to meet accepted standards.

To be more specific, freedom requires the rule of law and efficiency, the application of practical reason. In a model of decision-making similar to that followed in courts of law, regulatory agencies normally operate relatively independently from the partisan politics of legislatures and political executives. Their procedures are intended to provide for the gathering of intelligence on the direct and indirect impacts of regulatory decisions and to ensure that access is given to all affected interest groups. Regulations are generally based on reasoned decisions defensible by reference to the criteria established by law. Appeals of an agency's decision on procedural grounds involving errors of law and jurisdiction can be made to the courts. Appeals to the minister or the cabinet on the merits of an agency's decision may also be provided for by its enabling statute.

The growth of public regulatory agencies, boards, and commissions that operate independently of government departments has been a major element in the expansion of state activities in the twentieth century. These bodies have come to be used to redistribute income, allocate licences, plan for efficiency in production, make orderly arrangements in marketing, set prices and standards for goods and services, and control expansion, especially in those industries or markets that are subject to natural monopolies, destructive competition, limited information, uncertainties, or externalities.[20]

National Transport

One of the first regulatory agencies established in Canada was the federal Board of Railway Commissioners.[21] During the 1870s and 1880s it became obvious that the federal government would have to regulate destructive competition in areas served by several railways and monopolistic rates in areas served by only one railway. In the United States the Interstate Commerce Commission was established in 1887 to deal with similar problems; but in Canada Macdonald's Conservative government at first opted for controlling rates through the Railway Committee of the Privy Council, a subcommittee of cabinet. The upswing in railway activity that coincided with the election of a Liberal government in 1896 soon revealed the problems inherent in relying on the Railway Committee to develop a rational transportation policy – the members' lack of familiarity with railway problems, their political vulnerability, the lack of continuity in their membership, and the absence of any provision for wide public hearings.

To overcome these problems, the Board of Railway Commissioners was established in 1903 as an independent body whose three members were appointed for ten years and were eligible for reappointment. Its authority combined legislative, judicial, and executive functions over all railways within the federal legislative jurisdiction. In particular, it was empowered to introduce a general system of rate regulation and to create and administer a set of standards for the construction, safety, and operation of railways in Canada.

During the depression of the 1930s the impact of severely declining revenues made it impossible to regulate the railways without reference to other modes of transportation. In 1938 the board was renamed the Board of Transport Commissioners and charged with 'coordinating and harmonizing the operations' of all transport by railways, ships, and aircraft; but it had little success in its new mission. Truck and bus transportation was still excluded from the board's jurisdiction on the grounds that it was largely within the jurisdiction of the provincial governments; and after the Second World War important regulatory activities continued to be carried out by the Air Transport Commission, first established in 1919 and revived in 1945, and the Canadian Maritime Commission, set up in 1947.

The Royal Commission on Transportation was formed in 1959 to inquire into problems of railway transportation and rate structure. The royal commission reported in 1961 that the railways should be freed from the dead hand of restrictive rate regulation and permitted to meet the growing competition of road transportation. The achievement of a consistent national policy required a full commitment to intermodal competition and regulation. The royal commission expressed reservations about the effectiveness of a single regulatory authority to deal with all aspects of transportation; but in the preparation of the National Transportation Act (1967) the minister, J.W. Pickersgill, insisted on 'one unified organ of government divorced from any of these different modes of transport which will look at all of them, compare one with the another, and, when considering the regulation of one, would take account of what is happening in other fields and determine whether we are getting the best value by spending public money on railways, for example, or whether it would be better to scrap a branch of a railway and concentrate on a highway or an air line.'[22]

The Canadian Transport Commission currently performs regulatory and judicial functions with respect to almost all aspects of railway, commercial air, merchant marine, and commodity pipeline services; it is also responsible for studies and research in the economics of Canadian transportation. For example, the authority of the commission over railways includes engineering standards, location of lines, crossings and crossing protection, safety of train operation, operating rules, accident investigation, facilities for service, and abandonment of operations. In air and water transportation the CTC licenses all civil air services and fixes their rates, distributes subsidies to shipbuilders and shipping companies, licenses ships, and regulates tolls for most inland waterways.

None the less, the principle of intermodal regulation expressed in the National Transportation Act has been difficult to realize in practice. Oil and gas pipelines were not included in the CTC's mandate, and part III of the act, which would have made truck transportation subject to federal regulation, has never been implemented.[23] Within the CTC regulatory activities, such as setting rates or granting licences, are allocated to separate modal committees for air transport, commodity pipelines, motor vehicles, railways, and water transport. Each committee has its own staff, and there is relatively little contact between them.[24]

Radio and TV Broadcasting

Radio and television broadcasting in Canada is an industry that has been subjected to considerable public regulation and public ownership in order to protect important national cultural values from the vicissitudes of a private market. Privately owned radio stations began broadcasting in Canada in 1919, and a patchwork of commercial stations developed in the 1920s to serve urban areas. In the opinion of many nationalist critics, commercial radio stations were failing to realize the potential of radio as a medium for public education and national integration. In the absence of public intervention there was no means of ensuring that programming would have any Canadian content or character, and there was a strong likelihood that American commercial networks would come to dominate Canadian radio broadcasting.

These arguments found favour with the Royal Commission on Broadcasting (the Aird Commission). In 1929 the royal commission recommended the establishment of a national network governed by an independent public authority similar to the British Broadcasting Corporation. All local radio stations were to be owned and operated by one national public enterprise, and the core of the system would be seven fifty-kilowatt regional stations. The Aird Commission's recommendations for a government-owned system were taken up in turn by a well-organized public-interest group, the Radio League, and opposed equally vigorously by the Canadian Association of Broadcasters and the Canadian Pacific Railway, now also involved in radio. When the Radio League suggested public ownership of high-power regional stations and private ownership of low-power local stations, the Bennett government quickly adopted the compromise.

Speaking in the House of Commons in May 1932 on the bill to establish the Canadian Radio Broadcasting Commission, the prime minister clearly stated the protectionist goal that could only be achieved by public regulation and ownership; he also defended public ownership of radio broadcasting on the grounds of accessibility.

First of all, this country must be ensured of complete control of broadcasting from Canadian sources, free from foreign interference or influence. Without such control radio broadcasting can never become a great agency for communication of matters of national concern and for the diffusion of national thought and ideals, and without such control it can never be the agency by which national consciousness may be fostered and sustained and national unity still further strengthened ... Secondly, no other scheme than that of public ownership can ensure to the people of this country, without regard to class or place, equal enjoyment of the benefits and pleasures of radio broadcasting. Private ownership must necessarily discriminate between densely and sparsely populated areas.[25]

Difficulties in co-ordinating and administering broadcasting under the new commission led to its reorganization by the King government in 1936 so that general policy-making, including regulation of broadcasting, was assigned to a board of nine governors; responsibility for operations was given to a general manager. The Canadian Broadcasting Corporation continued to enjoy a monopoly on network privileges in Canada.

The leading student of Canadian broadcasting policy has concluded that the system created in the 1930s was not primarily the result of an ideological preoccupation with public ownership, a desire to follow the British model, or a choice for diversity in programming over commercial mass entertainment. If anything, according to Frank Peers, the predominant ideological preference was for private ownership and commercial broadcasting in the American pattern. 'The considerations which decided the political choice in the 1930s were nearly all national in character – bound up with the feeling that Canada should have an identity of its own, that its communications should not be subordinate to or dependent on the enterprise or the industry of another country.'[26]

The Royal Commission on National Development in the Arts, Letters and Sciences (the Massey Commission) argued that cultural development in Canada required much larger public expenditures and that Canadian culture needed governmental protection. The commission's studies of film production, radio broadcasting, and periodical publishing had revealed a formidable 'American invasion,' and some defensive measures to protect Canadian culture against excessive American influences obviously were justified.

There should be no thought of interfering with the liberty of all Canadians to enjoy [American films, radio, and magazines]. They widen the choice of the consumer and provide stimulating competition for the producer. It cannot be denied, however, that a vast and disproportionate amount of material coming from a single alien source may stifle rather than stimulate our own creative effort; and, passively accepted without any standard of comparison, this may weaken critical faculties. We are now spending millions to maintain a national independence which would be nothing but an empty shell without a vigorous and distinctive cultural life.[27]

On the specific question of protecting Canadian broadcasting against excessive American influence, the Massey Commission concluded that in spite of limitations and deficiencies, such as excessive commercialism, the national radio broadcasting system 'does much to promote a knowledge and understanding of Canada as a whole, and of every Canadian region, and therefore aids in the development of a truly Canadian cultural life.'[28] The CBC had 'exceeded all reasonable expectations,' and therefore provided the appropriate policy framework within which to regulate and operate television broadcasting. The royal commission accordingly rejected the pleas of private radio broadcasters to establish a regulatory agency separate from the CBC and to remove restrictions on the formation of private networks. The commission approved the federal government's interim decision in 1949 to give the CBC control of television broadcasting and to establish public production facilities and broadcasting stations as soon as possible. No private television broadcasting stations were to be licensed until the CBC had national programs available, and private stations were to be required to serve as outlets for national programs.

The federal government quickly accepted the Massey Commission's recommendation to apply the 1932 broadcasting policy to television, but over the next two decades the main instruments of policy changed from public enterprise to public regulation. Six publicly owned regional television stations were built in the 1950s, and broadcasting rights in the rest of the country were assigned to private operators.[29] In 1958, however, the Diefenbaker government remedied one long-standing grievance of the private broadcasters by accepting a recommendation of the Royal Commission on Broadcasting (the Fowler Commission) to divide the regulatory and operational functions of the CBC and set up the Board of Broadcast Governors, now the Canadian Radio-Television and Telecommunications Commission (CRTC), as an independent regulatory authority. Another grievance was removed in 1961 when privately owned television stations were given permission to form national networks under the regulatory authority of BBG/CRTC (radio broadcasting networks continued to be a CBC monopoly).

By the early 1970s it was evident that the federal government's goal of using radio and television to promote national consciousness and culture would be realized more by public regulation than by public enterprise. Under CRTC regulation most television stations were required to have an average of 60 per cent Canadian content between 6 a.m. and midnight. Between 6 p.m. and midnight privately owned stations were permitted to broadcast only 50 per cent Canadian content, but the CBC had to maintain a level of 60 per cent. As for radio, about 95 per cent of music broadcasting in Canada was non-Canadian before the CRTC issued Canadian-content regulations. In 1971 a 30 per cent Canadian content quota was imposed on music broadcasting over AM radio, and variable requirements were established for FM radio, ranging from 10 per cent Canadian content for classical-music stations to 30 per cent for country-and-western stations.[30]

The CRTC was set up to ensure that the ownership, control, and programming of broadcasting in Canada would reflect Canadian interests.[31] In the regulation of radio these objectives have been substantially achieved. Music broadcasting on CBC AM radio has about 60 per cent Canadian content, and the Canadian content of privately owned stations is well above the minimum.[32] The regulation of Canadian content also has had important spillover benefits; it has increased the business of Canadian record companies, refined Canadian production skills, and opened job opportunities for Canadian composers and popular singers. Similar benefits can be found in the regulation of Canadian content of television programming, but the achievement of national objectives is much less evident. In spite of CRTC regulation, strong viewer preference (especially in English Canada) for American comedy, drama, and variety shows, the high costs of domestic television production, and the competition that results from easy access to American stations by cable all ensure that television in Canada continued to be dominated by American programming.

The CRTC recognizes that Canadian content regulations in their present form do not work, for there are no requirements or incentives for private broadcasters to produce quality programming that would attract Canadian viewers. On the contrary, much of what passes for Canadian content – outside of news, public affairs and sports programs – encourages Canadians to seek something more substantial of foreign origin. Canada has failed, so far, in its efforts to mesh the profit-seeking motives of the private sector in broadcasting with the country's social and cultural objectives.[33]

Foreign Investment

Another threat to national values from the unrestricted operations of private markets is presented by American investment in Canada. Although Canada's dependence on the United States as its major trading partner and its main external source of development capital had been growing steadily over several decades, the rapid economic growth of the 1950s was stimulated primarily by a northward expansion of American business. That expansion resulted in a fundamental modification of Canada's economic structure from an east–west to a north–south integration, and Canada became a virtual economic province of the United States.

The political problem created by excessive dependence on American capital was given its first significant attention in the 1957 report of the Royal Commission on Canada's Economic Prospects.

At the root of Canadian concern about foreign investment is undoubtedly a basic, traditional sense of insecurity vis-à-vis our friendly, albeit our much larger and more powerful neighbour, the United States. There is concern that as the position of American capital in the dynamic resource and manufacturing sectors becomes ever more dominant, our economy will inevitably become more and more integrated with that of the United States. Behind this is the fear that continuing integration might lead to economic domination by the United States and eventually to the loss of our political independence.[34]

In the 1960s public opinion became less favourable toward reliance on American capital for Canadian economic development.[35] Much of the academic literature severely criticized the Canadian government for its failure to be more aggressively nationalistic in its economic policies vis-à-vis the United States;[36] and the reports of two committees of inquiry – the Watkins report on foreign ownership and the structure of Canadian industry (1968) and the Gray report on direct investment in Canada (1972) – recommended the introduction of governmental controls over foreign investment.[37]

As one approach to controlling foreign investment, legislation to require Canadian directors and shareholders has been gradually extended. In 1957 the Insurance Companies Act was amended to require that a majority of company directors be Canadian citizens resident in Canada. In 1964 insurance, loan, and trust companies with federal charters were required to appoint 75 per cent Canadian directors; in 1967 this rule was extended to banks; and the provinces of Ontario, Manitoba, and Alberta have applied it to provincially chartered loan and trust companies. Changes in the business corporations acts of Ontario (1972), British Columbia (1973), and Saskatchewan (1977) require corporations chartered by those provinces to have a majority of directors who are Canadian residents; and section 100(3) of the Canadian Business Corporations Act, passed in 1975, requires that a majority of the directors of all federally chartered corporations be resident Canadians.

With respect to shareholding in key sectors, the Broadcasting Act of 1958 limited foreign ownership in television broadcasting to 25 per cent, extended the rule to cover radio and cable systems in 1964, and then reduced the limit to 20 per cent of the voting shares in 1968. Foreign ownership in life insurance, loan, and trust companies has been limited since 1964 to 25 per cent of total shares, or the existing proportion where it exceeded 25 per cent, with a 10 per cent maximum for any shareholder; and the same rule has applied to banks since the 1967 revision of the Bank Act.

As another approach, provision has been made to screen certain categories of foreign investment. The corporate guidelines for foreign-owned firms issued by the minister of trade and commerce in 1966 failed to have much effect because there was no provision for enforcement other than moral suasion. In response to criticism in the Gray report on direct investment, the Foreign Investment Review Agency (FIRA) was set up in 1974 to review foreign takeovers of Canadian businesses, the establishment of new foreign-owned businesses, and the expansion of existing foreign firms into unrelated fields. According to the criterion established in the Foreign Investment Review Act, reviewable foreign investments should provide 'significant benefit' to Canada, such as more jobs, higher technology, or improved trade. In reviewing the foreign takeover of a Canadian business, for example (a procedure which was only activated for Canadian firms with gross assets of at least $250,000 or sales of $3 million), FIRA studied the benefits and costs of the takeover in terms of the 'significant benefit' criterion, bargained with firms to improve benefits accruing to Canada from the takeover, and made recommendations through the minister of regional industrial expansion to the cabinet, which had the final power to approve or reject the takeover.

The regulatory activities of FIRA produced quite different responses, depending on the value priorities of its critics. On the one hand, advocates of stronger economic nationalism in Canada argued that FIRA was too favourable in its reviews of foreign investment and that its jurisdiction is too limited to achieve its purpose. The act exempted from regulation the expansion of established foreign firms in their existing fields of business, and such non-reviewable foreign investment was 80 to 95 per cent of the total. Within the reviewable areas of foreign investment, FIRA each year recommended the approval of 85 to 95 per cent of the applications that were forwarded to cabinet for final decision.

On the other hand, advocates of an unrestricted market for capital who want to facilitate the flow of foreign investment into Canada were hostile to any attempts by FIRA to formulate a view of what investments were in the public interest and to impose corresponding limitations on exchange in the private market. These critics included Canadian and American businessmen whose capital operations were directly affected by the review process or who simply opposed in principle any government intervention in private investment decisions, the American government, and most of the provincial premiers, who saw unrestricted foreign investment as an instrument for economic recovery. In December 1984 the newly elected Conservative government introduced legislation to replace FIRA with a new agency, Investment Canada, which will have significantly reduced powers to review foreign takeovers and new foreign investment.[38]

Environmental Protection

Environmental protection is probably the most important contemporary instance of public regulation justified by the failure of private markets to take account of full social costs. The adverse consequences of private and public economic decisions based on market considerations that take no account of the impact on the natural environment have become increasingly well understood in recent years. The problems may be broadly categorized as depletion of renewable and non-renewable resources, pollution of the natural environment resulting from the disposal of waste effluents or chemical manipulation of natural systems to increase their yields, and environmental degradation caused by the introduction of synthetic substances such as plastics or DDT into natural systems.[39]

Around 1900 a conservation campaign that was much influenced by its American counterpart emerged in Canada to press for scientific management of forest resources.[40] The Laurier government sponsored a Canadian forestry convention in 1906 and established the Canadian Commission of Conservation, chaired by Clifford Sifton, in 1909, but this early conservation movement failed to have much effect on policy. In Ontario, for example, 'it raised feeling but did not rouse passion and had more impact upon rhetoric than policy ... it was the lumberman's rather than the professional forester's view of conservation that triumphed, and would for a long time to come.'[41] The Commission of Conservation operated mainly as a research and educational organization; when an attempt was made in 1921 to extend its jurisdiction to executive functions, the commission was dissolved.

During the 1960s a second campaign was begun to inject a concern for conservation into economic policy-making, and, like its predecessor, the campaign was strongly influenced by a similar movement in the United States. Perhaps the revival of conservation as a contemporary issue in Canada can be traced to the 1961 Resources for Tomorrow Conference.[42] As a result of the recommendations of that conference, a Canadian council of resource and environment ministers was established to act as a forum for federal–provincial discussions and co-ordination in the field of renewable resources and to undertake programs of public information.[43]

As the political demand grew for economic policies to take account of the need for environmental conservation, governments responded with a variety of organizational changes and substantive regulations. Legislation such as the 1970 Canada Water Act and the 1971 Clean Air Act endowed the federal government with new regulatory powers over the quality of the environment; provincial governments passed similar legislation. In 1970 the federal government created the Department of the Environment to administer all federal programs relating to the environment and renewable resources. The expansion of provincial departments of natural resources and the establishment of interdepartmental co-ordinating committees, semi-independent environmental commissions, and environmental advisory councils provide further evidence of the attempt to give institutional recognition to the growing importance of conservation.[44]

One important part of contemporary environmental policy development has been the introduction of environmental-impact assessment procedures, which require explicit consideration of the consequences of proposed public and private interventions into natural and human environments.[45] Here Canadian governments have followed the example set by the 1970 United States National Environmental Policy Act, which sets out environmental goals for federal agencies, directs all agencies to include environmental impact statements with policy recommendations, and authorizes the Council on Environmental Quality to administer the act.

Canada's national 'environmental assessment and review process' was established by a federal cabinet directive in December 1973 and placed under the jurisdiction of the Environmental Assessment and Review Office in the Department of the Environment. Using assessment panels and screening committees, federal departments and agencies are required to take account of environmental impacts in the design and implementation of all programs that involve federal administration, funding, or property. Assessments of potential environmental effects must be submitted for all major projects that will have a significant effect on the environment, and the results of the assessments and reviews must be incorporated in redesigning and executing programs.

In Canada much of the jurisdiction over environmental protection belongs to provincial governments, and by 1976 each province had adopted some type of procedure for environmental-impact assessment. Like the federal government, the provincial governments have preferred to introduce environmental assessment by administrative direction under existing statutes rather than by passing new legislation. Unfortunately, as Reg Lang observes, 'The Canadian approach is far less visible and considerably less accessible to the public, either directly through governmental processes or through the courts.'[46] An exception is Ontario's Environmental Assessment Act. Passed by the legislative assembly in 1975, it requires environmental assessments for projects of provincial agencies, municipal governments, and private enterprises. The sections covering municipal governments were not activated until 1980, however; and those covering private enterprises have not yet been proclaimed. Moreover, there are reservations about the effectiveness of the act. In the first five years of the act's existence, the Ministry of the Environment received only 68 formal assessment submissions compared with 206 projects that were exempted, and only three public hearings were held under the act.[47]

Environmental impact assessment is one policy approach to the problem of forcing some consideration of the environmental costs which are otherwise ignored in market transactions, but so far it exhibits some serious limitations. Assessment is carried out with minimal public participation; operating agencies have considerable autonomy in determining whether to submit projects for assessment; environmental agencies are weakly placed to serve as monitors or watch-dogs; many governmental projects, particularly the largest ones with the greatest impacts, are exempted from review; the private sector is scarcely touched by assessment programs; and the focus on discrete decisions overlooks the environmental damage that arises from the cumulative effects of many activities impossible to specify and assess in advance.

Former Prime Minister Pierre Trudeau forecast the coming of a 'conserver society'; and in a 1977 report the Science Council of Canada made an admirable attempt to analyse in a Canadian context the conceptual underpinnings of an alternative path of technological–economic development that would incorporate awareness and acceptance of ecological constraints 'from the limited carrying capacity of the biosphere and the finiteness of certain resources to limits set by competing claims on capital expenditures.'[48] According to the council, our growing problems of environmental conservation cannot be resolved without a basic change in our attitude toward non-human nature from one of unlimited exploitation to one of stewardship. 'We have to guard the natural environment against threats from ourselves. We have to be aware that cause and ultimate effect may be separated by decades, and we have to learn to recognize as early as possible signs of damage. Our concept of nature must change from seeing it as a shopping basket of unrelated goods that we can consume at will, to a set of living eco-systems from which we may take only that part that does not threaten the continued viability of the whole.'[49] If the need for stewardship were widely accepted and deeply entrenched, the costs of environmental depletion, pollution, and intrusion would be taken into account in market calculations. As yet, however, such an attitude is not sufficiently pervasive to act as an effective restraining influence on exchanges in private markets. In addition, the costs of conservation are usually immediate and concentrated while its benefits are prospective and diffused. In such circumstances, where private markets almost inevitably underestimate or even ignore altogether the benefits of conservation, public regulation to redirect market decisions has the potential to serve the double functions of protecting the environment for the short term and educating citizens in stewardship for the long term.

Private Markets and Public Regulation

In 1870 there were 25 federal and 125 provincial regulatory statutes. By 1978 there were 140 federal and 1,608 provincial regulatory statutes. One-half of the federal regulatory statutes were passed in four decades: 1900–19, 1930–9, and 1970–8. The introduction of provincial regulatory statutes was more distributed, as table 4.1 shows. Provincial governments passed an average of seven regulatory statutes a year from 1870 to 1909, fourteen regulatory statutes a year from 1910 to 1949, and twenty-three regulatory statutes a year from 1950 to 1978. About three-tenths of Canada's gross domestic product is now subject to some form of direct regulation.[50]

The growth of regulation in recent years, particularly the increases of the 1970s, resulted in a rising concern about the quality of public administration in regulatory policy-making and the burden it places on the private sector. The federal and provincial governments have undertaken a number of studies of the work of regulatory agencies, and these studies come to essentially the same conclusion: economic efficiency would be improved substantially by a much less restrictive regulatory regime.

The various studies of the regulatory process are very largely in agreement as to what should be done: *ex ante* review of proposed new regulations using cost-benefit analysis; improved, earlier and more extensive consultation; creation of a regulatory agenda; periodic *ex post* review of existing regulatory programs; the replacement of appeals to cabinet by government policy directives; clearer regulatory mandates in statutes and regulations; closer scrutiny of proposed new regulations and evaluation of existing ones by the legislature; and improved access and funding of 'public interest groups'.[51]

TABLE 4.1

Growth of Federal and Provincial Regulatory Statutes, 1870–1978

Period	Federal			Provincial		
	Number	Percentage	Cumulative percentage*	Number	Percentage	Cumulative percentage*
Before 1870	25	17.9	17.9	125	7.8	7.8
1870–9	9	6.4	24.3	59	3.7	11.5
1880–9	5	3.6	27.9	66	4.1	15.6
1890–9	2	1.4	29.3	71	4.4	20.0
1900–9	13	9.3	38.6	83	5.2	25.2
1910–19	16	11.4	50.0	133	8.3	33.5
1920–9	7	5.0	55.0	112	7.0	40.5
1930–9	16	11.4	66.4	154	9.6	50.1
1940–9	3	2.1	68.5	148	9.2	59.3
1950–9	12	8.6	77.1	177	11.0	70.3
1960–9	7	5.0	82.1	218	13.6	83.9
1970–8	25	17.9	100.0	262	16.3	100.2

*Cumulative percentages may not add to 100 per cent because of rounding.

SOURCES: Economic Council of Canada *Responsible Regulation* (Ottawa: Minister of Supply and Services 1979) 15

In spite of much political rhetoric and several policy studies, Canadian governments have done almost nothing to try to institutionalize regulatory reform.[52] In part this reflects the political effectiveness of those industries that are directly regulated and that benefit from its restrictions on competition. According to Michael J. Trebilcock, three myths about public regulation of economic activity need to be dispelled. First, our economy is not largely unregulated; in fact, very little of it is exempt from some type of regulation. Second, most regulation is not limited to technical questions that can be left to experts for answers; in fact, regulatory decisions impinge on issues of considerable social and political importance. Third, most major forms of regulation are not forced on unwilling producers by hostile non-producer groups. 'The fact is that the sheltered life of a regulated protectorate is likely to be more comfortable than life in a vigorously competitive marketplace.'[53]

The caution with which governments approach regulatory reform may also be attributed to their recognition of the permanent place that public regulation of private markets has won in the principles of modern liberal political economy. We can criticize the political effectiveness of regulators and regulatees in combining to protect their interests as well as the impediments to the smooth functioning and adjustment of private markets which result from wasteful, inept, and outmoded regulatory practices. Yet even a highly selective review of the historical development of regulatory policy-making with respect to restrictive trade practices, labour relations, agricultural marketing, national transportation, broadcasting, foreign investment, and environmental protection plainly reveals the essential contribution that public regulation has made to ensuring the continuing effectiveness and general legitimacy of private markets.

As Gilles Paquet has argued, from the heyday of laissez-faire to the present, regulation has provided 'a continuous and connected reaction to the failings of the market' and 'evolved to permit change without too much disruption and intolerable organizational instability.'

Because of the fact that these different forms of regulation were often brought about at different times and on a piecemeal basis as a result of circumstances and/or political bureaucratic expediency, and because of the rigidity built into the earlier regulation systems, the permanence of certain practices has demonstrably been detrimental to the good functioning of human economies. However, on balance, the workability of the human economies of the advanced industrial countries has been smoothed by regulation and the most recent period provides ample evidence of the role of regulation in steering the human economy between 'le probable et le souhaitable'.[54]

In the liberal political economy expounded by Adam Smith and his intellectual heirs, private markets dominate the social processes for allocating goods and services. Markets are honoured because they respect private property and individual preferences and reward economic efficiency and individual enterprise.

Markets can also fail. The beginning of industrialization set off recurring problems of socio-economic adjustment and organizational stability. The maturing of industrialization revealed persistent problems of monopoly power, consumer ignorance, and uncounted social costs.

Contrary to the tenets of liberal ideology, the industrializing experience demonstrated that neither efficiency nor liberty was necessarily the outcome of exchange in private markets. Given these anomalies between theory and experience, private markets could remain a fundamental of liberal political ideals only because their failures were alleviated, if not cured, by generous doses of public regulation. The simplicity of laissez-faire private markets has disappeared forever into the tensions, ambiguities, inconsistencies, and recriminations of publicly regulated markets.

5

Criminal Justice

Safety needs are basic in the hierarchy of human needs. In most definitions of the functions of governments, the protection of people's lives and property, the preservation of domestic social and political stability, and protection from external aggression are given the highest priority.

Not only is the maintenance of public order the most salient of governmental functions, it typically involves the full coercive power of the state. The principles guiding economic progress assign great importance to individual efforts and private organizations, thereby forcing governments to depend mainly on selective material inducements to manipulate individual economic behaviour; but the accepted principles that guide policies for public order all assign the leading role in conflict resolution to the state, clearly relegating individual efforts and private organizations to subordinate, supportive activities.

Just as the liberal political economy ascribes economic progress to individual effort and competition, the liberal conception of domestic public order focuses on the deviance of individuals.[1] The central problems of domestic public order are understood to be the control of individuals whose behaviour threatens the personal safety or property rights of others and the settlement of private disputes that arise from the pursuit of individual material interests. The simple liberal approach is to resolve these problems in a political community that maintains two sets of rules: the criminal law defines and outlaws deviant individual behaviour, and the civil law provides procedures for arbitrating private individual disputes. Then, to the extent necessary, deviation from the rules is controlled by overpowering isolated individuals with a physical force that is backed by the whole community.

The rule of law, criminal and civil, is the essence of justice in a liberal conception of social order. As it is customarily formulated in the Anglo-American tradition of political thought – by Dicey, for example – the rule of law binds governors to act within the limits established by two basic propositions: no person is punishable unless the law has been broken and is proved to have been broken in the ordinary courts of the land; and no person is above the law.[2]

If the rule of law is an effective element of the constitution, then obedience to the law duly established by legislature and courts is the duty of every citizen. A citizen's duty under the rule of law was clearly stated by John Beverley Robinson, then chief justice of Upper Canada, when he sentenced Samuel Lount and Peter Matthews to be hanged for their part in the 1837 rebellion. Robinson told the condemned men that it was their 'bounden duty' to support the constitution, and he portrayed the relation of liberty to authority in terms that convey the essence of the legalist principle: 'You were not the tenants of rigorous and exacting landlords; you were not burthened with taxes for the State, further than the payment perhaps of a few shillings in the year, to support the common expenses of the District in which you lived ... You lived in a country where every man who obeys the laws is secure in the protection of life, liberty, and property; under a form of government, which has been the admiration of the world for ages.'[3]

The rule of law assumes the existence of a community with a clear consensus on its basic values. In contrast with the pluralist position, which represents laws as the translation of specific group interests into public policies and views legal justice as mediation of competing interests,[4] the legalist principle understands laws as reflecting 'basically, the accepted moral standards of the day'[5] and legal justice as applying to particular cases universal rules derived from moral standards. Law will be narrower in its application than morality, which includes rules of social conduct imposed by public opinion and personal conscience, but law and morality should be consistent and reinforce each other as much as possible.

The rule of law also assumes the existence of political institutions capable of formulating rules to prohibit behaviour that is offensive to the community's shared values. Although other institutional arrangements are conceivable, the liberal position relies on a representative legislature authorized to make laws that incorporate the basic values of the community and hence obtain widespread legitimacy among its citizens. J.S. Mill expressed the liberal argument for representative government: 'Each is the only safe guardian of his own rights and interests,' and general well-being and a 'higher form of national character' are both promoted by political participation. However, 'since all cannot, in a community exceeding a single small town, participate personally in any but some very minor portions of the public business, it follows that the ideal type of a perfect government must be representative.'[6] To this add J.F. Stephen's assertion that with a representative legislature making the laws it is unnecessary to distinguish between the morality of the legislators and that of the people for whom the legislation is intended; the two can be assumed to coincide.[7]

Reliance on the rule of law as the foundation of public order requires a specialized administrative function to implement the law. A police force is needed to apprehend offenders and bring charges against them. A judiciary is needed to try accused offenders and sentence those who are convicted. Penal institutions are needed to carry out the sentences. Justice ordinarily requires that the enforcement of law be independent of the law-making, representative legislature and also that the administrative agencies responsible for arrest, trial, and punishment of offenders be independent of one another.

The punishments imposed on offenders depend upon prevailing assumptions about the motivations of offenders, the feelings of victims, and the security needs of the community. Convicted offenders may be punished to deter them and other potential offenders from committing crimes in the future; to demonstrate the repugnance of law-abiding citizens at the crime committed and to satisfy the desires of victims for vengeance; or to correct the social or personal conditions that resulted in criminal behaviour. These three justifications for punishment reflect different views of why people commit crimes and what public policy can do to prevent or control them. Each type of justification finds its place in the thinking about criminal justice at successive historical stages of Canadian policy development.

Criminal Justice as Deterrence

According to the supporters of the deterrence theory, the purpose of punishment is to inhibit offenders from repeating their offences in the future (individual deterrence) or to deter potential criminals from committing offences (general deterrence). The argument for deterrence assumes that the potential offender is a rational individual capable of balancing the benefits and costs of his actions in terms of personal pleasure and pain; the choice of law-abiding behaviour can be promoted by the existence of known costs for breaking the law. Increasing the probable cost of breaking the law by more effective threats of apprehension and punishment is expected to deter potential criminals. They will see the efficient apprehension, conviction, and punishment of others who engage in criminal behaviour, and will conclude that the probable costs of criminal behaviour outweigh the likely benefits.

As a justification for punishment, the deterrence theory is associated with liberal political philosophers. Locke advanced deterrence as one of the two grounds for punishment (the other was reparation) in his *Second Treatise on Civil Government*, but the classic statement is Beccaria's essay *On Crimes and Punishments*, published in 1764, attacking the barbarities and arbitrariness of European criminal justice in the eighteenth century.[8] The leading exposition of the deterrence principle in late eighteenth century English political thought was Jeremy Bentham's *Introduction to the Principles of Morals and Legislation*.

In English criminal justice, the end of the eighteenth century was an age of deterrence.[9] The existence of voluntary constabularies made detection and apprehension of offenders uncertain, and jails were institutions for short-term detention before a speedy trial followed, on conviction, by corporal or capital punishment. The law provided for severe punishments; over 200 crimes were capital offences, and lashing, branding, the pillory, stocks, and transportation were commonly imposed. As Bentham noted, 'Whenever then the value of punishment falls short, either in point of *certainty* or of *proximity*, of that of the profit of the offence, it must receive a proportionable addition in point of *magnitude*.'[10]

The English criminal law was introduced into Canada as a consequence of settlement in Nova Scotia (1758) and conquest in Canada (1763).[11] Its brutality was much reduced in a predominantly rural society that had no serious crime problem. A study of the records of the Court of Quarter Sessions for London District between 1800 and 1809 found fifty-one convictions, including twenty for assault, eleven for default as jurors, eight for profane swearing, and three for sabbath-breaking. Sentencing usually took the form of a fine, on average about five shillings. There was one sentence of twenty lashes in a conviction for petty larceny; and William Rice, who was convicted of pushing over the district stocks, was put in them for half an hour.[12]

In urban colonial society the application of the English criminal law was more severe. The records of the Court of King's Bench in Montreal show that 293 offenders were sentenced to be hanged between 1812 and 1840, including 105 for treason, eleven for murder, fifty-one for burglary, twenty-five for larceny, and fifty-nine for horse, cattle, or sheep stealing. Among the fifty-four persons actually hanged were seven for murder, twelve for treason, twelve for burglary, thirteen for horse, cattle, or sheep stealing, two each for shoplifting, larceny, sacrilege, and rape, and one each for robbery and forgery.[13]

By the middle of the nineteenth century heavy reliance on deterrence as a justification for punishment was ending in Canada. The Consolidated Statutes of Canada in 1859 still provided the death penalty for nine crimes, but with few exceptions after 1840 execution was carried out only for murder and treason. For example, the Court of King's Bench records in Montreal show that twenty-two persons were sentenced to be hanged from 1840 to 1886, including eighteen for murder, one for larceny, one for housebreaking, and two for felony; ten were actually hanged, all for murder.

A necessary condition for the reduction in the use of capital and corporal punishment was the increasing likelihood of detection and apprehension of offenders that accompanied the establishment and improvement of police forces. Voluntary constabularies were replaced by full-time police forces in Toronto in 1835, in Montreal in 1838, and in Quebec City in 1843. Voluntary constabularies survived in towns and rural areas into the twentieth century, but they were gradually replaced by the Royal Canadian Mounted Police or by provincial police forces. In Ontario, for example, the first salaried provincial constable was appointed in 1875 to aid rural constables; the Ontario Provincial Police was formally established as a force of forty-nine officers in 1909; and the force grew from forty-nine in 1920 to 401 in 1940, by which time the OPP had become the exclusive law enforcement agency for rural Ontario.[14]

Deterrence remained an objective of the post-war criminal-justice system. Policies were implemented to improve policing by means of larger forces, more professional training, more efficient communications, and better organization. Deterrence is still a consideration in law-making and sentencing. For example, advocates of capital punishment often base their argument on its alleged deterrent effect; and the heavy sentences attached to offences under the Narcotics Control Act (1961) were evidently meant to deter potential offenders. But the view usually reflected in modern policy is that expressed by the Canadian Committee on Corrections:

It is most difficult to ascertain the extent of the deterrent effect of legal prohibition, arrest, trial, conviction and sentence, and under what condition it operates. It has been suggested that the likelihood of detection, arrest and conviction is the best deterrent and that the nature of the sentence that follows conviction is of less importance. For the established member of the community, the risk of public trial is no doubt also a deterrent. However, the Committee is of the opinion that risk of punishment is a deterrent in certain areas of behaviour where the offender is motivated by rational considerations. The Committee is further of the opinion that removal of profit from crimes that involve financial gain would also serve as a powerful deterrent if made effective in practice.[15]

Criminal Justice as Retribution

Punishment of criminals may be justified as a form of retribution, the intentional infliction of a degree of suffering on an offender that is scaled roughly to match the quantity and quality of the victim's injury and the harm done to society. Breaking the law is assumed to evoke a sense of injustice that demands revenge for the victim, denunciation of the offender, and reassurance to the law-abiding. Consider the argument of James Fitzjames Stephen, an influential member of the 1879 British Criminal Law Commission whose work was to provide the model for the Criminal Code of Canada.

Whatever may be the nature or extent of the differences which exist as to the nature of morals, no one in this country regards murder, rape, arson, robbery, theft, or the like, with any feeling but detestation. I do not think it admits of any doubt that law and morals powerfully support and greatly intensify each other in this matter. Everything which is regarded as enhancing the moral guilt of a particular offence is recognized as a reason for increasing the severity of the punishment awarded to it. On the other hand, the sentence of the law is to the moral sentiment of the public in relation to any offence what a seal is to hot wax. It converts into a permanent final judgement what might otherwise be a transient sentiment. The mere general suspicion or knowledge that a man has done something dishonest may never be brought to a point, and the disapprobation excited by it may in time pass away, but the fact that he has been convicted and punished as a thief stamps a mark upon him for life. In short, the infliction of punishment by law gives definite expression and a solemn ratification and justification to the hatred which is excited by the commission of the offence, and which constitutes the moral or popular as distinguished from the conscientious sanction of that part of morality which is also sanctioned by the criminal law. The criminal law thus proceeds upon the principle that it is morally right to hate criminals, and it confirms and justifies that sentiment by inflicting upon criminals punishments which express it.[16]

Punishment serves as a symbolic response to public indignation and resentment toward those who break the laws of the community and to public uneasiness and insecurity about the fragility of the social order. Paul Weiler has described the criminal trial as a morality play with appropriate robes, ritual, and priestly terminology.

The source of [the trial's] dramatic interest is the presence in the wings of the prison sentence, the typical means through which the Canadian community now expresses 'its hatred, fear, or contempt for the convict.' When this process is put into operation, when we convict and sentence an offender to jail, we reinforce these basic standards of morality, drive home again to the waiting public the lesson that 'crime does not pay.' At the same time we try to repair the wound in the social fabric by reassuring the citizenry that its officials are able to do something about the crime problem, and so their own willingness to abide by the law continues to be a good bet.[17]

When criminal justice is seen as retribution, the moral foundation of the law not only justifies the punishment of offenders, but also provides a standard for the scale of punishment different from the expediential calculus assumed under the theory of deterrence. To exact retribution, the punishment must fit the crime. According to John Stuart Mill, who equated criminal justice with retribution, 'The principle, therefore, of giving to each what they deserve, that is, good for good as well as evil for evil, is not only included within the idea of justice as we have defined it, but is a proper object of that intensity of sentiment, which places the just, in human estimation, above the simply expedient.'[18] Mill added that most of the common maxims of justice derive from the purpose of retribution: 'that a person is only responsible for what he has done voluntarily, or could voluntarily have avoided, that it is unjust to condemn any person unheard, that the punishment ought to be proportioned to the offense, and the like, are maxims intended to prevent the just principle of evil for evil from being perverted to the infliction of evil without that justification.'

The achievement of Confederation in 1867 placed the criminal law within the jurisdiction of the federal Parliament, the significance of which was not lost on at least one of the founders. Speaking in February 1865 during the debates on Confederation, John A. Macdonald had compared the Canadian approach to the criminal law with that of the United States.

The criminal law too – the determination of what is a crime and what is not and how crime shall be punished – is left to the General Government. This is a matter almost of necessity. It is of great importance that we should have the same criminal law throughout these provinces – that what is a crime in one part of British North America, should be a crime in every part – that there should be the same protection of life and property as in another. It is one of the defects of the United States system, that each separate state has or may have a criminal code of its own, – that what may be a capital offence in one state, may be a venial offence, punishable slightly, in another. But under our constitution we shall have one body of criminal law, based on the criminal law of England, and operating equally throughout British America, so that a British American, belonging to what province he may, or going to any other part of the Confederation, knows what his rights are in that respect, and what his punishment will be if an offender against the criminal laws of the land.[19]

After Confederation provincial criminal law was gradually consolidated by a succession of federal statutes. The Criminal Code passed in 1892 followed in its basic conception the 1879 British draft code prepared by the royal commission led by James Fitzjames Stephen (and later rejected by the British Parliament). The Canadian Criminal Code offers a striking revelation of the deep-seated belief in the principle of retribution that governs the Canadian criminal justice system.

Implicit in the 1892 Criminal Code was the assumption that individuals chose freely between right and wrong. If a person chose to do wrong, he was responsible, guilty, and deserved punishment. Offences were defined by the code, and punishments were attached to them that varied with the seriousness of each offence. Murder was among the most serious offences, and if a person chose to commit this crime the maximum punishment was death. Treason was considered equally serious and deserving of the same punishment. Manslaughter was less serious than murder because intention and guilt were less readily established, and the maximum penalty was life imprisonment. Robbery, deemed still less serious, carried a maximum punishment of fourteen years plus whipping; but if the offence was an aggravated robbery, life imprisonment might be demanded.[20] The offence considered objectively, not the offender in a particular case, was the determinant of punishment.

Custodial prisons were an important instrument of retribution. The English reformer John Howard's vision had been to establish correctional institutions that would substitute detention for corporal and capital punishment and provide an environment for offenders to become 'penitents.' In Canada, however, any hope that penitentiaries would serve to rehabilitate offenders was frustrated by the weight placed on detention for the purpose of punishment.

The first penitentiaries were established in the United States early in the nineteenth century, and the first custodial prison in Canada, which opened at Kingston in 1835, was modelled on Auburn Prison in New York State. Brutality did not suddenly disappear from the system. The early records of Kingston Penitentiary reveal a heavy reliance on corporal punishment, and unspeakable cruelty was discovered by George Brown's royal commission of investigation in 1848–9. None the less, the very appointment of the royal commission and the subsequent forced resignation of the warden tend to confirm that a significant shift in the conception of the purpose of punishment had occurred.[21]

After the first brutal years at Kingston Penitentiary, the overriding objective of Canadian prisons became incarceration to punish. The federal Penetentiaries Act of 1869 did require that each penitentiary serve the purpose of 'confinement and reformation' of convicted offenders, but the reference to reformation proved to be strictly symbolic. For nearly a century, from the 1850s to the 1940s, the only effective policy developments in Canadian prisons were directed at better security and improved sanitation.

During the 1870s a major building program created a national system of penitentiaries. St Vincent de Paul (1873), Manitoba Penitentiary (1876), British Columbia Penitentiary (1878), and Dorchester Penitentiary (1880) were all typical examples of the 'Auburn system,' under which the standards of good penal policy did not extend beyond the maintenance of safe and sanitary buildings.[22] The Royal Commission to Investigate the Penal System reported in 1938 that buildings were old but clean, cells were adequate with modern sanitary equipment, food was ample but not extravagant, libraries were fairly well stocked (although censorship was stringent and puerile), and medical care varied widely in quality.

The commission also made it plain that policies for the physiological welfare of inmates did not extend to their rehabilitation. There was no effective segregation of prisoners, classification was designed for greater security and suppressing agitation rather than promoting reformation, work was insufficient and monotonous, and the education of inmates was almost completely neglected.[23] Provincial reformatories and prison farms differed from the penitentiaries only in that they were newer and therefore better designed and better equipped than the federal institutions.[24] The commission concluded that 'there are few, if any, prisoners who enter our penitentiaries who do not leave them worse members of society than when they entered them,'[25] and urged a new commitment to rehabilitation as the proper goal of criminal punishment.

Criminal Justice as Correction

Growing knowledge of the complexity of the human personality has provided the grounds for challenging both retribution and deterrence as justifications for punishing offenders. Theories of deterrence and retribution both assume that criminal behaviour is voluntary and rational; but according to modern psychological and sociological studies, much criminal behaviour is involuntary or irrational, caused by social or psychological conditions that are beyond individual control and hence beyond individual responsibility; the most effective approach to protecting society from criminal behaviour is to treat and rehabilitate those who commit crimes. Deterrent and retributive aspects of punishment should be subordinate to the goal of correcting the offender; punishment should fit the criminal, not the crime. This approach means that each offender must be seen as a person who requires individual treatment. It means organizing the provisions of the Criminal Code, police enforcement, courtroom sentencing practices, and treatment and rehabilitation procedures in the penal system so that they are flexible enough to include the variety of options necessary to meet the different needs of different offenders.

After the Second World War federal and provincial penal systems (increasingly referred to as correctional systems) began to introduce policies directed at rehabilitating convicted offenders. Attempts were begun in 1947 to develop vocational training facilities and better recreational opportunities. Positions for classification officers were established in the federal penitentiary services after 1947 and in the provincial systems of Ontario, Saskatchewan, and British Columbia after 1950. A permanent federal staff training college was opened in 1952 in Kingston, and additional colleges were opened in Quebec and British Columbia in the early 1960s.

Possibilities for segregating offenders improved markedly in 1959–60 with the opening of two medium-security institutions (Joyceville and Le-Clerc) and three minimum-security correctional camps (William Head, Valleyfield, and Springhill). The expansion continued throughout the 1960s and into the 1970s. In 1956 there were eight federal penitentiaries; by 1969, when the Canadian Committee on Corrections issued its report, there were thirty-seven federal penitentiaries; a decade later there were sixty-one. Fifteen maximum-security penitentiaries (including three regional psychiatric centres) and fifteen medium-security penitentiaries each hold 44 per cent of the federal prison population, fourteen minimum-security institutions hold 10 per cent, and about 2 per cent are held in seventeen community correction centres.[26]

An essential step toward using the penal system for correction was the establishment of the Remission Service and its eventual replacement by the National Parole Board in 1959. Conditional release from prison had existed since 1899 under the Ticket-of-Leave Act; but its criterion was clemency – the mitigation of retributive penalties in the light of extenuating circumstances – rather than rehabilitation. During the 1950s the Remission Service, assisted by the growth of voluntary after-care services,[27] began to shift its orientation toward rehabilitation, for example, by opening regional offices to investigate applications and supervise offenders after their release. The number of conditional releases granted did not increase significantly, however, until the Parole Act, passed in 1959, gave the new National Parole Board powers to 'grant parole to an inmate if the Board considers that the inmate has derived the maximum benefit from imprisonment and that the reform and rehabilitation of the inmate will be aided by the grant of parole.' The strongly rehabilitative orientation of the National Parole Board was evident in the growing number of paroles granted during the 1960s; a peak of 5,259 was reached in 1970–1 (compared with 994 in 1958). Thereafter, the number of paroles was cut back to about 2,500–3,000 a year because of increasing parole violations and strong public criticism of the board's apparent leniency.[28]

Assuming that correction and rehabilitation were the primary justifications for incarceration had some positive results. In its 1977 report to Parliament the Subcommittee on the Penitentiary System in Canada concluded that the rehabilitative philosophy had changed prison conditions for the better.

Unlike 100 years ago, [inmates] are out of their cells for most hours during the day, engaged in recreation, work and educational activities (although inmates in dissociation or in institutions where there has been a recent disturbance are subject to restrictions). There are also opportunities for psychological and social counselling. Inmates in most institutions are permitted to keep many of their personal effects such as rings, watches, lighters, electric shavers and even typewriters, although alarm clocks, television sets, and pets are not permitted. Correspondence with family and friends is encouraged although it is inspected and may be censored. There is a grievance procedure, inmate committees, a correctional investigator and more access to staff. Inmates are permitted to engage in hobbies if they do not constitute a nuisance or a danger to security.[29]

Nevertheless, the impact of rehabilitative thinking on policy development from the 1950s to the 1970s should not be exaggerated. The committee to inquire into the Remission Service reported in 1956 that penal institutions were overcrowded and understaffed and that too much time and attention was required for custodial supervision.[30] In the mid-1960s John Fornataro concluded that the 'prisonizing process' in Canada was 'characterized by the social and emotional regression of the inmate and his progressive capitulation to a system that erodes his individuality,' and that the system was 'substantially unchanged despite official pronouncements of "new deals" and the introduction of some changes calculated to improve the work of the prisons.'[31] William Mann's analysis of Guelph Reformatory presented a revealing case study of how an overriding concern for security and its attendant authoritarianism completely undermined hesitant rehabilitation programs.[32] Continuing high rates of recidivism also cast doubt on the effectiveness of current penal programs in realizing the goal of rehabilitation.[33]

Outside the penal system, the rehabilitative approach had limited implementation. Sentencing statistics show a decrease in the use of imprisonment and an increase in the use of fines and suspended sentences with probation. The report of the Ontario Task Force on Policing (1974) and the establishment of the British Columbia Police Commission both indicated a growing concern about the problems of fitting police discretionary powers into the contemporary criminal-justice system. Perhaps most important, the efforts of the Law Reform Commission of Canada in several research studies and working papers seemed to offer the promise of a searching look at 'Stephen's monument.' Yet the system remains a long way from fulfilling the ambition of the Canadian Committee on Corrections to cover the law, courts, police, and corrections with an integrated philosophy of criminal justice. The observations of one critic of corrections can be extended to the whole system of criminal justice: 'in Canada we have done very little more than *talk* about a new approach.'[34]

Failure to adopt rehabilitation as the main justification for punishment under the criminal law should not be surprising. It simply underlines the power in Canadian policy of the legalist principle with its corollary of retributive punishment. Changes in the Criminal Code have not altered its nineteenth-century liberal foundations. 'Tampered with and tinkered with, it remains the monument of the eminent Victorian, Sir James Stephen,' wrote Alan Mewett in 1967. 'The sad conclusion is that the criminal law has not progressed in one hundred years nor can it progress beyond a slight shuffling within boundaries as long as those boundaries are accepted as absolutes.'[35] Within those boundaries, as Paul Weiler has pointed out, the criminal law remains punitive.

It functions in an atmosphere of heightened moral fervour, fuelled by our attitude to the laws the offender has broken and the harm he has caused. When he is convicted through the solemn ritual of the criminal law and sent to jail, the outcome is an enduring stigma for the 'criminal' whose consequences are almost impossible to shake off. When the battery of treatment measures are only then brought to bear on the moral outcast, it should not be surprising that they face insurmountable obstacles.[36]

The relatively high rates of imprisonment in Canada (and in the United States) compared with those in Western Europe provide another indicator of the strong persistence of a retributive orientation to punishment.[37] Policemen's attitudes appear to be strongly affected by the view that 'justice' means giving an offender his just desserts – punishing an offender in accordance with the severity of his crime[38] – and many judges also hold this view.

Perhaps there is no stronger indicator of the importance of retributive justice in the Canadian public philosophy than the public support for capital punishment that persists despite the absence of positive evidence of its deterrent effects and despite the sizable élite opinion that supports abolition. Public criticism of such reform measures as reduction in pre-trial detention, greater use of probation and suspended sentences, and more lenient procedures in granting parole also are consistent with the survival of the retributive principle. Typical of such criticism is the statement of one of the founders of Victims of Violence – an association that provides moral support to the families of victims and presses for a hardening of the justice system – upon discovering that her daughter's murderer, sentenced to life imprisonment, could be freed on parole in ten years: 'My feelings are that when someone goes out and takes a life, they give up the right to life. I would like the death penalty to come back. My daughter is dead and gone and the man has been sentenced, so revenge has nothing to do with me personally. But it's justice that I feel is not being done.'[39]

Liberal Justice and Public Order

Although it may be a necessary instrument for creating and preserving public order, physical coercion or the threat of it does not guarantee justice. A just public order must be founded on principles that are widely, if not universally, recognized as fair and accepted as binding in a political community.

In retrospect, the critical step in the evolution of a system of criminal justice in Canada was the abandonment of the deterrent orientation and the excessive brutality of eighteenth-century English criminal law in favour of retributive justice and the rule of law. The idea of a value consensus among rational, morally responsible individuals who choose to live together in a political community with legal rights and corresponding civic obligations became the foundation for building a just public order. None the less, the principle of deterrence was not banished from policy thinking. Consistent with Bentham's utilitarian calculus that balanced the 'certainty' and 'proximity' of punishment against its 'magnitude,' deterrence was progressively subordinated to retributive justice in criminal sentencing, but it found alternative application in the organization of more effective police forces.

The legalist paradigm of codified law, individual responsibility, efficient policing, and retributive punishment for criminal acts survived virtually unaltered and unquestioned until the mid-twentieth century, when it encountered broader perspectives on human nature. The concept of diminished responsibility has long been recognized, as in the cases of juvenile or insane offenders; but modern psychological and sociological theory identified a wide range of personal and societal variables purporting to explain criminal behaviour that seemed to undermine any general assumption of individual responsibility. At the same time, these theories suggested general objectives for correctional programs.

If it were predominant, the corrections orientation would have significant implications for every stage of the criminal-justice process. The Canadian Committee on Corrections, for example, expressed its belief 'that the rehabilitation of the individual offenders offers the best long-term protection for society, since that ends the risk of a continuing criminal career'; but the committee added that segregation of dangerous offenders and deterrence by sanctions and prohibitions were also necessary to protect society.[40] Nevertheless, the purposes of retribution and rehabilitation are fundamentally opposed to each other in a way that retribution and deterrence are not. As George Herbert Mead predicted in his classic 1918 essay,

The two attitudes, that of control of crime by the hostile procedure of the law and that of control through comprehension of social and psychological conditions, cannot be combined. To understand is to forgive and the social procedure seems to deny the very responsibility which the law affirms and on the other hand the pursuit by criminal justice inevitably awakens the hostile attitude in the offender and renders the attitude of mutual comprehension practically impossible.[41]

Retributive justice evidently remains one of the basic operative ideals of the Canadian public philosophy, but its meaning has been confused and its legitimizing power correspondingly weakened by advocates of rehabilitation who equate retribution with vengeance. The Canadian Committee on Corrections, for example, rejected retribution understood as vengeance as a goal of modern criminal justice: 'The satisfaction of a desire for vengeance is a very expensive, and in our view fruitless, luxury. The cost to the community of incarceration and the damage to and the subsequent danger from an individual punished for vengeance make the execution of vengeance totally unacceptable to any rationally motivated community.'[42]

Such an argument not only misunderstands the moral basis of retributive justice and the symbolic significance of retributive punishment under the rule of law in a liberal democracy; it also undermines the legitimacy of the legalist social order. The advocates of rehabilitation contend that their approach has never been fairly tried as a principle of justice in Canada. Although the accuracy of this argument may be conceded and its importance recognized as a consideration in any humane administration of justice, rehabilitation can never serve as the paramount organizing principle of justice in a liberal social order because it denies the assumption of individual moral responsibility that is the foundation of liberal political thought.

Our consideration of the fundamentals of Canada's criminal-justice system has described the limitations of the rehabilitative approach, but those limitations should not stop the search for alternative approaches that would enhance the substantive teaching effects of the law while softening the 'hatred, fear, or contempt for the convict' that so often distorts retributive punishment. One possible avenue of reform suggested by the Law Reform Commission of Canada is to restore restitution as an important purpose of punishment.[43] Another possibility, recommended in 1977 by the House of Commons Subcommittee on the Penitentiary System in Canada (the Mac-Guigan Committee) in its Report to Parliament, is to recognize that imprisonment can only be justified as retributive justice, but consistent with that purpose the correctional system can and must provide offenders with opportunities for 'personal reformation.'

In the Middle Ages, before the theory developed that crime was an offence against the state, restitution was the main purpose of punishment in the countries of Western Europe.[44] In Anglo-Saxon England, for example, when an individual suffered damage because of another person's wrongful action, the matter was settled by private mediation or taken before a tribunal for arbitration. Restitution was the order of the day, and other sanctions were rarely used.[45]

In general, modern systems of criminal justice give little place to the victims of crime and make few provisions for restitution. The Canadian system is no exception.[46] Under current Canadian law, restitution may be required as a condition of probation, it may be ordered in the form of an additional penalty not exceeding fifty dollars in minor offences of damage to property, or the court may, in passing sentence for an indictable offence, concurrently order the offender to compensate the victims for loss of or damage to property as a result of the crime. In practice, none of these provisions has been much used.

In its 1974 working paper on restitution and compensation the Law Reform Commission of Canada proposed that the responsibility of the offender to make restitution to the victim should become a central consideration in sentencing and dispositions. The commission admitted that there are offences for which restitution is useless or impossible and the most appropriate sanction may be prolonged imprisonment, but it concluded that for the majority of offences restitution is appropriate 'punishment.' Restitution might be supplemented, where justice demanded it, by additional sanctions such as fines or probation: 'What is anticipated is a range of sanctions ranging from relatively light to severe, with restitution receiving consideration in most offences.'[47]

The argument for restitution rests on a specific theory of the nature of crime. Other approaches view crime as wrongful conduct to be punished, pathological behaviour to be treated, or self-interested actions to be deterred; but the principle of restitution derives from acceptance of the inevitability of crime as an aspect of social living. Torts and breaches of contract are accepted in civil law as normal features of social life, and may even serve the social purpose of clarifying different value positions. The Law Reform Commission has proposed that this view should be restored to the criminal law. Sentencing policy should make clear what values are at stake in a conflict and affirm 'in a tolerant but firm way those values which have the support of the community' rather than seek to suppress crime through severe sanctions. The offender should be viewed as a responsible person, thus encouraging reconciliation and redress rather than rejecting the offender as 'a parasite on the body politic.'[48]

Making restitution a central consideration in sentencing and disposition implies an important change in understanding and dealing with crime; but unlike rehabilitation, restitution appears to be compatible with a continuing commitment to retributive justice. The restitution philosophy begins with an affirmation of community values and individual moral responsibility, elevates the teaching function of the law beyond the awful symbolism of retributive punishment to describe a process for achieving just reconciliation, and tries to balance the state's duty to defend the community's social order with the rights of victims to procure a just redress. Such a recommendation presents a striking challenge to the policy-making élites and the Canadian people to shift their view of crime and punishment. So far the response has been discouragingly uncreative.

The Royal Commission to Investigate the Penal System (the Archambault Commission) was established in 1936 in the wake of several riots in Canadian penitentiaries. The commission's report was largely responsible for initiating the policy of rehabilitation that was developed and implemented after the war. The policy circle was closed in 1975 and 1976, when there were sixty-nine major incidents of violence in federal penitentiaries compared with a total of sixty-five over the previous four decades. In October 1976 a subcommittee was established by the House of Commons Standing Committee on Justice and Legal Affairs with instructions to prepare a report to Parliament on the Canadian penitentiary system.

In its report the subcommittee concluded that 'a crisis exists in the Canadian penitentiary system. It can be met only by the immediate implementation of large-scale reforms.'[49] According to the subcommittee, these reforms should be based on an 'opportunities' philosophy. They should assume that individual prisoners ultimately are responsible for their own reformation, but that the penitentiary system has an obligation to provide appropriate supportive opportunities for those who want to reform.

Like the Archambault Commission and the Canadian Committee on Corrections, the MacGuigan Committee argued that 'the best protection society has is for those who offend to come out of prison, not as a greater danger to the community, but as law-abiding, productive and tax-paying instead of tax-draining.' Unfortunately, 'there is little in the system to stimulate inmates to reform, to correct the behaviour and morality that brought them into prison.'[50] Again like the earlier commissions, the MacGuigan Committee recommended such basic policy reforms as better professional training for correctional officers, smaller penal institutions, and more work and educational opportunities for inmates.

The MacGuigan Committee differed from its predecessors in its effort to fit reformation into a system of retributive justice. In stating its principles, the committee held that 'there must be a clear distinction made between punishment and vengeance. Punishment is the means by which society expresses its disapproval of the behaviour of one of its members. Vengeance is a much more primitive and illogical reaction to offensive behaviour, and has no place in the correctional practices of an enlightened nation.'[51]

Imprisonment can be used to serve the purpose of punishment, but it is not a universal solution to the problems of crime in our society. It cannot be expected to serve the purpose of rehabilitation.

We do not recommend imprisonment for the *purpose* of rehabilitation. Even the concept is objectionable on several grounds. It implies that penal institutions are capable of adjusting an individual as if he were an imperfectly-operating mechanism, and, through acting externally on him, can make him over into a better person. In addition, it is misleading to judges, offers a false sense of security to the public, is the source of confusion to correctional service personnel as to their role, and is a false promise to inmates and their families.[52]

In the view of the subcommittee the courts should not attempt to determine whether an individual needs 'rehabilitation' and then impose a prison sentence for that purpose. However, once a decision to imprison has been taken, correctional practices should be aimed at encouraging and assisting the inmate's efforts toward 'personal reformation.' To do this the penitentiary system must provide each inmate with essential supportive conditions: discipline, justice, work, academic and vocational training, social therapy, and community involvement. 'Only the wrongdoer can bring about reform in himself since he is responsible for his own behaviour; but the penitentiary system must be structured to give positive supports to his efforts at reform.'[53]

Budgetary constraints since 1977 have gravely impeded the implementation of the reforms proposed by the Subcommittee on the Penitentiary System. That surely is a worrying indicator of the strength of public commitment to a more effective and humane system of criminal justice, but it does not diminish the subcommittee's substantial achievement in beginning an official rethinking of the possibility of reconciling punishment and reformation. That reconciliation means insistence on the traditional liberal principle of individual responsibility and the justice of retributive punishment; it also means acceptance of the modern liberal optimism about individual potential for positive personality change. Such a reconciliation is evidently not easy to make in practice, as correctional policies of the past three decades illustrate; but it is imperative if criminal control based on a modern ethical liberalism is to obtain public legitimacy and justice is to be done and seen to be done.

6

Public Schools

The issue in educational policy-making is who learns what, and how. The answers to those questions require both a theory of learning and a philosophy of education. A theory of learning is needed to assess the effectiveness and efficiency of instruction. It should provide understanding of the growth of individual capacities and the contribution specific learning experiences make to educated behaviour. It should also facilitate predictions about the effects of potential governmental interventions – for example, new policies on teacher training or classroom organization. A philosophy of education is needed to help resolve the inevitable political issues concerning the extent and distribution of schooling. It should clarify the social purposes of education, allocate responsibility among the social institutions – family, church, state – that will carry out instruction, and differentiate learning experiences among particular social groups.

A liberal theory of the aims of public education can be built on each of the three general functions of government. First, public education can be designed as 'civic education' to serve the preservation of social order. Under a liberal conception of public order based on representative government, the rule of law, individual responsibility, and retributive punishment, public education is assigned the vital task of teaching the moral standards of the community and the duties of democratic citizenship. The emergence together of public schools, responsible legislatures, professional police, and custodial prisons in the period from the 1840s to the 1880s is not a coincidence. These institutions formed a vital complementarity in nineteenth-century liberal thinking about the requirements of public order.

Second, public education can be designed to serve the requirements of industrial expansion. An industrial economy needs workers able to apply the latest advances in modern technology, managers with specialized professional education and skills necessary to organize production, and researchers who can create new technology. The widespread concern that developed among educators, businessmen, and politicians about the quantity and quality of industrial and technical education at the turn of the century attests to the contribution schools were expected to make to Canadian industrial expansion;[1] and the acceptance in the 1960s of higher educational expenditures as an investment in human capital that promised a high rate of economic return for the country shows the vitality of this purpose in the design of school policies.

Third, public education can be designed to serve the growth of each learner's unique capacities. Just as a liberal political economy ascribes economic progress to individual effort and competition, and just as a liberal social order achieves security by controlling individual deviance, so a liberal society conceives of individual development primarily in terms of opportunity for individuals to attain self-respect and self-development. Of course, what the realization of individual opportunities is understood to require in the way of specific public policies varies over time and among liberal societies.

Historically, the Canadian political community assumed that opportunity depended mainly on policies that promoted economic progress and preserved social order. Access to land and natural resources, opportunities for investment and employment, and protection of life and property were the essential elements of opportunity, at least until the first decades of the twentieth century. From that perspective schooling served the cause of social order, but was not expected to make an important contribution to increasing individual opportunity.

With industrialization came demands for reforms that would fit public schooling to the new occupational structure. The main purpose of the public school system was no longer merely the education of virtuous citizens; it was now responsible for the distribution of occupational opportunities. At the same time, the liberal idea of economic opportunity was redefined to include educational opportunity, and the availability of educational advantages to anyone able to benefit from them came to be regarded as an integral part of the meaning of equal opportunity.

Most recently, modern 'ethical' liberalism has challenged the traditional norms of 'economic' liberalism, which narrowly defined individual opportunities in terms of material enrichment and private initiative. Ethical liberal hopes for universal individual development presuppose the creation of an 'educative society.' According to Jean-Marc Leger, 'this educative society will be quintessentially a creative society which awakes in each man all his possibilities and facilitates their expression. The individual who consumes culture (which is often degraded by its commercial environment) will make way for the citizen-creator ... It won't be just that all will have access to cultural goods ... but more important is that all will participate in cultural creation.'[2] Given the goal of an educative society and an assumption of the state's responsibility to find public policies that will achieve it, the liberal ideal of educational opportunity must be extended accordingly.

Public Schooling as Civic Education

Civic education became the leading issue in Canadian politics between the 1840s and the 1870s.[3] This was a critical period in building the Canadian nation. In the 1830s colonial politics were élitist, corrupt, and oppressive; brief rebellions occurred in 1837 in both Quebec and Ontario. In the next three decades responsible self-government and liberal democracy were achieved in each of the colonies, and a difficult experiment with federal government in the two central colonies was developed into a continental federation. The fundamental change in the relationship of state to school proposed during this period owed much to the American example. In the end, compromised by the ambiguities of Canadian nationality and the political and constitutional position of Catholic education, civic education would be less dominant in Canadian public policy than it was in the United States. None the less, the American example remained relevant to Canadians because democracy and federation were bringing changes in the Canadian colonies which presented a nation-building problem comparable to that being experienced in the United States.

In her excellent study of the men who promoted public schooling in Upper Canada from the 1840s to the 1870s, Alison Prentice attributes to them a mixture of optimism and pessimism about human nature and their own society that strongly resembles the thinking behind the nineteenth-century reform of the criminal law.

The school promoters were essentially divided men, individuals who were at once fascinated and repelled by their rapidly changing environment. Their dominant feeling about the world seems, in the end to have been one of profound distrust. They claimed to believe in progress; indeed they promoted it. They hailed educational change as a great reformation in society. Yet one cannot ignore their even greater pessimism. The world, as they saw it, verged on chaos; the question uppermost in their minds often seems to have been how to tame rampant nature and the devil in men, and their real quest a quest for control. There was accordingly the desire, on the part of those who saw themselves as the reasonable, civilized and respectable elements of society, to exert control over the unreasonable, savage and disreputable at all social levels, but especially among the poor. The control, they hoped, would be exercised through the schools.[4]

According to Prentice, educators in Upper Canada promoted public schooling to subordinate the sensuality and self-indulgence of children to the restraints of intellect and morality, to protect children from the dangers of unsavoury social conditions, and to prepare them for living in a complex and troubled society.[5] The recurrent complaints of educators about Upper Canadian society focused on its excessive materialism, mass ignorance, increasing crime, and failure of public spirit. The schools were institutions that could cure these ills. Educators referred to the school system as 'a branch of the national police' intended both to 'occupy a large portion of the rising population' and to 'support and restrain many of the grown-up population,' and they defended public schools as 'the cheapest form of moral police' and as better public investments than penitentiaries or jails. The schools were instrumental in shaping what Egerton Ryerson called 'the state of the public mind.' He believed that 'it is on Canadian self-reliance, skill and enterprise – in a word, on Canadian patriotism – that depends Canadian prosperity, elevation and happiness.' Teaching such patriotic virtue was the great task of the public schools.

So that these ambitious goals of social order and national development might be achieved, school regulations stressed punctuality, orderly conduct, and industry.[6] The curriculum was to provide a 'practical education' for all children in traditional subjects such as arithmetic, language, and literature. The main instrument of political and social education seems to have been history. The only history course regularly taught in English Canada at mid-century was ancient history, which was available in the secondary schools. After Confederation, British and Canadian history courses appeared in all schools, and by the turn of the century had been introduced into all school grades except the lowest.[7]

In his report on the 1837 rebellions Lord Durham said, 'I entertain no doubts as to the national character which must be given to Lower Canada: It must be that of the British Empire; that of the majority of the population of British North America; that of the great race which must, in the lapse of no long period of time, be predominant over the whole North American Continent.' Durham's colleague Charles Buller recommended setting up a school system that 'would forward energetically the great national objects we have in view – uniting the two races and Anglifying the Canadian.'[8] Looking back on the founding of provincial school systems from the turn of the century, André Siegfried saw the inevitability of political division over state schools. 'In a country like Canada the schools must sooner or later become to a greater degree than elsewhere the principal stake to be struggled for by opposing forces, national and religious. Therein is the framework for the future. Catholics and Protestants, French and English, alike, ask themselves with anxiety what is being made of their children.'[9]

Denominational Schools

In the Canadian colonies the first schools were established by religious orders or denominational philanthropic societies, such as the Church of England's Society for the Propagation of the Gospel, the Benevolent Irish Society, and the Wesleyan Missionary Society. School politics were characterized in the early nineteenth century by competition among the denominational groups for grants from the colonial assemblies for their schools; and attempts to supplement these sectarian, voluntarist efforts with state-supported elementary and grammar schools either failed, as in Newfoundland and Lower Canada, or aimed unsuccessfully at the establishment of the Anglican doctrines of the ruling élites, as in the Maritimes and Upper Canada.[10]

The extension and rationalization of state support for elementary schools thrust the relationship of church and state to the top of the political agenda. Inevitably, the advocates of public schools found themselves in conflict with the supporters of the existing church schools. Which institution, church or state, should exercise ultimate authority over the guidance of learning? What was to be the primary social purpose of the schools? Compounding the conflict was the fact that in English Canada the public schools, although in principle non-denominational, in practice were firmly oriented to the values of Protestant majorities.[11]

Two provinces made no provision for denominational schools. The British Columbia public school system created by legislation passed in 1869 and 1872 was, in Canada, uniquely non-denominational; no serious campaign for public support for denominational schools developed in that province. In Manitoba, although a denominational system divided between Protestants and Roman Catholics was created by legislation passed in 1872, the Protestant population and its schools expanded much more rapidly during the 1870s and 1880s than the Catholic population and its schools; and in 1890 the Protestant majority in the provincial legislative assembly terminated the dual system in favour of a unified non-sectarian system.

In Quebec and Newfoundland, no effective efforts were made to set up non-sectarian schools. State-supported denominational systems divided between Protestants and Roman Catholics emerged in both colonies in the 1840s, and in Newfoundland, following a period of considerable acrimony, the Protestant denominations were also divided among themselves after 1874.

The public school systems in the remaining provinces all included some provision for state-supported denominational schools. In Canada West, Roman Catholic and Protestant dissidents in 1841 gained the right to set up separate schools. As compulsory local taxation gradually became the accepted approach to supporting the public schools, the Roman Catholic minority in Canada West, supported in the assembly by French-speaking Catholics from Canada East, was successful in extending the privileges of separate-school supporters. The crucial victory came in 1855 when separate-school boards were given the authority to tax, and separate-school supporters were exempted from paying public-school rates.

Provisions for Roman Catholic separate schools similar to those in Ontario were made in Saskatchewan and Alberta when their denominational systems, originally patterned after the Quebec system, were abandoned at the turn of the century; but in New Brunswick, Nova Scotia, and Prince Edward Island, intolerant Protestant majorities precluded any legislative recognition of separate schools. However, public support was given unofficially in the Maritime provinces; public school trustees rented Roman Catholic schools as part of the public school system, appointed teachers on the recommendation of the Church, and permitted Catholic children to attend those schools.

Language of Instruction

The language of instruction in public schools was not a major issue in school politics until late in the nineteenth century. Throughout most of the century the language of instruction was determined by local authorities, with the result that children from a minority ethnic group could be educated in their own language if the ethnic population was large enough to control the local school. Thus, English-speaking Catholics were a minority within the French-speaking Catholic school system in the province of Quebec, but the autonomy enjoyed by local school authorities ensured that a community with a majority of English-speaking Catholics would have an English-language school.[12] In Ontario in the 1850s French and German were accepted as languages of instruction in the schools of French-speaking and German-speaking communities. An 1841 act authorized the payment of grants to Nova Scotia schools using French, German, or Gaelic as the language of instruction. French was recognized as an official language of instruction in Manitoba after 1871 and in Alberta and Saskatchewan after 1878; in all three of these provinces, some of the schools were unilingual in French.[13]

The principle that Quebec's English-speaking Catholics were entitled to instruction in their own language was never questioned, although there were continual difficulties with its implementation. French minorities in the English-speaking provinces were not as fortunate as the English Catholics of Quebec. The British North America Act had attempted to balance the interests of English and French Canadians in the Maritimes, Quebec, and Ontario; but the influx of British and other non-French immigrants into Ontario, Manitoba, and the Northwest Territories upset the equilibrium and reopened the question of English–French coexistence in the English-Canadian provinces. After 1885 the change in ethnic composition resulting from European immigration raised fears among British Canadians for the preservation of the British character of Canada, and the potential fragmentation of public schooling became another rationale for questioning special privileges enjoyed by French minority groups.

The fears and tensions of the period were soon expressed in the schools. Previously permissive policies were altered to make English the language of instruction. In 1885 the Ontario government ordered that English be taught in all schools, and by 1890 bilingual schools were understood to be English-language schools in which French was taught only in the early years of school and then merely as a supplementary subject.[14] In Manitoba the French language lost its official status in 1890; in Saskatchewan and Alberta, in 1892. By the turn of the century a policy on bilingual schools similar to that in Ontario also had been adopted in Maritime school systems.

Two events in the early controversies over minority-language schooling established language of instruction as a political issue clearly separate from the question of denominational instruction. One was the proclamation of regulation 17 by the Ontario government in 1912; the other was the rescission of bilingual schooling rights by the Manitoba government in 1916. In a situation of rising tension between the English and the French in Ontario, regulation 17 reaffirmed the policy of 1890 which generally restricted the use of French as a language of instruction and communication to grades one and two.[15] When French-speaking trustees tried to protest by closing Ottawa's separate schools, an appeal to the courts by English Catholics established that section 93 of the British North America Act gave constitutional protection for minority rights to denominational schooling but did not confer any language rights in education.[16] In Manitoba the 1897 federal–provincial compromise over denominational schooling included a provision that in schools in which ten pupils spoke any language other than English, instruction should be bilingual. As Manitoba was settled over the next two decades by many immigrants with mother tongues other than English or French, school districts faced growing difficulties in providing adequate schooling in two or three languages besides English. The problem was compounded by the rise of ethnic prejudices during the First World War, and in 1916 the provincial assembly repealed the bilingual clause.

Central and Local Administration

In pursuing the goals of civic education the role of provincial governments was limited but definitive. School budgets were locally financed, but leadership from the provincial authorities was an essential condition for establishing compulsory local assessment. Provincial regulations with respect to textbooks and curriculum design determined the content of school lessons. Provincial training colleges educated teachers, and provincial licences were required to teach in the schools. To ensure that provincial regulations were respected, provincial inspectors regularly visited schools, observed and questioned pupils and teachers, and reported their findings to the provincial department of education. To ensure that young people attended school, provincial legislation set minimum requirements for school attendance. In 1871, for example, Ontario children aged seven to twelve were required to attend school four months a year; by the 1920s, all elementary-school children attended school for a full school year.[17]

The basic unit of school administration in the eight provinces that were most committed to civic education was the school section, essentially the attendance area of an elementary school. Even before the concept of civic education took hold, the section was the unit of administration for elementary schools in Upper Canada (1816), Prince Edward Island (1825), and Nova Scotia (1826). New Brunswick, however, continued to use the parish school district as its basic unit until 1871. Manitoba, under its 1871 act, at first used electoral district boundaries to define school districts, but the growth of population brought a shift to smaller sections well before the denominational system was terminated. In British Columbia (1872) and the Northwest Territories (1885) the first school laws set the minimum number of students in attendance for establishing school districts at between ten and fifteen.

Extensive systems of school sections flourished in the eastern provinces from the 1870s to the 1930s and beyond, and in the western provinces the number of school districts rose rapidly with settlement. New Brunswick, for example, was divided into 1,426 school sections by 1876, approximately the same number as existed in 1944. In Ontario there were 4,400 school districts operating in 1870 and over 6,000 in the 1930s. In Manitoba the number of districts was 774 in 1891 and 2,270 in 1936; in Saskatchewan there were 869 districts in 1905 and 5,146 in 1937.

The election of local school boards was an important feature of the system. In Upper Canada the Common School Act of 1816 provided for each school to be governed by three trustees elected by the residents of the school section at an annual meeting (although grammar-school boards were appointed until 1872). In the Maritime colonies the acts introducing election of rural school boards came later, as part of the gradual movement toward comprehensive state control over schooling – in 1847 for Prince Edward Island, 1850 for Nova Scotia, and 1858 for New Brunswick.[18] In each of the western provinces the first school acts provided for the election of local trustees.

Local property taxes financed the public schools and ensured that local trustees would have substantial discretion in making school policy. In Ontario, compulsory local assessment was included in the 1850 act as an alternative to fees and voluntary subscriptions; and largely as the result of a forceful, persistent campaign by the provincial superintendent of education, Egerton Ryerson, 96 per cent of Ontario's 4,400 school sections had voluntarily adopted compulsory assessment by 1871, when provincial legislation finally terminated the local option. Provincial grants for teachers' salaries in Prince Edward Island were conditional on the adoption of compulsory local assessment after 1852, although the condition was not strictly enforced until 1877. In New Brunswick the option of compulsory assessment included in the 1852 act was little used, and even after the 1872 act made compulsory assessment the required method for local school finance, difficulties in implementing the law continued for several years.

The goals of civic education – to instil moral standards and teach the duties of democratic citizenship – dominated Canadian school policies by the 1890s. Protestant denominationalism, which had been a strong force in nineteenth-century school politics in the Maritimes, Ontario, and Manitoba, was progressively eroded by or incorporated into the goals of civic education. What remained was a defensive Catholic denominationalism struggling to protect its sectarian view of education against the non-sectarian concept of civic education. Quebec and Newfoundland were the exceptions. In those provinces civic education made little headway in the face of strongly competing denominational and (in Quebec) ethnocentric interests. School districts were kept relatively large to accommodate schools for denominational and linguistic minorities. Provincial school administration remained weak and divided into parallel systems. Quebec did not have a provincial department of education from 1875 to 1964, and school attendance was not made compulsory in either Quebec or Newfoundland until 1942.

In sum, under civic schooling the public school systems were organized by the exercise of local democracy, but the quality of that grass-roots democracy should not be exaggerated or idealized. On the one hand, small school districts, local property taxation, and elected school boards provided an opportunity for citizen participation in the government of an essential public service to a degree probably unequalled in other jurisdictions or policy areas. The classroom of the public school undoubtedly was seen as a place for indoctrinating young people with appropriate national political values, but local school organization also was an instrument for educating adults in the responsibilities of democratic citizenship through discussion and voting in annual meetings, through service on school boards, and through taxpayers' responsibility for the maintenance of school facilities. On the other hand, many districts were non-operating. Trustees often failed to carry out their responsibilities. Majority opinion expressed in local government was often oppressive for minorities. Taxpayers' opposition to increased property taxation blocked educational progress. None the less, local school government provided an unparalleled opportunity for citizen participation in policy-making, an opportunity that disappeared with the movement to the larger units of school administration required by industrial expansion.

Public Schooling as Occupational Selection

There are occupational aspects to education in any school regime, and public schooling in North America has always emphasized 'practical education.' However, school policies in the twentieth century have been distinctive in their assumption that the main aims of schooling are to guide occupational selection and to prepare young people for earning a living. Schools are understood to provide general knowledge and skills as a base from which students can acquire specific knowledge and skills; and as the need for specific technical knowledge has grown with advancing technology, schools have been expected to provide students with both general and specific knowledge and skills. The aim of enlarging the content of specific technical knowledge in the school curriculum is most obviously evidenced by the development of commercial and technical training in secondary schools; but its influence has pervaded the entire curriculum from a decline in the teaching of ancient (and modern) languages to an emphasis on physical sciences, guidance, and 'life adustment.' Policy-making attention also has shifted from elementary to secondary and eventually to tertiary education, levels that are concerned with communicating occupation-specific knowledge and skills.

The North American public school carried with it the assumptions of agrarian democracy out of which it grew. Schooling was meant to produce virtuous citizens capable of personal and collective self-government. Economic advantages that might accrue to individuals were not considered to be significant; they could easily be acquired outside school by efforts at 'self-improvement.' As it became a major institution for occupational selection, however, the vocationally oriented school did bestow economic advantages on those individuals who attended it. Access to school, and particularly access to secondary school, became an increasingly important condition for access to jobs. That raised the issue of equal opportunity. Relative to elementary education, the quality of secondary vocational training turned out to be much more strongly correlated with school size – the larger the school, the greater the opportunity for specialized teaching and a broadened curriculum – and with the wealth of school districts. Wealthy, populous districts could afford the relatively expensive facilities for vocationally oriented education, while students in poor, small districts found less consolation in the virtues of self-improvement.

Thus, as the secondary school became an accepted societal instrument for occupational selection, a low level of public concern about inequalities among school districts, which had been the general attitude toward the original public elementary schools, was replaced by a rising concern that ecological factors – in particular, urban location and property assessment, both unrelated to individual merit – were exercising a strong influence over the distribution of educational and occupational opportunities. The result was pressure to reorganize school districts into larger units that could support the full array of services necessary for equal opportunity and to design provincial grants that would be related to the districts' differing financial capacities. From the 1930s onward, reorganization of school districts into larger units and establishment of provincial equalizing grants were central issues of school policies in Canada, culminating in a wave of educational reform during the 1960s that largely succeeded in realizing the goal of equal access to secondary schooling.

District Reorganization

The first experiments with consolidation of school districts were begun after 1903, the year in which the Macdonald Consolidated School Project was launched; but no effective movement toward larger units of school administration was made until the 1930s and 1940s when Alberta, Nova Scotia, Saskatchewan, and British Columbia each made significant progress in reorganizing their basic units of local school administration. In 1936 the newly elected Social Credit government in Alberta took up the unsuccessful legislative proposals of the preceding United Farmers goverment and created larger school units, each of which was made up of sixty-five to one hundred rural school districts. A 1939 report by the Nova Scotia Commission on the Larger Unit proposed that county school boards accept financial responsibility for a minimum program, employ teachers in special subjects, and operate rural high schools; that plan was adopted in 1942. The Larger School Units Act passed by the Co-operative Commonwealth Federation government elected in Saskatchewan in 1944 set up larger units similar to those in Alberta – a merger of approximately eighty districts into each larger unit governed by a board of five trustees and supported by locally elected boards that had largely advisory responsibilities. The next year, a royal commission on the financing and administration of education in British Columbia recommended reorganization into seventy-four districts. The plan was immediately advanced as an election promise by the incumbent Liberal government and was implemented by legislation the following April.

During the 1950s district reorganization was interrupted by administrative preoccupation with the problem of accommodating the post-war bulge in the elementary-school population. As these students began crowding into secondary schools, the goal of equal opportunity was reasserted and plans to enlarge school districts were pushed to their conclusion. In Manitoba, for example, the Royal Commission on Education recommended in its 1958 interim report that secondary education be administered by larger districts ('it is more apparent than ever that some substantial changes in the organization of our school districts must be made if the children of the province are to be provided with anything approaching equality of educational opportunity'); promptly responding, a new Conservative government introduced legislation that resulted in the formation of forty-five school divisions. Elsewhere, the Ontario government established county districts as the basic unit for rural secondary education in 1964 and for elementary education in 1968; 'Operation 55' saw the establishment of regional school commissions throughout the province of Quebec between

1964 and 1966; the New Brunswick school system was reorganized into thirty-three school districts, subject to a high degree of provincial control, beginning in 1967; and Prince Edward Island became the last province to reorganize its local administration when it consolidated 217 school districts into five regional units in 1971.

Provincial Equalization Grants

Another important approach to ensuring equal opportunity in occupational selection has been the development of provincial policies that attempt to equalize the ability of rich and poor school districts to provide programs and facilities. In the nineteenth century special funds were available to assist poor districts, but they were exceptional measures. Today equalization grants are an integral part of provincial school policy, and the main burden of paying for educational services is carried by provincial governments.

A weighted population grant was the instrument first used to promote equalization.[19] Such a grant commonly offers a fixed amount of aid for distribution by the provincial government. The amount distributed to each school district is divided according to a measure of population, such as number of pupils, classrooms, or teachers; and the population measure is adjusted to take account of local resources, usually by reference to the district's assessed property valuation per pupil compared to the average in the province. A good example is the weighted grant introduced in British Columbia in 1933 to replace the flat grant per teacher that had served as the provincial general grant since 1906. The new basic provincial grant to each district was the product of the number of teachers and the provincial grant per teacher ($780 for an elementary teacher, $1,100 for a junior-high-school teacher, and $1,200 for a high school teacher) less the yield of a one-mill (in cities 1.25 mill) tax in the district. In Alberta, a daily grant per teacher weighted by the value of local assessment was introduced as an addition to the flat grant for rural districts in 1942. The population base of the equalizing grant was changed to number of classrooms beginning in 1946, when towns became eligible for the grant. In 1955 a weighted grant per pupil was added; both continued in effect until a foundation program was introduced in 1961.

A more sophisticated instrument for attempting to equalize opportunities among local school districts is the foundation program, or fixed-unit equalizing grant, which establishes both the unit cost of an educational program to be provided equally in every school district and a mandatory local property tax rate to be applied to the equalized assessed valuation in every school district. The provincial grant paid to each district is the difference between its expenditure for the foundation program and its revenue from levying the mandatory tax rate.

Nova Scotia and British Columbia were the first provinces in Canada to use a fixed-unit equalizing grant. Under the Nova Scotia plan introduced in 1942, rural municipalities assumed financial responsibility for a 'minimum program of education' defined rather crudely by the province in terms of a minimum salary scale and maintenance rates of $125 to $150 per classroom. The department of education paid as an equalization grant the difference between the cost of the minimum program and the yield of a uniform school tax in each municipality. In 1955, following the recommendations of the Pottier Commission, the costs of providing the foundation program were redefined to include teachers' salaries, allowances for principals, and the cost of school maintenance, transportation, and tuition and boarding; the grant was extended to both rural and urban school districts. In British Columbia the plan recommended by the Cameron Commission in 1945 covered allowances for teachers' salaries, supervision, and maintenance; allowance for transportation costs was added to the basic grant structure in 1955. These allowances on current expenditures comprised the basic provincial program, and the share of each school district was the yield of a five-mill tax on real property. Fixed-unit equalizing grants were introduced to allocate provincial funding to school districts in Alberta (1961), Quebec (1965), Manitoba (1967), and finally Saskatchewan (in 1970 to replace the variable-percentage 'general formula grant' that had been used since 1957).

Ontario is the only province in Canada to use a percentage equalizing grant to finance its schools. The percentage equalizing grant defines a percentage of expenditures that will be paid by the central authority in a 'key district,' usually set up as a district with assessed valuation per pupil equal to the provincial average. The percentage of expenditures paid in other districts is adjusted according to the ratio of their assessed valuations per pupil to the assessed valuation per pupil in the key district. An approximation of the formula for this grant can be obtained by using schedules that set forth specific percentages of approved expenditures to be paid to districts in different wealth categories. Such schedules were used in Ontario from 1944 to 1964. In 1968, after an interlude in which a fixed-unit equalizing grant was used to finance ordinary expenditures, the province adopted a standard version of the percentage equalizing formula to determine the amounts of the provincial grants.

Analysis of the equalization formulas employed in each province would

TABLE 6.1

Current Revenues of Public School Boards from Provincial Grants and Local Taxation, 1890–1979

Year	Provincial grants, %	Local taxation, %	Combined revenue	
			%	Thousands of dollars
1890	17.8	82.2	100	7,032
1900	19.0	81.0	100	9,557
1910	17.2	82.8	100	22,787
1920	11.9	88.1	100	71,098
1930	14.7	85.3	100	115,638
1940	16.5	83.5	100	117,522
1950	35.3	64.7	100	307,526
1960	40.6	59.4	100	1,097,432
1970	56.8	43.2	100	3,966,774
1979	66.0	34.0	100	10,846,042

SOURCES: *Historical Statistics of Canada* edited by M.C. Urquhart and K.A.H. Buckley (Toronto: Macmillan 1965) 599; Dominion Bureau of Statistics *Survey of Education Finance 1959–60* (Ottawa: Queen's Printer 1963) 43; Statistics Canada *Financial Statistics of Education 1969–1970* (Ottawa: Information Canada 1975) 75–6; *Financial Statistics of Education 1979–1980* (Ottawa: Minister of Supply and Services 1982) 42–3

reveal much about patterns of influence in provincial school politics. Viewed from the perspective of equal accessibility, however, the important attribute of all of these provincial grants is their success, as tables 6.1 and 6.2 show, in shifting the main burden of financing elementary and secondary schools from local government (where the regime based on civic education had lodged it) to the provincial governments.[20] The financial support of the federal government also increased. Limited federal financial support for technical education was given under the Agricultural Instruction Act (1919), the Technical EducationlAct (1919), and the Vocational Training Co-ordination Act (1942). Undoubtedly, the single most influential instrument of federal support was the Technical and Vocational Training Assistance Act (1960), under which about $950 million in federal grants was expended between 1961 and 1968. By the time the program was terminated, the multilateral composite high school was irreversibly established in all provinces in both urban and rural areas, and occupational selection was the dominating orientation of provincial school systems.

Public Schooling as Individual Development

Because they emphasize the adjustment of the child to society (or, more precisely, to the economy) and imply a conditioning theory of learning,

TABLE 6.2

Public Expenditures on Elementary and Secondary Education by Source of Funds, 1950–1 to 1979–80

Year	Federal, %	Provincial, %	Municipal, %	Total %	Thousands of dollars
1950–1	3.6	37.8	58.6	100	339,721
1955–6	4.0	41.5	54.5	100	629,103
1960–1	4.1	43.5	52.4	100	1,245,833
1965–6	6.2	48.3	45.5	100	2,273,628
1970–1	5.9	57.4	36.7	100	4,677,353
1975–6	3.9*	66.4	29.7	100	8,101,911
1979–80	3.9*	67.7	28.4	100	12,970,645

*Contributions by the federal government under its Bilingualism in Education Program are included amounting to $98,612,000 in 1975–6 and $148,855,000 in 1979–80.

SOURCES: Statistics Canada *Historical Compendium of Education Statistics* (Ottawa: Minister of Industry, Trade and Commerce 1978) 183; *Financial Statistics of Education 1979–80* (Ottawa: Minister of Supply and Services 1982) 38–9

school systems that give priority to occupational selection may differ in curriculum from those that emphasize denominational instruction, ethnocentric education, or civic education, but they often differ little in school organization and methods. School systems that give priority in their policy development to child-centred education assume a dynamic theory of learning and express a deep commitment to the unique paths of individual development, and this orientation has significant implications for their educational programs.

In order to provide child-centred learning, schools in their methods and programs must fit the cycle of human physical, intellectual, and emotional growth; they also must be highly flexible in order to allow teachers to structure learning experiences to meet the needs of each child. Children are assumed to have the right to choose for themselves their courses of personal development, but they need help to acquire the capacity to choose freely and wisely. The child's impulses should be trusted, and personal discovery based on individual interests should be accepted as the basis of true learning. The teacher's job is to create an intellectual and psychological climate in which each child can attain self-realization.

Policies for child-centred learning shift the argument for accessibility from generally comparable occupational opportunities to individually specific developmental experiences. Schools are seen to contribute to individual development by providing learning experiences that meet the complex needs of each individual child and de-emphasizing the ranking and competition that inevitably accompany the function of selection. As it was expressed by the Provincial Committee on Aims and Objectives in the Schools of Ontario (the Hall-Dennis Committee),

> When schools exhibit a small selected honour role of students, a price is paid by those who did not make it. Concern should always be felt for the non-team members, the unhonoured, the absentees, and the corridor wanderers. Each child's development in the full sense should be appreciated and given consideration in the ideal school learning situation ... A school should serve all its children comfortably and humanely in its on-going child-centred programs and a learning experience should be found to match the needs to each.[21]

In its 1968 report the Hall-Dennis Committee showed its awareness of the inevitable interdependence of the worlds of work and learning, the need to reconcile civic and occupational education with the goals of individual development, and the potential conflict between the needs of individuals and those of the community: 'How to provide learning experiences aiming at a thousand different destinies and at the same time to educate toward a common heritage and common citizenship is the basic challenge to our society.[22] In its recommendations the committee attempted to resolve these difficulties by adopting John Dewey's ideal of 'the child in society'; but, consistent with its commitment to child-centred learning, 'where conflict remains, the committee tends to side with the individual.'

The goal of child-centred education was incorporated in the elementary and secondary school policies that accompanied two waves of educational reform in Canada. During the 1930s the provinces of English Canada all adopted new curricular guidelines for elementary schooling which reflected the influence of the progressive education movement. During the 1960s a renewed move toward child-centred learning in elementary schools was accompanied by the beginning of significant experiments in student-centred education in secondary schools.

School Programs and Organization

The ideals of American progressive education, with occasional reference to the reports of the Consultative Committee of the Board of Education in Great Britain (the Hadow reports), provided the model for curriculum change during the 1930s.[23] Beginning with Saskatchewan in 1929, significant revisions were made over the next decade in the official elementary programs of Nova Scotia (1930), Alberta (1936), Ontario (1937), and British

Columbia, Manitoba, and New Brunswick (1939). They signalled a shift from traditional formal elementary schooling toward greater concern for individual differences, more satisfying school experiences for children, and a conception of learning as an active developmental process.

The 1936 program of studies for elementary schools in Alberta changed school organization from an elementary-secondary to a primary-intermediate-senior division of grades; and it stressed an 'activity' or 'enterprise' approach in carrying out the revised courses of studies. The guidelines for the new curriculum in intermediate social studies stated that

the basic principle of procedure in this course is that learning is an active process. The outline abounds in activities that call for pupil experimentation, individual research, and creative self-expression. The social studies classroom instead of being a place where children 'learn' history, geography and civics, is to be a real laboratory, where co-operation, initiative, originality and responsibility are developed.[24]

Similarly, Ontario's *Program of Studies for Grades I to VI of the Public and Separate Schools*, published in 1937, assumed that 'knowing' and 'doing' were synonymous terms, each implying purposeful effort, and that each child's development was to be determined by individual needs and capacities. The school was expected to stimulate children and guide them into experiences that would help them to satisfy their own needs.[25] Accordingly, the program of studies proposed a flexible grade system, adaptation of the program by teachers to meet the interests and capacities of individual children, and enrichment or remedial programs for exceptional children.

Implementation of these revised aims of elementary schooling was impeded almost immediately by teacher shortages and expenditure constraints caused by the outbreak of war and by the enrolment increases of the 1950s. Moreover, even in the most progressive provinces of British Columbia and Alberta, the division between those defending teacher-centred, subject-oriented instruction and those advocating child-centred, activity-oriented learning persisted during the 1950s; curriculum changes were correspondingly modest. The outstanding contribution to the debate during the 1950s probably was Hilda Neatby's attack on progressive education in *So Little for the Mind*,[26] and at the end of the decade the reports of royal commissions in both Alberta and British Columbia advocated a greater emphasis on the traditional subjects and the intellectual development of the student.

The major educational reforms enacted during the 1960s were aimed at providing greater equality of access to secondary schooling; but in a reformist environment, the goal of more child-centred learning rapidly became the accepted assumption in policies for elementary schooling and began to gain some influence in the organization of secondary schooling. Recent advances toward child-centred learning are well illustrated by the revision of official aims of education to stress individual development and the redesign of public school systems to provide for the continuous progress of students.

Provincial government statements on the aims of education are typically vague and ambiguous and acquire some meaning only when they are studied in terms of details of departmental regulations and school practices. None the less, the general importance that is now assigned to individual development among the several aims of education is striking. For example, the stated philosophies of the governments of the four Atlantic provinces all express a belief in the dignity, worth, and right to self-realization of every person and an intention to nurture individual development. Their aim, as a 1972 New Brunswick document put it, is to help each child to become 'a happy, well adjusted, productive individual – the best person he is capable of becoming.'[27] In Quebec the official objectives of the reforms initiated in 1964 included the goals of making training more comprehensive and adapting the school to community needs; two other aims were 'to gear instruction toward *individual needs*' and 'to aim at a harmonious and integral development of the student's personality by promoting the concept of the *pupil-centred school*, rather than limiting the reform to intellectual development.[28] Similarly, a 1974 white paper on education in British Columbia expressed the belief 'that a major responsibility of the school system is to provide a measure of success for every student ... The opportunity for suitable education should be provided to all children.'[29]

In primary education the impact of the principle of child-centred learning is most easily illustrated by the widespread adoption of policies of continuous progress in ungraded systems. Consider, for example, the Atlantic provinces in the middle 1970s.

Many elementary schools in the Region are moving away from the rigid graded structures which encouraged conformity, stressed obedience, and fostered the cultural heritage of the majority. They are operating within a more open flexible non-graded structure based on the philosophy of continuous progress as a means of encouraging the development of individual potential. There is an increase in the use of those practices which encourage independent learning in a variety of social situations under teacher guidance.[30]

Primary schools in the western provinces also reorganized their programs to provide for individual differences among students; 'the concept of continuous progress, with its curricular corollary of units of work in place of units of time, is gradually replacing the traditional one-grade-one-year type of instructional planning.'[31] Significantly, the centralization and consolidation of small primary schools in rural areas of the west, a leading feature of earlier school reforms, was slowed down because 'the evolution of curriculum organization based on non-graded schools and continuous progress plans has enhanced the prospect of relatively small elementary schools located closer to the homes of the children.'[32]

Perhaps the greatest change occurred in the primary schools of Quebec. Regulation 1, issued by the Department of Education in 1965, ordered changes in school organization and curricula based on the fundamental principle that 'the pedagogical reorganization of the school system should be entirely centred on the child with a view of providing a well-rounded education and allowing each child to advance at his own pace.'[33] This policy meant replacing traditional grades by an ungraded primary program, individualized instruction, and greater autonomy and responsibility for teachers in guiding individual learning experiences.

In secondary schools, the influence of the principle of child-centred learning can be seen in the change that occurred during the late 1960s and early 1970s from separate academic, technical, and commercial streams to credit systems with subject promotion and individual timetables. In each of the western provinces, for example, secondary schooling became structured by a credit system that established various provincial requirements regarding general education and course distribution and that excluded vocational streaming either between different types of secondary schools or within different branches of composite schools. In contrast, the Atlantic provinces were slower to abandon vocational streaming. In Nova Scotia and Prince Edward Island, differences between 'academic' and 'vocational' students were reduced in comprehensive high schools. Both provinces continued to operate separate regional vocational schools, however, and in New Brunswick the majority of pupils continued to progress through senior high school in one of the three available programs: college preparatory, general educational, and occupational or practical.[34]

Changes in secondary school organization probably were most pronounced in Quebec and Ontario. In Quebec, regulation 1 replaced the former system of grade promotion, home-room teachers, and class timetables with subject promotion, discipline specialists, and individual timetables. As a result, students were no longer compelled to enrol in specific sections or schools determined by a particular program.[35] Ontario's reorganized program introduced in 1962–3 originally provided for three vocational branches (arts and science, business and commerce, and science, technology, and trades) with three programs (two-year, four-year, and five-year); but during the late 1960s the boundaries became increasingly blurred as students were permitted to build individual programs from all branches and courses. Between 1968 and 1971 circular HS1, which sets out provincial requirements for organizing secondary schools and conferring diplomas, provided for both the reorganized program and a new credit system. Schools were encouraged to transfer to the credit system, however, and most had done so by 1971–2, when all schools were required to adopt the credit system.

State Aid to Private Schools

School policy-making founded on a commitment to satisfy individual needs for belongingness, esteem, and self-realization gave a new context to old conflicts over state aid for private denominational schooling and state regulation of the language of instruction. Inherent in the tenets of ethical liberalism is a concern for freedom of individual choice in learning experiences, a concern that decisively undermines the exclusive prerogatives of a common state system. Consider, for example, J.S. Mill's classic argument against a state monopoly on education.

That the whole or any large part of the education of the people should be in State hands, I go as far as anyone in deprecating. All that has been said of the importance of individuality of character, and diversity in opinions and modes of conduct, involves, as of the same unspeakable importance, diversity of education. A general State education is a mere contrivance for molding people to be exactly like one another; and as the mold in which it casts them is that which pleases the predominant power in the government, whether this be a monarch, a priesthood, an aristocracy, or the majority of the existing generation; in proportion as it is efficient and successful, it establishes a despotism over the mind, leading by natural tendency to one over the body. An education established and controlled by the State should only exist, if it exist at all, as one among many competing experiments, carried on for the purpose of example and stimulus, to keep the others up to a certain standard of excellence.[36]

Commitment to individual development as the primary social purpose of education has only slightly altered the formal provisions for denominational instruction established by nineteenth-century compromises on 'the school question,'[37] but it has led to more generous public financial support for private schooling.[38] Since 1967 public funding has been available in Alberta to private schools that meet certain conditions: the Alberta curriculum must be taught, the teachers must have Alberta teaching certificates, the students must write provincial examinations, the schools must be open to regular inspection and must conform to provincial standards, and the parents of the students must be residents of Alberta. Grants to private schools can be as much as 75 per cent of the basic provincial foundation program. In 1968 Quebec began giving financial aid to private schools that were designated as operating in the public interest, a term defined primarily by the extent to which their curriculum coincided with the provincial curriculum. Such schools receive grants equal to 80 per cent of average per pupil costs in equivalent public schools, and schools not meeting the public-interest criterion may still be eligible for a 60 per cent grant. In British Columbia, following ten years of lobbying by the British Columbia Federation of Independent Schools, the Social Credit government in 1977 fulfilled its campaign promise to assist independent schools by paying part of their operating costs and their teachers' salaries. Public funding for private schools can be as much as 30 per cent of the grants made to public schools. Beginning in 1980, Saskatchewan granted private secondary schools 55 per cent of their average costs per pupil and, for those that had been in operation at least five years, 10 per cent of approved capital costs. Manitoba, after several years of providing assistance in kind for transportation, textbooks, vocational education, and even school facilities, in 1981 began to give private schools financial aid similar to that provided in the other western provinces.

Minority and Heritage Languages

The issues of language and culture surfaced again during the 1960s, partly because of the fundamental reconsideration of bilingualism and biculturalism that was taking place in Canada, partly because of the growing ascendancy of individualist over nationalist education. In its final report the Royal Commission on Bilingualism and Biculturalism argued that 'the school is a basic agency for maintaining language and culture and without this essential resource neither can be strong,' and that 'it must be accepted as normal that children of both linguistic groups will have access to schools in which their own language is the language of instruction.'[39] According to the commission, the exercise of that right required the establishment of parallel school systems in Quebec, Ontario, and New Brunswick, and parallel schools in the 'bilingual districts' of other provinces.

Provincial governments have responded to these demands for 'equal partnership' with varying degrees of generosity, but there has been a significant movement in several English-speaking provinces toward greater local autonomy in establishing English or French as the language of instruction in schools. For example, the Ontario government refused to create a parallel system of French-language schools, but in 1968 it did establish the right of Franco-Ontarian students, where their numbers warranted it, to receive instruction in French-language elementary and secondary classes or schools. In 1967 an amendment to the Manitoba School Act officially recognized French as an alternative to English as the language of instruction for up to one-half of the school day, and in 1970 Franco-Manitobans gained minority-language school privileges similar to those available to Franco-Ontarians. In Prince Edward Island the relatively small (one elementary school, one high school) Regional Administrative Unit Number Five has operated as a bilingual district since it was set up in 1972, and French is the operational language of the Argyle-Clare district school board in southwestern Nova Scotia.

In New Brunswick, where 34 per cent of the population has French as its mother tongue, the trend since the school reforms of 1967 has been to create parallel French and English systems. The first step was the appointment of separate English and French deputy ministers; that was followed by separate divisions of central educational services. At the local level, the Bathurst and Dalhousie school districts were replaced by unilingual districts with separate administrations in 1978, and by 1981 all school districts had been reorganized into parallel systems of English-language and French-language school districts.

In Quebec, where the language issue became a major expression of Quebec nationalism, school reforms tended to retreat from the long-standing concept of parallel systems and instead constrained English-language education. Bill 63, passed in 1969, made French the official language of Quebec, but preserved the minority right to choose English as the language of instruction. Bill 22, the 1974 Official Language Act, made French the official language of instruction in the public schools. School boards were permitted to provide instruction in English only to those pupils who already had a 'sufficient knowledge' of English; and an upper limit on English-language pupils was set at a number equal to the number of students enrolled in English-language schools in 1975. The act was attacked by immigrant groups as a device to force immigrants into the French sector; it was condemned by the English community in Quebec as an infringement of its historic rights; and it was derided by Quebec nationalists as totally inadequate to ensure the pre-eminence of the French language in Quebec.

The Charter of the French Language (bill 101), passed by the Parti Québécois government in August 1977, responded to this nationalist criticism. It abolished the language test of bill 22 and restricted entry to English-language schools to children who were residing temporarily in the province or who had at least one parent whose primary education was in English in Quebec. In spite of bitter criticism from non-French minority groups, the legislation stood without revision until September 1982, when the Quebec Superior Court ruled that the language charter's restriction on English-language instruction was unconstitutional. According to Mr Justice Jules Deschenes, 'the Quebec clause has been rendered of no force and effect as a result of the Canadian Charter of Rights and Freedoms.' Proclaimed in April 1982, section 23 of the Charter of Rights guarantees minority-language education, where numbers warrant, for children of all Canadian citizens educated in English or French anywhere in Canada. The Deschenes ruling was subsequently upheld by the Supreme Court of Canada and accepted by the Quebec government, but it may have little substantive effect as demographic trends and provincial emigration combine to shrink the English-language school population and threaten the viability of an English-language system.

In addition to English-French bilingual instruction, several provinces have implemented 'heritage language' programs intended to recognize and foster a multicultural Canada. In 1971 Alberta made it legal to teach in a language other than English for up to 50 per cent of school time; bilingual programs combining English with French, Ukrainian, Hebrew, or German have been developed.[40] Manitoba began an English-Ukrainian program in 1979, and since then has added English-German and English-Hebrew programs. Saskatchewan offers English-Ukrainian and English-German bilingual programs. The Ontario government has made grants since 1977 to school boards for instruction in forty-five heritage languages, but instruction is limited to $2^{1}/_{2}$ hours a week, carries no academic credit, and must be given outside regular school hours or by lengthening the school day. In 1978 Quebec offered to support one half-hour of daily instruction in minority languages beginning in first grade, and instruction during school hours is now given in Italian, Portuguese, Greek, and Arabic. Obviously, provincial policies differ markedly among the eastern, central, and western provinces. Yet, as William Johnson has concluded, 'the trend toward the recognition of heritage languages is running strong';[41] it is an expression of continuing commitment to a philosophy of educational diversity and individual development.

Of course the achievements of the movement toward child-centred learning should not be exaggerated. Many schools continue to be dull, depressing places unaffected by any anti-authoritarian orientation. Criticism from the public and from teachers has resulted in a slow retreat from unstructured credit systems. In Ontario, for example, secondary-school reorganization was hardly in place when the Ontario Teachers' Federation in 1973 presented a brief to the minister of education calling for a return to compulsory subjects because of 'the lack of any defined core of knowledge, skills or attitudes' in the new program. Beginning in 1974, Ontario secondary students were required to take six compulsory subjects (four English courses and two Canadian studies courses); in 1977 the compulsory core was increased to nine credits; and in 1984, beginning with the students who entered grade nine that year, sixteen of the thirty credits required for the new Ontario Secondary School Diploma became compulsory. Ontario has so far resisted pressures to reinstate formal provincial examinations; but in Alberta, where one of the first acts of the newly elected Lougheed government in 1971 was abolition of provincial examinations, students graduating in 1984 were required to take an examination that tested their knowledge in four major areas – language arts, mathematics, history and social sciences, and physical and biological sciences – covering work done during the final three years of school.

The achievements of child-centred learning should not be exaggerated, but neither should they be underestimated. The revisions of official statements of the aims of education are significant. So are the changes in school organization and programs which, regardless of the current tendency to focus on secondary schooling as job preparation, have been altered decisively and permanently by their expressed concern for individual development. In spite of budget constraints, school boards are expanding their programs to meet the particular needs of students who are physically or mentally handicapped, artistically talented, or intellectually gifted. Public funding for private schooling and heritage-language instruction demonstrate a recognition of the diversity of beliefs and cultures that nurture individual development in a pluralistic society. The prevailing liberal public philosophy attributes a high priority to individual opportunity through education; but now, despite the differences between 'economic' and 'ethical' liberalism, the meaning given to 'opportunity' recognizes in principle the diversity and complexity of higher needs for individual development.

Liberalism and Accessibility

Historically, economic progress and social order have been the dominant functions of the liberal state; and, assuming the criterion of gratification health founded on a hierarchy of basic human needs, they should be expected to take priority. None the less, individual needs for belonging-ness, respect, and self-actualization can be realized in part by public collective action. The argument that there are higher needs with corres-ponding political goods implies a shortfall in the realization of full human development if the purposes of governments are restricted simply to economic progress and social order. Hesitantly, federal and provincial governments in Canada have begun to recognize those higher needs and to commit themselves to a broader conception of the purposes of public policy. Accordingly, whatever they may contribute to the functions of economic progress and social order, at least some modern public policies have to be interpreted and assessed primarily in relation to a growing recognition of basic rights to individual growth and self-realization.

As a principle of educational policy, accessibility assumes that public or private distributional inequalities are the main barriers to individual dignity and creativity. Opportunities for self-realization can be equalized by policies that remove or at least substantially reduce inequalities in access to education, but individuals continue to be responsible for taking the initia-tives required to make the most of those opportunities. Accessibility thus is a policy principle consistent with traditional liberal ideological assump-tions about the priority of individual privacy and freedom. The goal is individual development; individuals have the right and responsibility to make the personal efforts required to realize their potentials; the state's obligation is limited to ensuring that unfair or unjust differences in oppor-tunities for self-developmental activities are minimized.

A hidden question concerns what constitutes the unfair or unjust differ-ences that ought to be remedied by the state. In Canadian educational policy, liberal thinking has been most comfortable attacking territorial inequities, such as low-quality secondary schooling in poor rural areas. Policy-making has appeared more tentative or has stalled completely when faced with institutional inequities that result from the dominant majority's value system – for example, the superior status of traditional academic secondary schooling or the assumption that all Canadians should speak English. Although options in school programs have been growing, espe-cially since the 1960s, educational policy still adopts a far more restricted view of what accessibility should mean than is required for the satisfaction of universal individual development in a pluralistic, multicultural society.

A more difficult problem with liberal policy thinking about accessibility is the assumption that equalizing opportunities meets the state's obliga-tions to further individual development. In fact, a combination of publicly promoted accessibility and privately generated initiative is necessary but not sufficient to ensure individual development, and certainly does not exhaust the state's potential contribution to individual development. To carry out self-developmental activities people need a combination of opportunity, capacity, and incentive. If opportunities for individual development are increased or even equalized, individual responses will still depend on the existence of individual capacities or resources and growth-oriented personal motivation. This implies a need for more far-reaching policies that will effect positive changes in people's capacities for and orientations toward self-realization. This also explains why the concept of child-centred education is so important in ethical liberal thought. People cannot be forced to be free, but perhaps they can be taught to be free. The difficulty, of course, is to devise appropriate educational programs; the danger is that in the process people might be manipulated. Yet if the potential of public policy to aid individual development is to be fully realized, that danger has to be met and surmounted.

7

Human Rights

A right is a claim made against the state authorities of a political community for some specified kind of treatment to be accorded to individuals or groups. In this sense we limit rights to claims that other persons are capable of fulfilling.[1]

Human rights can be conveniently divided into three broad categories.[2] First, political rights and freedoms include suffrage rights, freedom of expression, freedom of assembly and association, and freedom of conscience and religion. Second, legal rights include general security of life, liberty, and property; equal protection of the law; and the right to be informed promptly of the reason for arrest, to retain counsel, to have the remedy of *habeas corpus*, to have a fair hearing, to be presumed innocent until proved guilty, and to be protected against cruel punishment. Third, egalitarian rights are guarantees against private conduct or governmental action that distinguishes people for differential treatment according to their national origins, race, sex, or other unjustifiable demographic characteristics. Codes of human rights now commonly forbid such discrimination in offers of employment and in admittance to trade unions and professions; the use of public accommodations, facilities, and services; and entrance into contracts or covenants that involve, for example, private firms or individuals contracting with public agencies, obtaining credit, buying insurance, or selling property.

Unless it is stated in very general terms, neither a claim to a human right nor its guarantee can be taken as absolute.[3] Every right is subject to limitations. Rights claimed and given recognition change over time in political communities, and even those most committed to the protection and enhancement of human rights will disagree, often intensely, about priorities and trade-offs.

The protection of human rights is a field of public policy, although it is all too seldom recognized as such. As in other areas of policy, protecting human rights requires ongoing comparisons among legitimate objectives. The public policy of rights is, however, even more complicated than the others because persons and groups press their claims in an absolutist fashion with the assertion that qualifications of such rights are a denial of the first-order values of the community.[4]

Disagreements also arise among liberal supporters of human rights about the preferred strategy for recognizing and protecting rights in the constitution. On the one hand, the English liberal tradition places its reliance on ordinary law and elected parliaments. Popularly elected representatives are given ultimate responsibility for making laws that protect and enhance human rights, for settling disagreements over rights, and for adopting statutory provisions as concepts of fundamental rights change over time. In the English tradition, independent courts of law are vital institutions for the protection of human rights, but democratic parliaments are sovereign. On the other hand, the American liberal tradition relies primarily on a written constitution and judicial review. A charter of rights entrenched in a written constitution and enforceable through the courts is believed to offer a more effective way of opposing oppressive or arbitrary legislation than political pressures on the legislature. This is particularly true for minorities whose only protection without a charter of rights is the good will of the majority. The advocates of a constitutional charter also emphasize the efficacy of the courts in supervising administrative agencies, removing contentious issues of human rights from legislative politics to the non-partisan deliberations of the courts, and promoting public awareness of basic rights.

Two trends can be detected in the history of Canadian public policy on human rights. First, with respect to claims for fundamental rights, basic political and legal rights were recognized in the achievement of responsible and federal government from the 1840s to the 1860s; effective claims for egalitarian rights were not made until a century later following the Second World War. Second, with respect to the strategy for guaranteeing fundamental rights, the English constitutional tradition of parliamentary supremacy was adopted in the nineteenth century, although legislative powers were divided between federal and provincial legislatures; but as the concern for human rights intensified after the Second World War the American constitutional tradition of a written bill of rights gained increasing support. This trend culminated in the entrenchment of fundamental political, legal, egalitarian, and language rights in the Canadian Charter of Rights and Freedoms.

Political Rights

In liberal-democratic thought a just and free political order is achieved by creating the conditions for political competition. The twin foundations of political competition are political leaders winning public office by competing for the support of non-leaders and non-leaders having the opportunity to switch their support from the incumbents to their rivals.[5] The parallel between the liberal concept of economic market and that of political order is unmistakable.

In the economic model, entrepreneurs and consumers were assumed to be rational maximizers of their own good, and to be operating in conditions of free competition in which all energies and resources were brought to the market, with the result that the market produced the optimum distribution of labour and capital and consumer goods. So in the political model, politicians and voters were assumed to be rational maximizers, and to be operating in conditions of free political competition, with the result that the market-like political system produced the optimum distribution of political energies and political goods.[6]

If liberal democracy depends on free political competition, then democratic political rights are defined by the conditions required to support such competition. Robert Dahl has listed eight institutional requirements for liberal-democratic political competition: freedom to form and join organizations, freedom of expression, the right to vote, general eligibility for public office, the right of political leaders to compete for popular support, alternative sources of information, free and fair elections, and institutions for making government policies depend on votes and other expressions of opinion.[7] The history of liberal democracy in Canada is the struggle over two centuries to establish those institutional requirements as political rights.[8]

Colonial Authoritarianism

During the French colonial regime the authoritarian controls of state and church made impossible the development of political competition. Before 1690 the authorities experienced difficulties in enforcing some of their controls, particularly those directed at the trading activities of the coureurs de bois in the interior. After 1690 even that resistance disappeared as the French military presence on the frontier was strengthened, as the fur trade was brought under close control, and as the coureurs de bois became voyageurs.

The defeat of the French regime by the British did not immediately affect the authoritarian character of colonial government. An assembly was granted to Nova Scotia in 1758, but for three decades there was no opposition to the government. In Canada there was an even more determined effort than in Nova Scotia to maintain authoritarian government, and by 1774 governmental and ecclesiastical control was wider and stronger than it had been under French rule.[9]

Between 1790 and 1840 political oppositions were formed in the colonial assemblies, but they were subjected to continual harassment by governmental authorities. Opposition movements, such as those of James Glenie in New Brunswick (1789–1805), Cottnam Tonge in Nova Scotia (1792–1807), Louis-Joseph Papineau in Lower Canada (1807–37), and Robert Gourlay (1817–19) and William Lyon Mackenzie (1828–37) in Upper Canada, were met with suspension of the reformers from official positions, their expulsion from the assemblies, rejection of policies proposed by reformist assemblies, charges of seditious libel, and banishment from the colonies. In Nova Scotia, for example, Cottnam Tonge succeeded in building up the rudimentary organization of a popular reform movement and was elected speaker of the assembly in 1805; but after the election of 1806 the governor refused to accept Tonge as speaker, dismissed him from his post as naval officer, enforced an old law against town meetings to prevent demonstrations of public opposition, and suspended a number of justices of the peace who supported Tonge. In 1827 the governor of Lower Canada refused to accept Papineau as speaker, prorogued the legislature, and brought charges of seditious libel against the editor and printer of a newspaper carrying accounts of protest meetings. The following year fifty-seven bills passed by the first reform assembly in Upper Canada were vetoed by the legislative council, and the reform leader Mackenzie was expelled five times from the anti-reform assembly of 1830.

The subservience of newspapers to the government was taken for granted in British North America during the second half of the eighteenth century.[10] It resulted from their almost complete dependence on the financial support and patronage of the colonial ruling élite. In the early nineteenth century, however, editors began to print advertisements and sell subscriptions instead of depending on government patronage. Editorial comment on contentious social and political issues, especially on the struggle for responsible government, openly challenged governmental controls over news publication and resulted in many conflicts between editors and public officials. Coercion of newspaper publishers, editors, and journalists was common and at first effective; but it also tended to evoke public sympathy and opposition, as illustrated by the acquittal of Joseph Howe on criminal charges of libel in 1835, an important victory for freedom of the press.

Probably the most oppressive policy of the Canadian authorities was their tolerance of anti-reform mob violence. As a result of the activities of the reactionary Orange Order, 'something closely approaching gangsterism was introduced into the politics of Upper Canada, and mob violence came increasingly to be relied upon in the two years before the rebellion as a means of suppressing efforts to secure by free and open discussion a solution of public questions.'[11] Violence involving reformers and reactionaries after a mass meeting caused Papineau to leave Montreal in November 1837; but the government, believing the reformers to be on the verge of rebellion, issued warrants for the arrest of Papineau and other reform leaders. A series of bitter clashes followed and the insurrection was ruthlessly suppressed, as was a clumsy rebellion led by the reformers of Upper Canada.

The franchise acts that followed the granting of representative assemblies from 1758 to 1830 also contributed to the suppression of political competition by their highly discriminatory property, sex, and religious qualifications.[12] The freehold franchise prevalent in rural England was extended to the colonies of Nova Scotia, New Brunswick, and the Canadas, and freeholders, leaseholders, and householders were allowed to vote in Prince Edward Island. The colonies followed the British practice of disfranchising women by convention and the rule of the common law. The first franchises in the colonies also included religious disqualifications similar to those existing in Britain; these especially affected Roman Catholics, Quakers, and Jews.

Following the introduction of more liberal policies in Britain after 1749, legislation permitting an affirmation to be substituted for an oath of allegiance was passed by the assembly of Nova Scotia in 1759, New Brunswick in 1786, Prince Edward Island in 1785, Lower Canada in 1793, and finally Upper Canada in 1833; the colonial franchises and legislatures were thereby opened to Quakers, Moravians, Mennonites, and members of other religious sects who refused to swear an oath. Roman Catholics were first enfranchised in Nova Scotia in 1789. The Constitutional Act of 1791 granted all citizens in Lower and Upper Canada the rights of franchise and election to the colonial assembly regardless of their religious adherence, and New Brunswick passed legislation allowing Roman Catholics to vote in 1810. Finally, following the example of the Catholic Emancipation Act in Britain, Prince Edward Island opened its franchise and all elective offices to Catholics in 1829, and Nova Scotia and New Brunswick granted them the right of election the following year. The disfranchisement of Jews in British North America was an incidental effect of the policies intended to disfranchise Catholics, and as Catholics obtained the right to vote so did Jews, although indirect restrictions on their right of election remained in force in New Brunswick and Nova Scotia until 1846.

Although religious disqualifications ended, suffrage restrictions relating to sex and property ownership were being tightened. Disfranchisement of women was given statutory effect in Prince Edward Island in 1836, in New Brunswick in 1843, the Province of Canada in 1849, and in Nova Scotia in 1851. Until the 1830s the freehold property qualification was perhaps more significant in principle than it was in practice, but the end to grants of free land made the property qualification much more restrictive after the 1830s. At mid-century Prince Edward Island had the most liberal provisions; its occupancy franchise was extended after 1853 to include all citizens liable for statute labour on the roads – in effect, the entire male population. The most restrictive qualifications existed in New Brunswick, where the assessment franchise adopted in 1855 did not include the labouring class, which represented one-fifth of the male population, and in British Columbia, where a very complex franchise came close to producing manhood suffrage for whites only in a province with a large proportion of non-white residents. Property qualifications remained an important restriction until 1898, when the federal government returned to using provincial franchises for federal elections; and, since manhood suffrage had been adopted in all the provinces except Quebec and Nova Scotia, the notion that the franchise was a trust accompanying property rather than a right of citizenship soon disappeared from Canadian politics except at the municipal level.

Competitive Parties and Universal Suffrage

During the 1840s party competition came to be accepted as a part of responsible government, and executive oppression of opposition parties was replaced by governmental manipulation of electoral rules. The main methods used to improve the position of the governing party and to inconvenience the opposition were deferred elections, gerrymandering, and the alteration of franchise qualifications.

Voting was not simultaneous in all constituencies in the first three national elections of 1867, 1872, and 1874. The government was able to call the election first in favourable constituencies, and later take its campaign to marginal and dangerous constituencies. In 1878 simultaneous voting was established throughout the east for all but a few constituencies; Manitoba voted with the east in 1882, and by 1908 deferred elections had been discontinued in the majority of western constituencies.[13]

In 1872, 1882, and 1892 the governing party clearly abused its power to redistribute seats in the House of Commons by altering constituency boundaries so as to favour its re-election; this practice was especially flagrant in 1882, when forty-six constituencies in Ontario were gerrymandered.[14] The potential for abuse was greatly reduced in 1903, when the Laurier government assigned the task of redistribution to a select committee of the House of Commons that included representatives of both parties; and gerrymandering on a grand scale disappeared.

The most blatant example of manipulating the rules of voting eligibility was the Wartime Elections Act, passed just before the 1917 election. Under the 1917 amendments the franchise was granted to virtually all members of the armed forces including non-residents, minors, and Indians, to all women who had husbands, sons, brothers, or fathers in the Canadian or British armed forces, and to any men disqualified by provincial property or income qualifications who had sons or grandsons in the services. The disfranchised groups included conscientious objectors, Mennonites, Doukhobors, all naturalized British subjects born in an enemy country and naturalized after March 1902, and anyone naturalized after 1902 who habitually spoke an enemy language. Newly franchised soldiers and the fathers, grandfathers, wives, mothers, sisters, and daughters of soldiers were expected to vote for the government; the disfranchised naturalized aliens, according to their record between 1900 and 1911, were thought likely to vote for the Liberal opposition. As Ward has remarked, these changes produced 'the most remarkable franchise act ever passed in Canada and very possibly in the democratic world' and could hardly fail to return a majority for the Union government enacting it.[15]

The most important instance of party oppression in the early twentieth century occurred during the 'red scare' period at the end of the First World War. Fifteen radical associations were banned by order-in-council in 1918–19 under the authority of the War Measures Act.[16] Among the seven leaders of the Winnipeg Strike who were convicted of seditious conspiracy in 1920, four were also leaders of the radical Socialist Party of Canada and one was a Social Democrat. In 1919, following the strike, a section aimed at preventing unlawful association was added to the Criminal Code. Any organization

whose professed purpose or one of whose purposes is to bring about any governmental industrial or economic change within Canada by use of force, violence of physical injury to person or property, or by threats of such injury, or which teaches, advocates, advises or defends the use of force, violence, terrorism, or physical injury to person or property, or threats of such injury, in order to accomplish such change, or for any other purpose, or which shall by any means prosecute or pursue such purpose or professed purpose, or shall so teach, advocate, advise or defend shall be an unlawful association.

There were three reported instances of prosecutions and two convictions under this section, all against Communists, before the section was repealed in 1936.[17]

The following year the Quebec government passed the Communistic Propaganda Act, which empowered the government to close any house being used to propagate communism and to confiscate propaganda materials. It was not until 1957 in the case of *Switzman* v *Elbling and the Attorney-General for Quebec* that the Supreme Court of Canada declared the 'Padlock Law' to be unconstitutional. In a historic decision on legislative jurisdiction over political rights in Canada, five of the eight-member majority ruled that by making the propagation of communism a crime the Quebec act invaded the federal parliament's jurisdiction over criminal laws. The other three in addition rejected the provincial act as constituting a restriction of a fundamental political right. Referring to the preamble of the BNA Act, they held that without freedom of expression the democratic parliamentary system of government intended by the British North America Act would be impossible to achieve.[18]

In the second half of the nineteenth century attempts at governmental domination and manipulation of the press ended, and the limits of press freedom were set by public laws on censorship, sedition, defamatory libel, and contempt of court.[19] Except for the periods of the two world wars, restrictions on the freedom of the press in the twentieth century have been relatively few.[20] The most important attempt to censor the press was made by the Alberta Social Credit government in 1937.[21] The Act to Ensure the Publication of Accurate News and Information compelled newspapers to disclose the sources of their information and to print government statements correcting previous articles. Contravening the act could result in a ban on further publication. When it was referred to the Supreme Court of Canada by the federal government, the act was found to be an invasion of federal powers; but three judges put forward for the first time the argument based on the preamble to the BNA Act that 'a Constitution similar in principle to that of the United Kingdom' implies freedom of expression, including freedom of the press. In Mr Justice Cannon's opinion,

under the British system which is ours, no political party can erect a prohibitory barrier to prevent the electors from getting information concerning the policy of the government. Freedom of discussion is essential to enlighten public opinion in a democratic state; it cannot be curtailed without affecting the right of the people to be informed through sources independent of the government concerning matters of public interest. There must be an untrammelled publication of the news and political opinions of the political parties contending for ascendancy.[22]

Restrictions on the rights of Canadians to vote and run for public office were substantially removed in the twentieth century, beginning with the first legislation granting female suffrage in Manitoba in 1916. Similar legislation soon followed in other jurisdictions, and by 1922 women had the right to vote and seek election at the federal level and in all provinces except Quebec.[23]

After the adoption of female suffrage, the most serious remaining shortcomings of suffrage legislation were the discriminatory qualifications based on ethnic and national origins. Until 1948 Canadians of Chinese, Japanese, and East Indian origins had no vote unless they had served in the armed forces; and it was not until 1953 that all references to race were finally removed from franchise legislation in British Columbia. Doukhobors were enfranchised in British Columbia in 1953, and in 1955 Parliament repealed the federal provision that disqualified from voting any persons entitled to claim exemption from military service because of their religious affiliations. The provision of the federal franchise act that had prevented Eskimos from voting after 1934 was repealed in 1950. The federal disfranchisement of Indians living on reservations continued until 1960, and their provincial disfranchisement in Quebec until 1969.

In terms of the number of people who were previously disqualified, the most important changes in suffrage qualifications since 1920 have been those that increased the number eligible to vote and seek elective office by lowering the age limit from twenty-one to eighteen or nineteen. The first provinces to lower the age limits were Alberta (to nineteen in 1944), Saskatchewan (to eighteen in 1945), British Columbia (to nineteen in 1953), and Quebec (to eighteen in 1963). At the end of the 1960s similar changes were made in other jurisdictions. By 1973 the voting age had been lowered to eighteen for federal elections, to eighteen for provincial elections in Prince Edward Island, New Brunswick, Ontario, Manitoba, and Alberta, and to nineteen in Newfoundland and Nova Scotia.

Constitutional Rights

The first attempt to give comprehensive legislative protection to political rights in Canada was made in the Saskatchewan Bill of Rights (1947), which provided for the protection of basic political rights, including freedom of speech, religion, and assembly, and for a provincial election at least once every five years. The only other province to give such legislative protection to political rights is Quebec, which enacted its Charter of Human Rights and Freedoms in 1976.

The Canadian Bill of Rights was passed in 1960. The preamble of the bill affirmed 'that men and institutions remain free only when freedom is founded upon respect for moral and spiritual values and the rule of law.' Sections 1(c) to 1(f) recognized and guaranteed four specific political freedoms: freedom of religion, freedom of speech, freedom of assembly and association, and freedom of the press. The bill provided that federal statutes should be construed and applied so as not to infringe these rights except where Parliament specifically authorized an exemption. Apparently Prime Minister John Diefenbaker would have preferred a bill that was entrenched in the constitution, but believed that the provincial support necessary for a constitutional amendment was unattainable.[24]

Mainly because the Bill of Rights was not entrenched, the record of the Supreme Court in its review of the bill was disappointing. However, it was a desire to broaden linguistic rights and forestall a unilateral provincial initiative on constitutional review rather than the weak judicial record of the Bill of Rights that led the federal government to propose the entrenchment of basic political, civil, egalitarian, and linguistic rights in the constitution.[25] The first part of the 1968 white paper, *A Canadian Charter of Human Rights*, recognized and guaranteed freedom of conscience and religion, speech, assembly and association, and press, and the rights of each individual to life, liberty, security of person, enjoyment of property, due process, and equal protection of the law. The third part of the charter, which was based on existing provincial anti-discrimination codes, was soon dropped from active consideration, and two continuing federal–provincial subcommittees were struck to draft sections that would entrench political and linguistic rights in the constitution.

The resulting sections on political rights in the Victoria Charter recognized the fundamental freedoms of thought, conscience and religion, opinion and expression, peaceful assembly, and association. The charter also went beyond the Bill of Rights and the 1968 proposed charter in proclaiming the principles of universal suffrage and free democratic election to be fundamental principles of the constitution. No person should be denied the right to vote in a federal or provincial election or denied the opportunity to serve in the federal or provincial legislature by reason of race, ethnic or national origin, colour, religion, or sex. Each legislature should continue for no more than five years between elections, except in cases of real or apprehended war, invasion, or insurrection; and there should be at least one session of each legislature at least once in every year. The sections on political rights and corresponding sections on language rights were approved at the Victoria conference in June 1971, only to be nullified by the Quebec government's refusal, because of textual ambiguities concerning jurisdiction over social security and fears about the impact of the amending formula on provincial autonomy, to recommend the agreed articles to the National Assembly.

The apparent threat to Canadian unity created by the victory of the Parti Québécois in the 1976 Quebec provincial election inspired another round of constitutional deliberations, beginning with the federal government's Constitutional Amendment Bill introduced in June 1978 and followed successively by the report of the Task Force on Canadian Unity (January 1979), the Quebec government's proposal for sovereignty-association set out in its white paper, *Quebec-Canada: A New Deal* (November 1979), and the Quebec Liberal Party's plan for a renewed federalism (January 1980). Both the Task Force on Canadian Unity and the Quebec Liberal Party's constitutional committee recommended entrenchment of political, legal, egalitarian, linguistic, and aboriginal rights. The Task Force report pointed out that arguments against entrenchment simply failed to recognize the realities of contemporary political life,

the growing concern of individuals at the pervasive impact of government on their lives, the energetic assertions of native peoples and ethnic groups, and the desire of Quebecois for collective security and for assurances that the individual rights of French-speaking Canadians will be respected as much as those of English-speaking people. Furthermore, entrenchment would perform an educational and inspirational function by making Canadians more aware and more proud of the wide range of freedoms they do have. Above all, a sense of individual and collective confidence in the security of their rights would contribute to a positive attitude to Canadian unity.[26]

The Constitution Act was introduced in October 1980 as a resolution of the House of Commons and Senate addressed to the British Parliament. After prolonged debate and substantial revision in the House of Commons it was also subjected to intensive federal–provincial negotiations before its approval by the Canadian Parliament in December 1981 and by the British Parliament in March 1982. In addition to transferring all constitutional authority to enact laws for Canada from the British Parliament and establishing an amending formula that will govern future constitutional changes in Canada, the Constitution Act, 1981, included the Canadian Charter of Rights and Freedoms, which sets out guarantees for fundamental freedoms and democratic, mobility, legal, equality, and linguistic rights.

The freedoms enumerated in section 2 of the charter are freedom of conscience and religion; thought, belief, opinion, and expression, including freedom of the press and other media of communication; peaceful assembly; and association. Democratic rights (sections 3 to 5) comprise guarantees of universal suffrage, general legislative elections, and annual legislative sessions. These sections of the charter thus guarantee the basic freedoms and rights required to support the free political competition of a liberal democracy, but section 2 purports to do more than that. According to Peter Russell, the section 'is badly cluttered with extravagant phrases.' The charter asks judges to uphold open-ended guarantees such as freedom of conscience and religion and freedom of thought, belief, opinion, and expression without direction as to the purposes for which these freedoms should be protected.

This has the unfortunate result that the section fails to distinguish between those freedoms which are essential to the workings of parliamentary democracy and those which are not. Constitutional entrenchment of the former is more compatible with democracy, as it invites courts to consider whether the democratic process has been interfered with rather than whether the judges approve of laws resulting from the democratic process.[27]

This argument serves to emphasize the continuity in recent Canadian policy-making supporting an open-ended conception of freedoms. The 1960 Bill of Rights, the 1968 proposed charter of fundamental rights, the charter negotiated at Victoria in 1971, and three major drafts of the Charter of Rights and Freedoms have all stated open-ended guarantees of fundamental freedoms rather than restricting them to the narrower context of freedoms essential to the workings of parliamentary democracy. Such an open-ended conception of individual freedoms appears to be entirely consistent with a modern ethical liberalism that gives priority to the general societal requirements for self-development of each individual, not simply the specific political requirements for maintaining parliamentary democracy.[28]

Legal Rights

In the debates of the last quarter century over the entrenchment of human rights, legal rights have been explicitly defined and included in three federal codes: the Canadian Bill of Rights, the 1968 charter, and the Canadian Charter of Rights and Freedoms. The three documents differ in detail, but their main provisions reveal a fundamental consensus on legal rights in Canada.[29]

General Legal Rights: Fundamental Justice

The three statements of rights all guarantee the right to life, liberty, and security of person. The Bill of Rights recognized and declared 'the right of the individual to life, liberty, security of the person and enjoyment of property, and the right not to be deprived thereof except by due process of law.' The proposed 1968 charter used essentially the same language to recognize and guarantee 'the right of the individual to life, and the liberty and security of the person, and the right not to be deprived thereof except by due process of law' (section 1(e)) and 'the right of the individual to the enjoyment of property, and the right not to be deprived thereof except according to law' (section 1(f)). Section 7 of the Canadian Charter of Rights and Freedoms guarantees ('subject only to such reasonable limits prescribed by law as can be demonstrably justified in a free and democratic society') that 'everyone has the right to life, liberty and security of the person and the right not to be deprived thereof except in accordance with the principles of fundamental justice.' Although advocated by the opposition Conservatives and acceptable to the Liberal government, a legal right to enjoyment of property was omitted from the charter. Apparently this was the result of opposition from the New Democrats; they feared an entrenched right could become a conservative barrier to reformist economic regulation and their support was considered essential by the Liberals.[30]

In addition to the general right to life, liberty, and security of person, the charter entrenches three other general legal rights: the right to be secure against unreasonable search or seizure, the right not to be arbitrarily detained or imprisoned, and the right not to be subjected to any cruel and unusual treatment or punishment. Protection against cruel and unusual treatment or punishment was included in virtually identical language in both the 1960 and 1968 charters. Security against unreasonable searches and seizures was also recognized in the 1968 charter, but not in the Bill of Rights; protection against arbitrary detention, imprisonment, or exile was included in the Bill of Rights but not in the 1968 charter.[31]

The general legal rights consistently recognized in Canadian codifications of human rights have their origins far back in the history of English common law. Chapter 39 of the Magna Charta set out the general principle in 1215: 'No free man shall be taken or imprisoned, or disseised of his free tenement, or outlawed or exiled or in any wise destroyed, nor will we go upon him, nor will we send upon him, unless by the lawful judgement of his peers, or by the law of the land. To none will we sell, deny, or delay right or justice.'

The Magna Charta became a powerful symbol of successful opposition to the crown, and in the seventeenth century the forces of liberalism rallied around it.[32] In his commentary on the Magna Charta in 1628, for example, Edward Coke equated 'law of the land' with 'due process of law' and concluded that the provisions were intended to protect the subject from oppressive royal authority.[33] The Petition of Right (1628) from the British House of Commons to Charles I referred to a number of statutes and provisions in the Magna Charta and declared that arbitrary imprisonment was unlawful. The English Bill of Rights (1689) added 'That excessive baile ought not to be required nor excessive fines imposed; nor cruell and unusuall punishment inflicted.'

The Magna Charta and the classic documents of the seventeenth-century liberal struggle with the crown were the primary sources of the American Bill of Rights (1791). In general, the language used in the modern expression of Canadian legal rights has its origins in that great eighteenth-century liberal codification of rights. The Fourth Amendment declared that 'the right of the people to be secure in their persons, houses, papers, and effects, against unreasonable searches and seizures, shall not be violated'; the Fifth Amendment declared that no person shall be 'deprived of life, liberty, or property, without due process of law.'[34] The Eighth Amendment picked up the provision of the English Bill of Rights: 'Excessive bail shall not be required, nor excessive fines imposed, nor cruel and unusual punishments inflicted.'[35]

What do the terms 'due process' and 'fundamental principles of justice' mean in Canada? The leading case under the Bill of Rights is *Curr v The Queen*, decided in 1972.[36] Curr was charged under the Criminal Code with refusing without reasonable excuse to take a breathalyzer test. His claim that he had been denied due process was rejected, and his conviction on appeal was upheld by the Supreme Court of Canada. Speaking for the majority, Mr Justice Laskin asserted the need for great caution when applying the right of due process 'in negation of substantive legislation validly enacted by a Parliament in which the major role is played by the elected representatives of the people.' In addition, he was hesitant to read more into 'due process' from a procedural standpoint than he found in sections 2 (e) ('a fair hearing in accordance with the principles of fundamental justice') and 2(f) ('a fair and public hearing by an independent and impartial tribunal'). The inference is quite clear, however, that if a proper case could have been demonstrated, the Supreme Court would have been prepared to find that the Bill of Rights prevailed over otherwise valid legislation.[37] No doubt the Supreme Court would also have found the bill's due process clause to prevail over procedures not specifically cited in the bill if a case before it caused the members of the court to suffer sufficiently strong 'revulsion and shock of conscience.'[38]

Given the Supreme Court's hesitancy in defining due process, perhaps the best working definition is that of Mr Justice Rand, given in 1960 after his retirement from the Supreme Court. He defined due process as 'a limitation on law which to a degree of unreasonableness affects personal liberties or property.' This interpretation may be especially pertinent to an understanding of the provisions of the Charter of Rights and Freedoms.

What, on its face, is indicated by the [Bill of Rights] is the setting up for all law infringing rights, privileges and liberties, a standard of rational acceptability in the regulation of human conduct and relations. Pertinent to that would be those considerations: the existence of an evil to be curbed or a benefit to be provided, in the public interest; the appropriateness of what is proposed as regulation to the end sought; the extent to which individual privileges and liberties are encroached upon; and the relation between the degree of imposition and the good achieved.[39]

Specific Legal Rights: Criminal Procedure

Section 10 of the Charter of Rights and Freedoms guarantees everyone specific rights in the event of arrest or detention: '(a) to be informed promptly of the reasons therefore; (b) to retain and instruct counsel without delay and to be informed of that right, and (c) to have the validity of the detention determined by way of *habeas corpus* and to be released if the detention is not lawful.' Each of these rights was also recognized and guaranteed in virtually identical language by section 2(c) of the Canadian Bill of Rights and by section 2(b) of the proposed 1968 Charter of Fundamental Rights.[40]

The most ancient of these legal rights is the right to have the validity of detention determined by a writ of *habeas corpus*. The writ, which originated in the Middle Ages, was issued by courts of common law to bring before them persons committed by inferior courts. Later it was used against the royal courts of requests and Star Chamber, but not until the seventeenth century was *habeas corpus* used to resist crown attempts to imprison people without trial. The writ was given statutory recognition in the Habeas Corpus Act of 1679. According to that act, a judge was obligated to issue the writ unless the prisoner obviously had been committed by lawful means.

The instructions to Governor Carleton in 1775 included a direct reference to provision for the writ of *habeas corpus* in Canada: 'Security to personal liberty is a fundamental Principle of Justice in all free Governments, and the making due provision for that purpose is an object the Legislature of Quebec ought never to lose sight of; nor can they follow a better example than that, which the Common Law of this Kingdom hath set in the provision made for a writ of Habeas Corpus, which is the right of every British Subject in this Kingdom.'[41] Carleton determined not to obey this instruction, however, and the legal status of the writ remained in doubt until an ordinance passed in April 1784 established the right of *habeas corpus* for criminal but not civil cases.

Another major grievance of 'the English party' after 1774 was the denial of a right to choose trial by jury under Quebec civil law, although trial by jury was available in criminal cases. In criminal trials in Canada at the end of the eighteenth century, the most noticeable aspect of procedure, as Hilda Neatby has pointed out, was 'the way in which the dice were loaded against the prisoner.'

The witnesses were called in turn, and their depositions, prepared beforehand, were read aloud in court. The prisoner, who had not seen the depositions beforehand, was allowed to cross-examine each individual, but it is not surprising if he made little use of the privilege. He was not allowed the assistance of a lawyer. One man who asked for it was told that such aid was unnecessary, since it was the duty and desire of the whole court to do him justice. At the conclusion of the evidence for the crown the prisoner was allowed to make his own defense and to call witnesses if he so desired, but whether he had the power to compel their attendance is not certain. The conclusion of the defense was followed by the judge's charge to the jury, the verdict, and the sentence.[42]

Independence of the judiciary is an essential condition for a fair hearing.

Under the British colonial regime the power to appoint judges belonged as a matter of royal prerogative to the imperial government, which delegated the authority to colonial governors. The Act of Settlement, 1701, which guaranteed tenure during good behaviour for the British judiciary, did not apply to the appointment of colonial judges, whose tenure was only 'during pleasure.' Chief justices served as members of the governor's executive council, and judges were eligible for election as representatives to the colonial assemblies.

Judicial independence was established by degrees in the first half of the nineteenth century.[43] In 1811, for example, the assembly of Lower Canada made King's Bench judges ineligible for election as representatives. In 1831 the chief justice of Upper Canada ceased to sit on the executive council and retired from the legislative council in 1838. Legislation that disqualified all judges from holding legislative offices was passed first in Nova Scotia and Prince Edward Island in 1848, in the Province of Canada in 1857, and later in British Columbia (1871), Newfoundland (1872), Manitoba (1875), New Brunswick (1877), Saskatchewan, (1906), and Alberta (1909). An 1834 statute of Upper Canada prescribed tenure during good behaviour for superior court judges, and this principle was extended to cover Lower Canada's Queen's Bench judges in 1843 and other superior-court judges in 1849. Nova Scotia bestowed tenure during good behaviour on its superior-court judges in 1848. With the achievement of responsible government the power to appoint judges passed to elected colonial ministries on whose advice the governor was obliged to act. The British North America Act gave the federal government the power to appoint judges to superior, county, and district courts; and the tenure of superior-court judges during good behaviour was constitutionally guaranteed.

The liberal reforms of criminal procedure that occurred in nineteenth-century England were followed in Canada, and certain specific rights to a fair hearing were given statutory guarantees. Under English law after 1696, accused persons were allowed counsel in trials for treason, but not until 1836 were they allowed counsel in felony trials. An 1848 British act (11 & 12 Vict., c.42, generally known as Jervis's Act) required that during preliminary hearings witnesses should be examined in the prisoner's presence and should be liable to cross-examination. The accused was also to be permitted to call witnesses and was entitled to have copies of depositions.

Canada's Criminal Procedure Act, 1869, gave statutory recognition to the accused person's rights to a full defence and the advice of counsel and the rights to inspect all depositions and hear the indictment; these rights were continued in the 1892 codification of Canadian criminal law. On the presumption of an accused person's innocence until guilt has been proved, the 1869 act stated, 'It shall be understood that such a person shall only be deemed guilty of such offence and liable to such punishment after being duly convicted according to law.' This provision was inserted in the 1892 Criminal Code as section 931, and is found in slightly revised form in the current code.

Sections 11(c) and 13 of the Charter of Rights and Freedoms follow the Bill of Rights and the 1968 proposed charter in establishing protection against self-incrimination. Compulsory examination under oath was not part of the English legal tradition, except in the notorious Star Chamber and the Court of High Commission, and the 1848 British act established that the pre-trial examination should be preceded by a warning that it might be used in evidence and that the prisoner need not make a statement. The Canada Evidence Act passed in 1893 did not compel an accused person to testify; but once having taken the stand, no person was excused from answering any question 'upon the ground that the answer to such question may tend to incriminate him, or may tend to establish his liability to a civil proceeding ...' Where a witness or accused person objected, the answer could not be used as evidence against him in any future proceeding other than a pro- secution for perjury. The provisions of section 5 of the 1893 act are found in the current Canada Evidence Act. No case decided after 1960 has indicated that the protection against self-incrimination in the Bill of Rights modified the provisions of the Canada Evidence Act,[44] and the same conclusion probably will apply to sections 11(c) and 13 of the new charter.

Public policy on legal rights has developed in three stages in Canada. The first stage began with the introduction of English criminal law and its corresponding rights into the Canadian colonies in the eighteenth century. It encompassed the reforms erected in English law in the nineteenth cen- tury, and it ended with the consolidation of criminal-law procedure in federal statutes, especially in the Criminal Procedure Act of 1869. From the 1860s to the 1960s legal rights in criminal matters remained essentially unchanged. Writing in 1967, Alan Mewett concluded, for example, that 'the law of evidence and the law of procedure have remained remarkably static over the past century but this is due less to the courts than to the legisla- ture.'[45] In particular he noted that the procedural rules still stemmed largely from the Criminal Procedure Act of 1869 and that there had been little judicial development of those rules. A third stage of renewed concern about legal rights began with the passage of the Bill of Rights in 1960. This stage was marked by the criticism of the excessive powers of police to arrest and of the stringent policies on granting bail that was voiced by the

Canadian Committee on Corrections in 1969, and it includes the implementation of the committee's recommendations in the Criminal Law Amendment Act, 1971.

The guarantee of legal rights in the Charter of Rights and Freedoms has the potential to open the way to a further period of significant judicial development. Whether judicial policy-making in the years ahead will expand legal rights remains to be seen. However, one early survey of cases decided in lower courts across the country concluded that judges appeared unwilling to adopt more liberal interpretations of citizens' rights. Mr Justice Zuber of the Ontario Court of Appeal expressed his cautious approach by saying, 'The Charter does not intend a transformation of our legal system or the paralysis of law enforcement. Extravagant interpretations can only trivialize and diminish respect for the Charter.'[46]

Egalitarian Rights

Individual needs for acceptance, respect, and creativity require the achievement of a society that is flexible in its application of rules and standards, unwilling to make narrow-minded judgments about non-conformist behaviour, and consistently disapproving of unequal treatment of any of its members. Public policies that are guided by the principle of tolerance seek this ideal society by attempting to eliminate or, more realistically, to reduce public and private actions that are perceived to discriminate unfairly against members of minority groups.

Because discrimination can occur in so many areas of private and public conduct, effective protection of minority rights requires positive legislative enactment and a careful balancing of regulation and education as instruments of public policy. The mere absence of discriminatory laws and administrative practices does not ensure the protection and promotion of egalitarian rights, as Walter Tarnopolsky has pointed out: 'Without legislation forbidding it, the private individual, group, or trade union or corporation, may discriminate in employment, in public service industries, in accommodation, even in the sale of property, on the ground of the applicant's or consumer's race, colour, creed, religion, age, or sex. A constitutional safeguard against discriminating legislation is not enough.'[47]

Nor can legislation protect human rights simply by prohibiting specific discriminatory actions and applying appropriate penal sanctions. Programs of education are required to undermine prejudice and affirm tolerance in the community. According to Daniel Hill, a former director and chairman of the Ontario Human Rights Commission, modern-day human rights legislation is predicated on the theory that the actions of prejudiced people and their attitudes can be changed and influenced by the process of verification, discussion, and the presentation of socio-scientific materials that are used to challenge popular myths and stereotypes about people ... Human Rights on this continent is a skillful blending of educational and legal techniques in the pursuit of social justice.[48]

Similarly, Gordon Fairweather, the chief commissioner of the Canadian Human Rights Commission, has explained the 'double-barrelled strategy' of the federal commissioners.

On the one hand, they must implement the legal aspects of the legislation and, on the other, they must educate the Canadian public about the necessity of human rights for all. This dual approach reflects the distinction between prejudice, which is an attitude based on bias against a group or groups, and discrimination, which is an external manifestation of biased opinion. Legislation is the short-term solution to ending discriminatory practice. But it is only through a continuous program of public education that entrenched prejudices can be uprooted.[49]

Court Decisions

In constitutional theory, Canadian courts are a potentially formidable instrument of public policy for discouraging public or private discriminatory behaviour. In practice courts have proved reluctant to use their powers to strike down discrimination in public law, public administration, or private conduct. The main exceptions to this trend have involved jurisdictional disputes over the legislative powers of provincial governments.

When the British Columbia legislature passed statutes in 1884 that prevented Chinese Canadians from acquiring crown land, imposed an annual tax on every Chinese person over age fourteen, and prohibited Chinese from entering the province, the provincial courts ruled that they were measures affecting naturalization and aliens and thus outside the jurisdiction of the province under the BNA Act. The British Columbia Coal Mines Regulation Act of 1890 prohibited the employment of women and girls, boys under twelve, and men of Chinese origin in mining; the act was upheld in the provincial courts but was overturned on appeal to the Judicial Committee of the Privy Council because it encroached on federal jurisdiction. However, in 1903 and again in 1914 the judicial committee did uphold a British Columbia statute that disfranchised Asian residents of the province, and refused to interfere with a provincial government condition in granting timber licences that prohibited the licensees from employing Chinese and Japanese labour. A 1912 Saskatchewan law that prohibited the employment of a white woman in an apartment, laundry, or other place of business owned or managed by an Asian also was upheld in the Supreme Court of Canada, and leave to appeal to the Judicial Committee of the Privy Council was denied.

Two more recent examples of the courts' feeble treatment of discriminatory governmental action involved the deportation of Japanese Canadians at the end of the Second World War and restrictions of Hutterite land purchases in Alberta. In 1946 the Supreme Court of Canada upheld three orders-in-council issued under the War Measures Act authorizing the deportation of Japanese nationals over sixteen who had requested repatriation and had not revoked their request. The judicial committee not only confirmed this ruling but approved its extension to include the wives and children of those being deported. Fortunately, public criticism caused the government to alter its policies; none of the 3,964 Japanese people who were repatriated appears to have been forcibly deported. When the Alberta Communal Property Act (1947), designed to control land purchases by Hutterite colonies, eventually was tested in the courts, the Supreme Court of Canada held that the law was not directed at the profession of Hutterite religious beliefs but at the use of Alberta lands as communal property and hence came within provincial legislative competence. The Alberta government repealed the act in 1972; but provincial governments still apparently 'have legislative jurisdiction to regulate landholding by groups even if distinguished by religion, and presumably any other distinguishing characteristic such as race, or national or ethnic origin.'[51]

Attempts to use the courts to prevent discriminatory private conduct in public places have not met with much success in Canada. According to D.A. Schmeiser, the earliest reported case was *Loew's Montreal Theatres Limited* v *Reynolds* in 1919.[52] The respondent sued for damages on the grounds that the appellant had refused to sell him an orchestra seat because of his colour, but the court held that 'the management has the right to assign particular seats to different races and classes of men and women as it sees fit.' In 1924 in the case of *Franklin* v *Evans* an action against a London restaurant-keeper who refused to serve a black man was dismissed on the basis that there was no authority supporting it. In 1939 the Supreme Court of Canada decided in the case of *Christie* v *York Corporation* that a licensed tavern-keeper was within his rights in refusing to serve a black man, at least under the civil code of Quebec. The following year in the case of *Rogers* v *Clarence Hotel Co. Ltd*, which involved the refusal of a beer-parlour operator in British Columbia to serve a black man, the provincial court of appeal ruled that the *Christie* decision also applied to the common-law provinces. 'Thus by 1940,' concludes Ian Hunter, 'it was clear that Canadian courts regarded racial discrimination as neither immoral or illegal ... The judiciary had not lacked opportunities to advance equality but had preferred to advance commerce; judgements had adumbrated a code of mercantile privilege rather than a code of human rights.'[53]

Categorical Legislation

An international movement emerged in the liberal democracies during the Second World War that advocated a larger, more democratic conception of human rights and aspirations. These ideals won expression after the war in the Universal Declaration of Human Rights. Set against the historical reluctance of Canadian courts to use existing constitutional, criminal, or civil law to strike down discrimination, they gradually influenced Canadian governments to enact legislation designed to protect citizens from specific types of public and private discrimination.

The first Canadian anti-discrimination statutes, Ontario's Racial Discrimination Act (1944) and the Saskatchewan Bill of Rights (1947), were quasi-criminal statutes that made certain discriminatory practices illegal and provided for enforcement by the regular machinery of police and courts. The Ontario act merely made it an offence to publish or display signs, symbols, or other representations expressing racial or religious discrimination. Saskatchewan's Bill of Rights was more ambitious. Besides providing for the protection of political and legal rights, it granted specific egalitarian rights – the right to engage in any occupation or business, the right to buy or sell property, the right to become a member of any trade union or other occupational association, and the right to obtain an education – to be enjoyed without discrimination because of race, creed, religion, colour, or ethnic or national origin.

Walter Tarnopolsky has described the weaknesses of quasi-criminal legislation such as the Racial Discrimination Act and the original Saskatchewan Bill of Rights, which attempted to extend a narrow legalist approach to the protection of minority rights.

There is reluctance on the part of the victim of discrimination to initiate the criminal action. There are all the difficulties of proving the offence beyond a reasonable doubt, and it is extremely difficult to prove that a person has not been denied access for some reason other than a discriminatory one. There is reluctance on the part of the judiciary to convict, probably based upon a feeling that a discriminatory act is not really in the nature of a criminal act. Without extensive publicity and promotion, many people are unaware of the fact that such human rights legislation exists. Members of minority groups who have known discrimination in the past tend to be somewhat skeptical as to whether the legislation is anything more than a sop to the conscience of the majority. Finally, the sanction in the form of a fine does not really help the person discriminated against in obtaining a job or home or service in a restaurant.[54]

To remedy the weaknesses of this legalist approach, Ontario passed a Fair Employment Practices Act in 1951 which was modelled on legislation passed in New York State in 1945. On the one hand, the act prohibited discrimination by employers and trade unions on grounds of race, national origin, or religion in employment or trade-union membership and set out the fines to be levied on conviction for infractions. On the other hand, an educative, persuasive orientation was apparent in its provisions for the investigation of complaints by a public official and for the appointment of conciliation boards, with prosecution undertaken only as a last resort. The Ontario model soon was followed by six other provinces – Manitoba in 1953, Alberta and Nova Scotia in 1955, and British Columbia, New Brunswick, and Saskatchewan in 1956 – and somewhat later by Quebec in 1964.

Categorical legislation similar in design to the fair employment practices acts also was passed in several provinces during the 1950s and early 1960s to promote fair accommodation practices and equal pay and to prevent sex and age discrimination. Fair accommodation practices acts in Ontario (1954), Saskatchewan (1956), New Brunswick and Nova Scotia (1959), and Manitoba (1960) prohibited discrimination because of race, religion, and national or ethnic origin in public accommodation and residential occupancy. British Columbia's Public Accommodation Practices Act (1961) affected only public lodgings and services such as hotels and restaurants. A 1963 amendment to the Quebec Hotels Act made it an offence for the keepers of hotels, restaurants, and camping-grounds to discriminate in their provision of lodging, food, or other public services against any person because of race, beliefs, nationality or origin. Equal pay acts were passed in Ontario (1951), Saskatchewan (1952), British Columbia (1953), Manitoba and Nova Scotia (1956), Alberta (1957), Prince Edward Island (1959), and New Brunswick (1960); but until recently they had little effect because of difficulties in proving that the law had been broken.[55] Alberta in 1955 and British Columbia in 1960 provided that no one could be disqualified by sex or marital status from exercising a public function, holding public office, carrying on a profession, or gaining admission to an incorporated society. The Quebec Discrimination in Employment Act (1964) prohibited discrimination in employment on the basis of sex. Following the lead of a 1960 amendment to the British Columbia Fair Employment Practices Act, Ontario's Age Discrimination Act (1966) prohibited employers from refusing, because of age, to hire, promote, or continue to employ a person who was forty or more, but less than sixty-five, years of age.

The federal government followed the provincial governments in legislating egalitarian employment rights for workers coming within its jurisdiction. The Canada Fair Employment Practices Act (1953) was similar to the Ontario statute; it prohibited discrimination on the grounds of race, national origin, or religion in employment and trade-union membership. Applying only to businesses operating in the federal jurisdiction, including federal crown corporations, the act provided the customary machinery for an inquiry into complaints, remedial orders by the minister that were binding on the parties, and fines if the act or the minister's orders were violated. The Federal Employees' Equal Pay Act was passed in 1956. In the federal territories, the Yukon Fair Practices Ordinance (1963) and amended Labour Standards Ordinance (1973) and the Northwest Territories Fair Practices Ordinance (1966) prohibited discrimination in employment and public accommodation and legislated equal pay for equal work.

Comprehensive Codes

The categorical human rights statutes passed by most provincial governments during the 1950s were converted during the 1960s and 1970s into unified codes administered by human rights commissions. Ontario continued to lead the way. In 1958 the Ontario Anti-Discrimination Commission was set up to administer the existing statutes on fair employment practices, fair accommodation practices, and equal pay. The Ontario Human Rights Code (1962) consolidated and extended previous legislation, and the Ontario Human Rights Commission was given responsibility not only for enforcing the code but also for promoting equality through public information, educational programs, and research.

The other provinces have set up similar human rights codes and commissions. Nova Scotia's three categorical statutes were consolidated in its 1963 Human Rights Act, and a commission responsible for enforcing the act was created in 1967.The Alberta Human Rights Act (1966) prohibited discrimination because of race, religion, ancestry, or place of origin in accommodation, employment, and trade-union membership; the administrator who originally enforced it was replaced by a commission in 1972 when the act was revised and renamed the Individual's Rights Protection Act. The consolidation of fair employment and accommodation practices acts into human rights acts with commissioners to administer the acts also was carried out in New Brunswick (1967), British Columbia (1969), and Manitoba 1970. Prince Edward Island, which previously had only an equal pay act, enacted a comprehensive human rights code in 1968, and Newfoundland, which had no categorical rights legislation, passed a human rights act in 1969. Following the recommendation of the Commission of Enquiry on the Position of the French Language and on Language Rights in Quebec, in June 1975 Quebec became the last province to pass a comprehensive human rights act. The Quebec Charter of Human Rights and Freedoms prohibits discrimination because of race, colour, sex, civil status, religion, political convictions, language, ethnic or national origins, or social condition in employment, public accommodation, public transportation, and advertising.

In the federal jurisdiction, the Canadian Bill of Rights (1960) recognized the existence of basic political and legal rights in Canada 'without discrimination by reason of race, national origin, colour, religion or sex.' The two leading cases in the Supreme Court of Canada on the anti-discrimination provisions of the bill involved the Indian Act.[56] Laws passed prior to the enactment of the Canadian Bill of Rights had been upheld even when they were in conflict with its provisions. The Supreme Court reasoned that parliament intended such laws to operate notwithstanding the Canadian Bill of Rights; otherwise it would repeal them. Then, in *The Queen* v *Drybones* (1970), the Supreme Court declared inoperative a section of the Indian Act that prohibited Indians from being intoxicated outside a reserve. This section, it was held, created an offence that applied only to Indians, and hence failed to meet the requirement of the Bill of Rights for racial equality before the law. However, in *Attorney-General for Canada* v *Lavell* (1973) the Supreme Court ruled that another apparently discriminatory section of the Indian Act did not contravene the Bill of Rights. Under the section in question Indian women lost their Indian status when they married non-Indians, but Indian men who married non-Indians did not. The majority of the court held that the impugned section involved only 'the internal administration of the life of Indians on Reserves' and that it did not deny equality of treatment in the administration and enforcement of the law between Indian men and women. Walter Tarnopolsky rightly complains that the court's reasoning is difficult to follow.

How can it be denied that Indian women who marry non-Indians are not equally treated before the ordinary courts of the land, when in the administration and enforcement of the law the courts must deny them property rights, status, and access to their native territory, because of a provision which applies to them and not to Indian men? Surely this is a greater inequality before the law, more fundamental and more drastic, than the relatively minor inequalities dealt with in the *Drybones* case. One must conclude, therefore,that Mr. Justice Laskin must be correct when he states: 'It appears to me that the contention that a differentiation on the basis of sex is not offensive to the *Canadian Bill of Rights* where that differentiation operates only among Indians under the *Indian Act* is one that compounds racial inequality even beyond the point that the *Drybones* case found unacceptable.[57]

In its 1968 white paper, *A Canadian Charter of Human Rights*, the federal government proposed to entrench basic egalitarian rights as well as political, legal, and linguistic rights. Part 3 of the proposed charter followed existing provincial codes of human rights in prohibiting discrimination because of race, national or ethnic origin, colour, religion, and sex with respect to employment, membership in occupational and professional associations, education, property rental and ownership, contracting with public agencies, use of public accommodation and services, and eligibility to vote and hold public office.[58] These anti-discrimination provisions were not included among the articles approved at the Victoria conference in June 1971. After the failure of the Victoria Charter the Trudeau government returned to the precedent set by the provincial governments and created a human rights code and commission to protect egalitarian rights in the federal jurisdiction.

First promised in December 1973 and finally passed in July 1977, the Canadian Human Rights Act prohibits discrimination in all matters within the federal jurisdiction on the grounds of race, national or ethnic origin, colour, religion, age, sex, marital status, physical handicap, or conviction for an offence for which a person has been pardoned; and it requires the government and any employers doing business with the government to give their employees equal pay for work of equal value. Hate messages that are recorded and transmitted over federally regulated telephone systems also are prohibited. Like its provincial counterparts, the federal human rights commission has the power to investigate complaints, seek conciliation, issue restraining orders, and prosecute violations of the act; it also places a heavy weight on long-term programs of public education to combat prejudice.

Constitutional Guarantee

Section 15(1) of the Canadian Charter of Rights and Freedoms provides a constitutional guarantee of rights against discrimination. This section came into effect in April 1985, three years after the proclamation of the Canada Act. Section 15(1) states that 'every individual is equal before and under the law and has the right to the equal protection and equal benefit of the law without discrimination and, in particular, without discrimination based on race, national or ethnic origin, colour, religion, sex, age or mental or physical disability.'[59]

An assessment of the implications of section 15 for anti-discrimination policies in Canada must await the revision of statutes, regulations, and practices by governments and the decisions of the courts. In the meantime, four aspects of the implementation of section 15 deserve comment.

First, as Donald Smiley has complained, section 15 confuses two types of discriminatory distinctions.[60] There are distinctions of race, national or ethnic origin, colour, and religion that should virtually never be used (except in affirmative-action programs) as legal categories in determining how people should be treated. There are also distinctions that are justifiable but that may be used for indefensible discrimination. Federal and provincial laws, for example, on school attendance, voting rights, criminal responsiblity, driving permits, and alcohol consumption make many defensible distinction on the basis of age and physical or mental disability. Peter Russell has concluded that 'the specification of prohibited forms of discrimination will require judges to distinguish reasonable from unreasonable forms of discrimination in the law. It is simply inconceivable that judges will treat all these prohibited forms of discrimination as absolutes.'[61]

Second, section 15 requires that there be no discrimination in the protection or benefits provided by the law. The nine prohibited categories are not intended to be exhaustive. Obviously, several additional egalitarian claims are being advanced in Canada, and some of them already have statutory recognition in federal and provincial human rights codes.[62] For example, the Ontario Human Rights Code includes prohibitions on discrimination in employment because of marital status, family status, and offence record. An important question about judicial policy-making under section 15 is the willingness of the courts to expand the protection of section 15 beyond the nine specific prohibitions. Unless the courts are so willing, excluded minority groups will have to rely on federal and provincial human rights codes for statutory protection against discrimination.

Third, the extent to which section 15 will be applied to limit discriminatory private conduct is uncertain. The section prohibits discrimination by governments and by agencies under government jurisdiction, but how far that jurisdiction will be extended will depend upon judicial policy-making. Even with a generous interpretation, much private conduct will remain outside the ambit of section 15 leaving the provincial human rights codes as the main instrument of rights protection.

Finally, the Canadian Charter of Rights and Freedoms strengthens the regulatory instruments to promote egalitarian rights in Canada; but it does nothing beyond the admittedly useful teaching of the charter to balance regulation with education. In our multicultural society the work of provincial and federal human rights commissions will continue to be crucial in combatting prejudice, reforming attitudes, and realizing respect and dignity for all individuals who are identified with minority groups.

Human Rights and the Liberal State

The modern understanding of politics as founded upon basic human rights enjoyed equally by all individuals is the legacy of liberal political philosophers and liberal political movements. The concept of human rights rests on a tradition of political thought that began with Spinoza and Hobbes and matured in the works of Locke, Montesquieu, Rousseau, and Kant.

These men were the first to teach that all legitimate government derives its authority solely from the consent of the governed; that each sane adult, as an independent individual, must be understood to possess certain claims or rights that cannot be taken away, and for which he is beholden to no human authority; that far from being indebted to government or political society for these rights, the individual has joined with other individuals in creating, transforming, or maintaining government as an instrument whose major purpose is to protect and foster his preexisting rights.[63]

Traditional conservative political thought has no such concept of individual human rights. Political authority in conservative theory was not based on popular consent, but on divine right and superior ability to govern. In practice, an élite laid claim to political authority on the basis of such criteria as age and experience, moral virtue, religious custom, superior wisdom, aristocratic birth, or great wealth. By its superior ability to govern the political élite assumed responsibility to guide the community in a particular way of life determined by them as the good or proper way.

Ordinary citizens had a duty to obey; their rights arose from their duties as subjects. In this collectivist conception of political order, as Clifford Orwin and Thomas Pangle have put it, 'an individual's political dignity was thought to be grounded in his belonging to larger social wholes of which he was necessarily a part.'[64]

This traditional conservative conception of political order prevailed in New France, as it did under the absolutist monarchs of imperial France during the seventeenth and eighteenth centuries. At the time of the British conquest of New France liberal political ideas were in the ascendancy in Britain, but for a time basic political and legal rights in the Canadian colonies remained in jeopardy. The struggle for responsible government against the opposition of British imperial authorities and conservative colonial élites eventually established in Canada the essential principle of a liberal state: political authority rests on the consent of the governed. The popular base of government, the practice of competitive politics, and administration under the rule of law continued to have substantial imperfections, notably represented in restrictions on suffrage; but the principle was clearly established and so was the course of political and legal reform.

Basic egalitarian rights did not become an important part of public policy on human rights until after the Second World War. The economic liberal view of human rights focused on political and legal rights that would protect individual enterprise against the arbitrary exercise of state power. Ethical liberal thought focused on the needs of every individual for respect and opportunities for self-development, and it showed that barriers to individual development resulted not only from state intervention but also from prejudicial private conduct. In the idealistic and innovative era of reconstruction during the war and immediate post-war years, ethical liberal ideas affected policy-making for economic stability, social welfare, criminal justice, and educational opportunity, and began to affect policy-making for human rights as well. The protection of individuals against discrimination in the first quasi-criminal statutes, the Ontario Anti-Discrimination Act and the Saskatchewan Bill of Rights, was imperfect; but the principle of a right to tolerance was clearly established and the course of progressive reform toward comprehensive codes of human rights was set.

The greater weight given in Canadian policy-making to ethical liberal ideas focused more attention on human rights policy, and it also gradually changed the strategy for protecting individual rights. Historically, Canadian public policy had adopted the English liberal constitutional tradition of protecting basic political and legal rights by parliamentary supremacy and the rule of law. In the 1938 Alberta Press Bill reference and again in the

1950s, minority judgments in the Supreme Court of Canada held that the preamble of the British North America Act gave a written guarantee of basic civil liberties. The Canadian Bill of Rights was only an ordinary statute applying to the federal jurisdiction, but it expressed an aspiration and created a precedent for constitutional entrenchment of a charter of rights. The proclamation of that charter in April 1982, whatever may be its outcome in the courts, obviously marks the beginning of a new era in human rights policy-making.

This triumph of ethical liberal ideas and American liberal strategy should not cause us to overlook the shortcomings of Canadian thinking about the protection of human rights. As a principle of public policy the ethical liberal concept of tolerance shares a basic ideological harmony with the ethical liberal concept of accessibility in education, and it has the same deficiencies.

First, anti-discrimination policies have been designed to respond to specific cases where individuals allegedly have been denied employment or accommodation because of their race, religion, ethnicity, sex, or age. Such cases are assumed to produce a complainant and a defendant, charges can be made and investigated, differences can be mediated, and orders can be issued and enforced if necessary to terminate discriminatory practices. The need for general public education is recognized in principle, but in practice most human rights commissions have had to concentrate their scarce resources on dealing with specific complaints. As a result the persistent patterns of discrimination in the society and the more elusive but potentially highly damaging effects of institutionalized prejudice tend to escape public exposure and remediation. The liberal tendency to see the problem of discrimination in terms of conflicts between identifiable individuals avoids the issue of the social-group context of their conflict and its crucial implication that any permanent resolution of individual discrimination requires a transformation of the social-group environment within which prejudice is learned.

Second, like accessibility, the principle of tolerance implies that creating opportunities for self-realization will free private initiative; but it cannot be taken for granted that people who are given such opportunities also will have the personal capacities and incentives to make use of them. This should not be taken as a criticism of human rights policy itself. Combatting prejudice is obviously a vital element of any comprehensive policy for individual development. Rather, it is a comment on liberal thinking about the requirements for individual development and the contribution that public policy can make to its realization. If capacities and incentives as well as opportunities must be the subject of public policy, then tolerance, like accessibility, is still too restricted a principle to serve as the dominant guide to policy design.

Third, the limitations of liberal thinking on human rights can be seen in its difficulty in coming to terms with economic and social rights. Socialist conceptions of human rights invariably extend to include rights to employment, health, housing, and education. Ethical liberal thinking promotes remedial legislation to satisfy basic economic and social needs, but it resists bestowing enforceable claims to guaranteed status in those areas. In contrast with the primacy given to equality of condition in the hierarchy of socialist values, liberals give their allegiance to equal opportunity, which implies the possibility of failure. With respect to employment, for example, liberals may want full employment and may be prepared to implement programs to assist unemployed workers with grants for relocation or retraining; but some workers may still not succeed in finding jobs. Liberals may be prepared to offer greatly subsidized or free tuition for education above the compulsory school age, and to assist students with scholarships, bursaries, and loans, but some students may still be unable to afford to extend their formal education. Obviously, economic liberals and ethical liberals will differ vigorously among themselves about how generous public programs to remedy inequalities of opportunity really should be, but they are agreed on the liberal idea of human rights as equality of opportunity, not as equality of conditions, results, or outcomes in life.

What [individuals] make of life on the basis of these rights, together with their other distinct endowments (and what life makes of them), is not determined by the rights. The doctrine of human rights begins from awareness of, and strives to maintain respect for, human inequality and diversity; human rights are intended to foster the conditions within which individuality, creativity, and excellence can become manifest.[65]

8

Public Policies and
Political Development

If the purpose of government is the satisfaction of human needs, then political development can be understood as changes in public policies and political organization that contribute to human well-being and growth. Political development is the growth of a political community in which the realization of individual potential is the unfailing standard of its public policy and the unchallenged norm of its political constitution. It implies conceptions of public purposes that are dedicated to the satisfaction of basic needs by collective action. It means furthering and applying knowledge of the natural and human environment so that people are able to identify, understand, and remove deficiencies in need satisfaction and establish the socio-political conditions for self-actualizing behaviour. It means improving the political and administrative organization that produces and distributes political goods.

Many factors contribute to the development of Canada – its demographic composition, physical geography, level and distribution of material wealth, rate of technological innovation, threats to national security, cohesion of family life, dignity and creativity of work, and cultural integrity and vitality. Many of these factors are difficult to affect by public policy; none of them is impervious to some degree of public intervention, however modest, that can enhance beneficial trends or mitigate trends deleterious to human survival and growth. Thus choices about public policies also are an essential factor in determining the level of need satisfaction in Canada and in other countries affected by Canadian policies. Canadians' ideas of political good and the proper functions of government, their knowledge of human behaviour and the natural environment that is used to guide public policy-making, and their principles of government are crucial determinants of political development. All are subject to analysis, appraisal, debate, and change.

Trends of Public Purpose

In the appropriative political economy that existed from the seventeenth century to the nineteenth century the priorities of Canadian governments necessarily were national defence and public security. Material prosperity was thought to be dependent primarily on private group ventures and individual initiative. Governments would act whenever possible to facilitate such ventures and initiative, but the imperatives of external defence and internal stability pressed hard on colonial and imperial resources. In any case, the provision of external and internal security was agreed to be the most important contribution either colonial or imperial government could make to the achievement of material prosperity in the new world.

Under the French and English colonial regimes social order was the priority and deterrent power was the primary means of achieving it. To protect the Canadian colonies from external aggression, the imperial governments and their colonial administrations relied on military and naval defences to deter aggression and to repel invasion when deterrence failed. To preserve internal law and order the colonial governments resorted to severe corporal and capital punishment, which was expected to deter political and criminal violence.

Colonial governments also made an important contribution to economic development based on resource appropriation through land grants, immigration, internal transportation, and property rights. Still, the virtues of individual work and voluntary association were powerful norms that justified restrictions on public powers and encouraged private initiative. Small public grants were made for the relief of poverty, the provision of schooling, and the founding of cultural institutions; but private initiative and voluntary association were the dominating assumptions of original colonial principles of social policy.

As the American military threat to national security disappeared and as the Canadian economy began to industrialize in the late nineteenth century, the primacy of social order gave way to mounting pressure for more state intervention in economic development. The industrialization of Europe and America and the wars that followed impressed upon policy-makers the crucial implications of building economic power in order to preserve national security. Industrialization offered a greater range of opportunities for productive state intervention in building transportation and communication facilities, protecting infant manufacturing industries, encouraging domestic saving and foreign investment, and supplying public services essential to the urban development that was counterpart to industrialization. Industrialization pitted business owners against workers and farmers and metropolitan centres against peripheral regions; its impact on latent, organizable economic interests was so disruptive that extensive state regulation was needed to preserve domestic political stability. For all these reasons the accumulative political economy in the twentieth century became a publicly subsidized and publicly regulated political economy, and the state's responsibility for economic progress came to weigh equally with its traditional concern for social order.

The main principles of the colonial policy-making system (deterrence, appropriation, voluntarism) were altered gradually during the nineteenth century to fit the changing political economy. The first change was the displacement of the deterrent physical brutality of eighteenth-century English criminal law in favour of retributive, proportionate punishment as the operative principle for achieving criminal justice and public security. Attainment of responsible government and federal union created a stable, self-governing political community that provided a popular moral foundation for the rule of the majority's law. Public schools taught the virtues of good citizenship, and custodial prisons punished criminal deviance.

This legalist democratic regime provided an accommodating political environment for economic industrialization. Sometime in the late nineteenth century policy orientations shifted from resource appropriation to capital accumulation as the master principle of material prosperity. By the early twentieth century an array of public policies supported individual and especially corporate business enterprises by public investment, regressive taxation policies, high tariff protection, and positive inducements to foreign investment; both federal and provincial governments were irretrievably committed to building an industrial capitalist economy.

The distributive inequities of industrial capitalism created strong political and moral pressures to find principles of policy-making that would alleviate its worst excesses. The poverty of urban industrial society led to policies of income redistribution, at first by means of niggardly categorical assistance and workers' compensation, and after the Second World War by more comprehensive programs of income maintenance and social services. The intensified class conflict of an industrial capitalist economy also forced governmental regulation of private markets, for example, at first by means of minimal legislative protection for trade-union organization and later through wider legal recognition of the general role of protective economic associations and regulated bargaining in resolving conflicts among economic producer groups.

State responsibility for individual development had virtually no legitimate standing in Canadian policy-making before the Second World War. Public schools contributed toward equalizing individual opportunities for self-development, while poverty-stricken museums and art galleries struggled to advance collective cultural development. However, the main considerations in making these pre-war policies for education and culture were their anticipated impacts on national integration, public order, and economic growth.

The traditional policy-making pattern that rigidly privatized the potential state function of individual development was broken during the reconstruction period of the Second World War. Along with redistribution of wealth to alleviate material poverty and regulation to achieve economic stabilization, post-war policies advanced accessibility and tolerance as legitimate principles of policy-making for individual development. In the 1950s and 1960s equal opportunity in education, protection against discrimination, recognition of language rights, and support for cultural development became acknowledged priorities of public policy-making.[1] They asserted individual dignity and self-fulfilment as proper ends of government that required fresh approaches to state interventionism in order to bring them into balance with the historical ends of social order and economic progress.

The consensus that during the 1950s and 1960s gave a high priority to individual development met hard times in the 1970s and 1980s. Habitual expectations of economic progress were dimmed by the frustrating persistence of inflation and unemployment and the puzzling failure of Keynesian policy to correct them, by the seeming permanence of hard-core poverty in the face of general unwillingness to pay the huge cost of universalist income-maintenance programs, and by the prospective burden of implementing effective energy conservation and environmental protection (or the even heavier burden of failing to do it). Habitual expectations of social order were upset by growing fears of criminal violence, by inconsistencies between élite and popular conceptions of criminal justice, by entrenchment of uncompromising economic and regional interests, and by the demoralizing eclipse of Anglo-American domination of world affairs.

The difficulties of maintaining previously assumed levels of material prosperity and physical security have rejuvenated the most basic issues of human needs and political good – physiological and safety needs, welfare, and security. Given a public philosophy that has not thoroughly legitimized the individual – developmental function, the argument for a retreat to the traditional narrow conception of state responsibilities can be persuasive. Yet rejecting the higher priority given so recently to individual development could result in failure to recognize appropriately the authenticity of higher human needs for belongingness, esteem, and creativity. It carries the risk of failing to realize the long-term potential of a society that better serves the needs of all its members, and others outside it, for full human development. In the face of this crisis it is scarcely surprising that public policy-making in the 1970s and 1980s has revived fundamental questions about the nature of the Canadian public philosophy.

Patterns of Public Philosophy

Five basic ideological positions or doctrines have formed the elements of the Canadian public philosophy: traditional conservatism, anti-democratic liberalism, protective liberal democracy, developmental liberal democracy, and non-Marxist social democracy. In recent years students of Canadian political culture have engaged in vigorous arguments about the relative importance of each of these positions. In general they have agreed on the paramountcy of traditional conservatism in French-speaking Quebec, beginning with the ethos of New France and ending with the quiet revolution of the 1960s. They also have agreed on the considerable importance of liberal doctrine in English-speaking Canada, although at least three different interpretations of its relative weight have been advanced. One interpretation assigns to liberalism a paramountcy in English-speaking Canada similar to that enjoyed by conservatism in French-speaking Quebec. A second interpretation weighs the impact of conservative and socialist doctrines on Canadian liberalism and concludes that the resulting public philosophy is best understood as a symbiosis of conflicting ideologies. A third interpretation finds that a persistent conservatism in English-Canadian political thought and practice has made a vital contribution to building a nation while preserving regional particularities.

Looking simply at the evidence of what federal and provincial governments have done to promote economic development, relieve poverty, regulate markets, control crime, build school systems, and protect human rights, the conclusion is clear: liberalism is not just the core, it is the essence of the Canadian public philosophy. Traditional conservatism and socialism make distinctive though limited contributions to the substance of Canadian public policies; but after the French colonial regime and the first few years of the British regime, public policies in Canada were based overwhelmingly on liberal ideas, beliefs, and values. If the historical record of public policies can be treated as evidence of what went on in the minds of those who created them, then Canadian policy-makers have found the answers to their deepest questions about human needs and political goods in liberal political ideology.

For liberals, economic progress depends on a capitalist economy. It depends on private markets, private enterprise, and private property. This assumption has determined most Canadian economic policy since the early nineteenth century.

The liberal state has functioned in the first place to facilitate agricultural, commercial, and industrial prosperity. Public economic policies have opened and protected access to natural resources. They have facilitated the growth of the labour force and regulated the allocation of property rights. Public investments in transportation, communication, health, and education have been made in order to create economic and social conditions favourable to the expansion of industrial society and the growth of private investment. Private investment also has been encouraged by public subsidies in the form of expenditure, fiscal, and regulatory policies favourable to business enterprises.

The liberal state has functioned in the second place to regulate economic competition and income distribution. Liberal policy-makers are strongly biased against state intervention to regulate exchange in private markets, but they have accepted that under some conditions economic efficiency and individual liberty normally attainable in private markets may not be realized. Market competition may be weakened or destroyed by oligopolies or monopolies, information essential for rational decision-making about production and consumption may be missing, important interests may be excluded from market exchange, or the process of market adjustment may be excessively volatile. Under such circumstances state regulation is essential in order to preserve the values of efficiency and liberty and the long-term legitimacy of private markets.

Liberalism defends a capitalist economy; it also accepts a class-divided society. Each worker is responsible for earning a living for himself and his dependents. Economic stratification is simply the inevitable result of unequal outcomes to economic competition; liberal policy-makers, fortified by their belief in work and private property, have a strong bias against state intervention to redistribute income. However, just as failures of competition, information, inclusiveness, or adjustment may justify public regulation of private markets, the existence of 'undeserved' poverty on a scale beyond the help of voluntary charity may justify public redistribution of income in order to protect each individual's rights to survival and citizenship.

The history of redistributive programs in Canada shows changing perceptions of poverty and changing criteria for income redistribution as the Canadian economy evolved from its original reliance on appropriation to an advanced industrial society. Public charity has always depended on the application of a means test or the pre-payment of insurance contributions. Usually it has required the occurrence of contingencies – such as unemployment, sickness, disability, or death – that are plainly beyond the control of individuals. On occasion there has been recognition of whole categories of persons, such as the young or old, many of whose members deserve public assistance. Whatever the combination of tests used, at every stage liberal beliefs in individual responsibility, private property, income inequalities, and public charity for the deserving poor have determined particular policy responses.

The state must be satisfied that a person is not individually responsible for his poverty before dispensing public charity; conversely, the state must prove an individual's responsibility for breaking the law before he can be punished. The two classic liberal justifications for state punishment of criminal deviance both take individual responsibility for granted. Adherents of the deterrence theory understand individuals as being capable of calculating the benefits and costs of obeying or breaking the law. Effective detection of criminals is combined with punishments that are graduated expediently in order to raise the costs of law-breaking and increase the probability of law-abiding behaviour. Adherents of the retributive justice theory hold individuals morally responsible for breaking democratically established laws, and punishments weighted according to the harm done to society are imposed to express the community's repugnance at the violation of its law.

In the twentieth century, knowledge of the sociological and psychological determinants of criminal behaviour has worked to undermine the traditional liberal assumption of individual responsibility, and it has had some impact on the substance of penal policy. Yet the long-standing liberal legalist order, which includes the rule of law, individual responsibility, efficient policing to deter crime, and retributive punishment of criminal acts, has survived. Indeed, the failure of rehabilitation as a principle of criminal justice simply confirms the powerful liberal doctrine at the heart of the Canadian public philosophy. Rehabilitation cannot be accepted as the paramount organizing principle of social order in Canada because it denies the assumption of individual moral responsibility, which is a fundamental of liberal political thought.

Public elementary schools in Canada were established in the middle of the nineteenth century in order to educate young people as subjects and citizens of a new nation founded on principles of liberal democracy. As the economy became more industrialized, both national economic development and individual economic opportunity were seen to depend on higher, more technical schooling. After the turn of the century, secondary schooling received appropriately greater attention from policy-makers, and since the 1930s territorial and financial inequalities that determine individual access to secondary schools have been a major target of school policies in all provinces.

Public schooling as political socialization for liberal democracy or individual economic opportunity in an industrialized capitalist economy clearly springs from liberal ideas about the proper aims of public education. Progressive education, which aims to educate the whole child, is a manifestation of liberal political thinking. However, in contrast with the economic or protective orientation of civic education and occupational selection as purposes of school policies, child-centred education expresses an ethical liberal view that education should be designed to serve each child as creator, exerter, and developer of his or her individual talents.

Liberal concepts have defined the public problem of human rights in Canada and have completely dominated policy responses. The seventeenth-century liberal revolution in England established political and legal rights that could not be long denied to Canadians under the British colonial regime. By the middle of the nineteenth century the basic political and legal rights that are requisites of protective liberal democracy had been established, and political and legal reform over the next century completed the details of the model.

In the 1950s legal guarantees of fair employment and accommodations practices began to reverse what had previously been at best laissez-faire and at worst sometimes very restrictive public policies on egalitarian rights. During the 1960s and 1970s more comprehensive codes of individual rights were based on the liberal principles of individualism, tolerance, and equality of opportunity. With the Canadian Charter of Rights and Freedoms Canadian policy-makers have adopted the classic American liberal instrument, a written bill of individual political, legal, and egalitarian rights enforceable in the courts.

Turning to the contribution of traditional conservatism, we see that it has had two distinct but limited impacts on public policy-making in Canada. First, while conservatism held sway as the public philosophy of Quebec, the introduction of liberal political and social reforms was substantially impeded in that province. Second, conservatism produced a compromise in denominational education in public school systems that is unique in the Anglo-American countries.

The traditional conservative ideology of French-speaking Quebec aimed to preserve a French Catholic community based on an autarkic, agrarian economy against the expansive industrial economy and the secular, multiethnic society of English Canada.[2] As a result, public policies in Quebec historically were much slower to respond to the public agenda of liberal social and political reforms. For example, the rationalization of public assistance to voluntary charitable organizations occurred in 1921 through the Quebec Public Charities Act, nearly fifty years after a similar but more extensive act covering charity aid was passed in Ontario. Quebec continued to rely much longer than other provinces on institutional care for indigent poor and orphans. In 1931 Quebec became the last province in Canada to adopt a compulsory public workers' compensation scheme, and Quebec was also last (along with New Brunswick in 1936) to subscribe to the provisions of the 1927 Old Age Pensions Act. A compulsory school attendance law was enacted in Quebec in 1942, at least two decades after the other provinces (except for Newfoundland, which also passed a similar law in 1942) and fifty years after an attendance law was passed in Ontario. Quebec retained a property qualification in its provincial election law until 1936, and women did not gain the right to vote in the province until 1940.

The quiet revolution that began in 1959 was in part a revolt of French-speaking Quebeckers against threats to their culture and domination of their economy by English Canada, but it was also a belated liberal revolt against the predominant conservatism of the Quebec public philosophy. Since the 1960s the public philosophy of Quebec has been predominantly liberal and strongly nationalist in its orientation, and it has transformed the role of the state in Quebec society.

Liberal policies of public schooling that aim to educate citizens for liberal democracy or to train workers for industrial capitalism take a ruthlessly secular view of public education. Public schooling for individual development may be more sympathetic to denominational instruction, but simply as one among several aspects of the cultural foundations for individual growth. Traditional conservatism, however, makes denominational instruction the core of public education. The nineteenth-century compromise on denominational schooling continues to be the greatest manifestation of conservative doctrine in contemporary Canadian public policy. Significantly, that compromise depended on the support French-speaking Catholics of Canada East gave to the Catholic minority of Canada

West in the assembly of the united Canadas after 1840. Without that constitutional union at a critical juncture in the development of public schools, it seems certain that Ontario, and presumably the prairie provinces, would have followed the strong preference of Egerton Ryerson for a liberal, secular school system similar to those created in the United States, Australia, and New Zealand.

Leaving aside the impact of socialist ideology on the political organization of workers and farmers in Canada and looking simply at its manifestation in public policies, the record shows an impact at least as significant as that resulting from conservative doctrine. Manifestations of socialism also appear to be highly concentrated in public ownership of economic enterprises and public insurance of health services.

The programs of public ownership of minerals, fur marketing, insurance, transportation, and forest products which were undertaken by the CCF government in Saskatchewan from 1944 to 1947 certainly depended to a considerable extent on the social democratic ideology of the governing party. Similar ideological influences can be detected in the creation of several public corporations by NDP governments in Saskatchewan, Manitoba, and British Columbia, notably the public insurance corporations in Manitoba (1970) and British Columbia (1973) and the Saskatchewan Oil and Gas Corporation (1973) and Potash Corporation of Saskatchewan (1975).

Except for the few enterprises set up by CCF and NDP governments, Canadian public enterprises have had pragmatic rather than ideological origins. Interpretations of the Canadian public philosophy that emphasize the impact of conservative and socialist doctrines on Canadian liberalism sometimes hold that the greater degree of state intervention in the Canadian economy (in particular, the greater extent of public ownership) is a manifestation of a strong collectivist orientation that is absent from the American political tradition. Such an interpretation underestimates the role of the state in American economic development, and it misrepresents the ideological origins of most Canadian public enterprises. On the one hand, the public policies that contributed to Canadian economic development in the nineteenth and twentieth centuries, such as public subsidies for private investments, land grants, immigration, favourable fiscal and regulatory policies, and public investment in the economic infrastructure, were also commonly employed in the United States. On the other hand, public ownership of railway, airline, broadcasting, and petroleum enterprises, which appears to distinguish Canadian from American economic policies in the twentieth century, is best understood as a pragmatic response to the twin problems of national development in a small, dependent economy and national integration in the face of persistent threats from American economic domination. As Lloyd D. Musolf has argued,

Canadian public enterprise ... is complex in character and not lacking in paradoxical elements. It occupies only a modest segment of the economy, but it literally links the nation together. Although it has had a long history, it has never won the emotional allegiance of Canadians. Without an ideological drive to sustain it, it has still achieved a vital place in the economy because of its decisive importance in the continuing task of nation-building. Exceedingly pragmatic as Canadian enterprise appears to be, the consistency with which it is used in situations involving challenges to national economic unity virtually gives its motivating factor the status of a theory.[3]

The commitment of CCF and NDP governments in Saskatchewan to social democratic ideals resulted in that province's leading the country in the introduction of public insurance of health services. The Douglas government gave the province the first public hospital insurance program in 1946, and the Lloyd government extended coverage to physicians' services in 1961 after a tough political battle with the Saskatchewan College of Physicians and Surgeons. The Blakeney government introduced a dental care program for school children in 1974, in part to fulfil the long-standing objective of a comprehensive health services policy.

The Saskatchewan plans eventually became important precedents for national programs of hospital insurance (1957) and medical insurance (1966), but those national health insurance programs also have origins in liberal policy thinking. Comprehensive public insurance for health services was part of the design for an ethical liberal welfare state that emerged from the reconstruction planning of the Second World War, and national health insurance was a major element in the federal government's 'Green Book' of 1946. Evidently there was no incompatibility in principle between public insurance of health services and modern liberal social policy. The social democratic commitments of CCF and NDP governments in Saskatchewan gave health-policy development in Canada a direction and priority that might otherwise have been lacking, but the establishment of national insurance programs depended ultimately on the long-term commitment of liberal policy-makers.

Interpretations of the Canadian public philosophy that give a greater weight to conservatism have tended to emphasize the absence of a Canadian revolution and the persistence of a British connection which continues, though somewhat attenuated, to the present. As long as such conservatism is understood to mean a reluctance to cut historical ties, it is obviously true; certainly a favourable orientation to Britain has been an important element of English-Canadian political thinking. It is important to understand, however, that in the context of public policy, at least, the Canadian heritage from Britain is overwhelmingly liberal.

Parliamentary democracy and legal rights as they exist in Canada are a heritage of seventeenth-century English liberalism. The establishment of parliamentary democracy and federal union was deeply influenced by the analysis and recommendations of an eminent political advocate for the reformers' model of protective liberal democracy, Lord Durham. The Canadian Criminal Code is based on the work of a British royal commission headed by another eminent English liberal, Sir James Stephen. Unemployment insurance legislation in Canada adopted wage-related rather than flat-rate benefits, but it was modelled on the legislation passed in 1911 by a British Liberal government. The Canadian approach to economic stabilization and income security in the post-war period was deeply influenced by the policy theories and prescriptions of two great modern British liberals, John Maynard Keynes and William Beveridge.

Once the influence of British liberalism on Canadian public policy is conceded, there remains an enormous Canadian debt to American liberal policy examples. The Dominion Lands Act of 1872, for example, was inspired by the United States Homestead Act which had been introduced ten years earlier to facilitate settlement of the American frontier. The Board of Railway Commissioners (1903) was based on the example of the United States Interstate Commerce Commission set up in 1887, and regulatory policy-making ever since then has been much more influenced by American examples than by those of any other country. Both Canadian and American police forces benefited from the organizational example set by Sir Robert Peel in London in 1829. On the whole, however, Canadian police organization, operations, and professional development have been more influenced by American experience. Kingston Penitentiary was built in 1835 and became the model for the Canadian penitentiary system. It followed the design of Auburn Prison in New York State. The workers' compensation program which was introduced in Ontario in 1914 and became the model for other provinces was part of an American policy trend that saw the introduction of a number of similar programs in various American states after the turn of the century. Mothers' allowances were introduced to Canada by the province of Manitoba in 1916, but the precedent was set by the state of Illinois in 1911. American educational theory and practice have been overwhelmingly the most important external influence on the development of Canadian public school systems. That influence is evident in the establishment of common elementary schools in the nineteenth century, in the development of comprehensive high schools, larger school districts, and grant equalization, and in the reorganization of schools and curricula to reflect the ideals of progressive education. In the area of human rights, the legislation on fair employment and accommodations practices introduced by Ontario followed the example of legislation passed in New York State in 1945; and the Canadian Charter of Rights and Freedoms follows the precedent of constitutional entrenchment and judicial protection of human rights established by the American Bill of Rights.

Interpretations of the Canadian public philosophy that stress the differences between Canadian and American liberalism are correct. The differences reflect the influence of Canadian conservatism and socialism; more important, the differences reflect the influence of British liberalism on Canadian political thought. Both American and British liberal political thinking and policy examples have been powerful external influences on Canadian public policies. The American liberal influence is perhaps more quantitatively extensive and clearly has been in the ascendancy since the Second World War but British liberalism has made vital contributions to Canadian approaches to constitutional and legal development and social welfare. There seems little point in trying rigorously to separate the relative importance of the two; it is their coexistence that matters.

Liberalism and Political Development

Canadian concepts of public purpose, policy theories, and principles of political and administrative organization have been drawn overwhelmingly from the doctrine of liberalism. Canadian public philosophy is a liberal public philosophy. It has been shaped decisively by the British and American liberal traditions. It has been influenced by Catholic conservatism and non-Marxist socialism. It also has been divided within itself.

One division between anti-democratic liberalism and protective liberal democracy was terminated by the achievement of responsible government in the 1840s and federal union in the 1860s. Near the turn of the century a second division appeared between protective liberal democracy or economic liberalism and a developmental or ethical liberal democracy; in the 1980s it remains the basic ideological division in Canadian political life.

An accumulative political economy and a legalist political order were the ideological pillars of an economic liberalism grounded on a materialist possessive individualism. In spite of stubborn dissent from disadvantaged social groups and grudging steps toward political and economic reform, the ideas of accumulation and legalism easily retained their domination of policy thinking until the Great Depression. During the 1930s and 1940s, however, the misery of the depression followed by the political idealism of the war made narrow economic liberalism untenable as a public philosophy. Canadian liberalism emerged from the Second World War with a stronger commitment to ethical developmental individualism, a tentative recognition of the state's function of individual development, and a reconstructed paradigm of policy principles.

The post-war policy-making system has been governed by a tenuous conjunction of economic and ethical liberalism. Accumulation and legalism have remained the predominant guides to policy-making, but they have been heavily qualified by the norms of redistribution and regulation while admitting accessibility and tolerance as additional principles of policy development.

Its policy achievements in terms of human need-satisfaction are apparent, but the internal contradictions of this post-war public philosophy reveal its limitations as a basis for long-term policy development aiming at higher levels of need satisfaction. Accumulation has created material prosperity by private bureaucratization, frustrating individuals' aspirations for identification, dignity, and creativity in their work; and it ignores the limits of the natural environment. Social security policies have alleviated the worst distributive consequences of an industrial capitalist economy but their remedial design stops far short of significantly reducing, let alone actually removing, the causes of poverty. Pluralist regulation has stabilized the domestic social order by accommodating the interest conflicts of whatever social groups prove too powerful to be coerced, with a consequential clouding of the test of social justice. Finally, policies aimed at furthering accessibility and tolerance have reduced individual instances of discrimination but on the whole have failed to confront the institutionalized class inequality, sexual bias, and racial prejudice from which individual cases originate.

Judged against an ethical liberal ideal of a government fully committed to a conserver national economy, a just social order, and universal individual development, the policy consequences of the modern Canadian public philosophy leave no room for complacency. Judged against the economic liberal argument for a retreat to more traditional, harder principles of policy, the search for a generous and consistent combination of principles becomes imperative. Can the conflicting ideas, beliefs, and values of the liberal political tradition be reconciled and adapted successfully, or must Canadians turn to other assumptions?

The progressive adaptation of political institutions, innovations in policy theories, and especially the historical enlargement of conceptions of public purpose all show an essential capacity for change and growth in Canadian liberalism. With all its tensions and contradictions, a liberal public philosophy has proved a good guide to Canadian political development. Perhaps this is because liberalism contains within itself the contradictions of the human condition. On the one hand, liberalism still shows its original tendency to see people as selfish, calculating, atomistic individuals who are motivated primarily by their material interests. On the other hand, liberalism assumes in principle the worth and dignity of each person and aspires to provide each person's basic needs for welfare, safety, belongingness, respect, and freedom. The hope for a creative society and the heritage of individual materialism form the bench marks from which Canadians can act to preserve their present achievement and strive for higher levels of political development for themselves and for those who live in less fortunate political communities.

The dialectic of economic and ethical liberalism is nothing new in the Canadian political tradition. If the contradictions of liberalism constitute the essence of the present crisis of public policy, the historic values and potential growth of liberalism continue to present the best hope for future political development.

Notes

ACKNOWLEDGMENTS

1 See Ronald Manzer *Canada: A Socio-political Report* (Toronto: McGraw-Hill Ryerson 1974).
2 See *Education and Development in Atlantic Canada* edited by Eric Ricker (Halifax: Dalhousie University Department of Education 1978) 97–127.

CHAPTER I

1 For a review of material prosperity, physical security, and human rights in Canada using a variety of social indicators to measure their provision, see Ronald Manzer *Canada: A Socio-political Report* (Toronto: McGraw-Hill Ryerson 1974). More recent evidence is available in Statistics Canada *Perspectives Canada III* (Ottawa: Minister of Supply and Services 1980).
2 For an argument that satisfying human needs is the conclusive justification of government, see Christian Bay 'Needs, Wants and Political Legitimacy' *Canadian Journal of Political Science* I (September 1968) 241–60.
3 See Abraham H. Maslow *Motivation and Personality* (New York: Harper and Brothers 1954) chapters 5, 12.
4 James C. Davies, *Human Nature in Politics* (New York: John Wiley and Sons 1963) 31
5 Maslow *Motivation and Personality* 91
6 Christian Bay has argued that two additional basic needs are a need to preserve conditions for collective survival and a need for personal freedom, including a sense of personal competence and power. See Christian Bay 'Human Needs and Political Education' in *Human Needs and Politics* edited by Ross Fitzgerald

(Rushcutters Bay, NSW: Pergamon Press 1977) 8–13. Undeniably these are basic needs, but the first appears to be covered by Maslow's categories of physiological and belongingness needs and the second by his categories of esteem and self-development needs. This seems to be the case at least when Maslow's list of needs is translated into a list of political goods.

7 For an elaboration on the connection between human needs and political goods, see Manzer *Canada: A Socio-political Report* chapter 1.

8 Ibid. 20–1

9 William Christian and Colin Campbell *Political Ideologies and Political Parties in Canada* (Toronto: McGraw-Hill Ryerson 1974) 20

10 Samuel H. Beer 'In Search of a New Public Philosophy' in *The New American Political System* edited by Anthony King (Washington: American Enterprise Institute for Public Policy Research 1978) 5. The term 'public philosophy' was used by Walter Lippmann in *The Public Philosophy* (Boston: Little, Brown 1955), but he used it specifically to refer to a liberal public philosophy based on natural law and articulated in a bill of rights. Beer's use of the term is analytical, as is that of Theodore J. Lowi in 'The Public Philosophy: Interest Group Liberalism' *American Political Science Review* 61 (March 1967) 5–24, and in *The End of Liberalism: Ideology, Policy and the Crisis of Public Authority* (New York: Norton 1969). As an analytical term public philosophy refers to certain political ideas, beliefs, and values that are also covered by definitions of political culture; but public philosophy focuses on orientations, both élite and mass, to public problems and governmental policies and omits reference to such individual psychological orientations as sense of political efficacy, degree of political trust, and level of political interest, which have been central concerns in contemporary studies of political culture. See, for example, the classic study by Richard Simeon and David J. Elkins, 'Regional Political Cultures in Canada' *Canadian Journal of Political Science* 7 (September 1974) 397–437.

11 Beer, 'In Search of a New Public Philosophy' 6

12 Kenneth D. McRae 'The Structure of Canadian History' in *The Founding of New Societies* edited by Louis Hartz (New York: Harcourt, Brace and World 1964) 219

13 Ibid. 222

14 Ibid. 234

15 Gad Horowitz 'Conservatism, Liberalism, and Socialism in Canada: An Interpretation' *Canadian Journal of Economics and Political Science* 32 (May 1966) 64

16 S.D. Clark *The Developing Canadian Community* (Toronto: University of Toronto Press 1962) 189

17 Reg Whitaker 'Images of the State in Canada' in *The Canadian State: Political*

Economy and Political Power edited by Leo Panitch (Toronto: University of Toronto Press 1977) 35–6

18 Ibid. 43

19 Thomas Hockin *Government in Canada* (Toronto: McGraw-Hill Ryerson 1975) 13

20 Ibid. 66–7

21 C.B. Macpherson *The Life and Times of Liberal Democracy* (Oxford: Oxford University Press 1977) 48

22 In addition to the 'protective democracy' of Jeremy Bentham and James Mill and the 'developmental democracy' of John Stuart Mill and such twentieth-century liberal democrats as Ernest Barker, A.D. Lindsay, Robert MacIver, John Dewey, and L.T. Hobhouse, Macpherson outlines two other models. 'Equilibrium democracy,' first formulated by Joseph Schumpeter in 1942, abandoned the ethical liberal moral vision as unrealistic and offered a theory of democracy as a competition among élites which produces equilibrium without much popular participation. More recently, 'participatory democracy' has envisaged a combination of industrial democracy and substantial citizen participation in governmental decision-making. Obviously, equilibrium democracy is closely aligned with the assumptions of the older model of protective democracy, while participatory democracy shares the same moral vision as developmental democracy. Here I shall deal with the four models as manifestations of two conflicting traditions of modern liberalism.

23 Ibid. 1

24 The process of making public policies includes the selection of issues for the political agenda of the community, the creation of alternative policy designs that promise to resolve the issues, the choice of one design as the preferred course of action, and the implementation of that preferred design. Public policy-making may be understood as a process of political exchange in which policies are the outcome of successive political bargains struck by its various participants, or it may be conceived as a process of rational choice in which policies result from collective deliberation by a responsible group of political authorities. However the process is understood, making public policy involves the application of power; but it also is necessarily an exercise in political thought.

25 Alfred Schutz *The Phenomenology of the Social World* translated by George Walsh and Frederick Lehnert (Evanston, Ill.: Northwestern University Press, 1967) 136

CHAPTER 2

1 Harold A. Innis *Essays in Canadian Economic History* (Toronto: University of Toronto Press 1956) 321

2 Harold Innis *The Fur Trade in Canada* (Toronto: University of Toronto Press 1930; revised edition 1956) 390

3 *Northern Frontier, Northern Homeland: The Report of the Mackenzie Valley Pipeline Inquiry* vol. 1 (Ottawa: Minister of Supply and Services 1977) 117. See also K.J. Rea's account of the fur trade and northern development in *The Political Economy of the North* (Toronto: University of Toronto Press 1968) 73–9.

4 A.R.M. Lower 'The Trade in Square Timber' in *Approaches to Canadian Economic History* edited by W.T. Easterbrook and M.H. Watkins (Toronto: McClelland and Stewart 1967) 45

5 Hugh G.J. Aitken 'Defensive Expansionism: The State and Economic Growth in Canada' in *Approaches to Canadian Economic History* 191

6 Ibid. 203

7 Lower 'The Trade in Square Timber' 29–35

8 The description here is based on Chester Martin *'Dominion Lands' Policy* (Toronto: McClelland and Stewart 1937; reprinted 1973). New Brunswick, Nova Scotia, and Upper Canada each pursued lavish and chaotic policies of free grants from the 1780s to the 1820s, after which efforts were made to follow a more orderly policy of settlement based on land sales (ibid., 128–36). The essentially appropriative character of prairie settlement is indicated by James Mavor's estimate in 1904 of the capital required to begin farming: yoke of oxen costing $180; wagon, $20; milch cow, $30; breaking plow, $14; and household furnishings as the settler might regard necessary. Mavor estimated that settlers accustomed to a European peasant's standard of living could establish themselves for $250 to $350, and that $1,500 or more would provide 'for more ample and comfortable settlement.' Cited in David C. Corbett *Canada's Immigration Policy: A Critique* (Toronto: University of Toronto Press 1957) 30–1. Corbett observes that the picture here is one of a modest capital outlay for a settler to start farming in western Canada.

9 Martin *'Dominion Lands' Policy* 156

10 Chester Martin *The Foundations of Canadian Nationhood:* (Toronto: University of Toronto Press 1955) 483–4

11 W.G. Smith *A Study in Canadian Immigration* (Toronto: Ryerson Press 1920) 54–5

12 The relative importance of these inducements can be judged from the evidence that from 1905 to 1909 commissions were paid on 6 per cent of u.s. emigrants to Canada, on 16 per cent of British immigrants, and on 11 per cent of European immigrants. Dominion expenditures on immigration amounted to $6.8 million for the fiscal years from 1898 to 1908, with 37 per cent of the total spent on entrance regulation and 63 per cent on external promotion (ibid. 58–9).

13 Both countries excluded the insane, feeble-minded, deaf and dumb, dumb, blind, or infirm; people with loathsome or contagious diseases; and paupers, vagrants, or anyone likely to become a public charge. The Canadian law differed from the American law in that it did not exclude polygamists, anarchists, and contract labourers.

14 Ibid. 72, 125–6

15 See, for example, Gordon W. Bertram 'Economic Growth in Canadian Industry, 1870–1915' *Approaches to Canadian Economic History* 74–98.

16 Kenneth Buckley *Capital Formation in Canada 1896–1930* (Toronto: University of Toronto Press 1955) 54

17 Richard E. Caves and Richard H. Holton *The Canadian Economy* (Cambridge, Mass.: Harvard University Press 1961) 71

18 Don Gracey 'Public Enterprise in Canada' in *Public Enterprise and the Public Interest* edited by André Gelinas (Toronto: Institute of Public Administration of Canada 1978) 25. See also the excellent discussion by M.J. Trebilcock and J.R.S. Prichard, 'Crown Corporations: The Calculus of Instrument Choice' in *Crown Corporations in Canada: The Calculus of Instrument Choice* edited by J. Robert S. Prichard (Toronto: Butterworths 1983) 46–74. Among the fields of economic activity in which public ownership has been a dominant although not exclusive instrument of intervention Trebilcock and Prichard include the provision of capital funds, promotion of national security and security of supply, integrating the country by making infrastructure investments, and providing essential services that private business is unable or unwilling to provide. They also include several additional fields in which public ownership tends to be used primarily as an instrument of economic regulation: natural monopoly regulation, moderating the effects of economic transitions and stabilizing income, creation of a yardstick competitor, control of externalities, and developing a national identity and preserving Canadian control over certain services and sectors of the economy.

19 Allan Tupper 'The State in Business' *Canadian Public Administration* 22 (Spring 1979) 130–2

20 Task Force on the Structure of Canadian Industry *Foreign Ownership and the Structure of Canadian Industry* (Ottawa: Queen's Printer 1968) 18; Mira Wilkins *The Emergence of Multinational Enterprise: American Business Abroad from the Colonial Era to 1914* (Cambridge: Harvard University Press 1970) 142

21 Michael Bliss *A Living Profit* (Toronto: McClelland and Stewart 1974) 109

22 For example, Ontario municipalities offered free sites, money bonuses, loans, and tax exemptions to attract new business. The Patent Acts of 1872 and 1903 required American manufacturers to set up Canadian branches or license a Canadian manufacturer or else forego the Canadian market. See Wilkins *The*

Emergence of Multinational Enterprise 142–3. On the manufacturing condition in Ontario, see H.V. Nelles *The Politics of Development* (Toronto: Macmillan 1974) 48–107.

23 John H. Perry *Taxes, Tariffs, and Subsidies* (Toronto: University of Toronto Press 1955) 107,123,135

24 This conclusion is based on estimates of the impact of taxes for various income groups on 'pre-government' income, that is, before taxes and government transfers and expenditures. For comprehensive studies of the impact of taxes see W. Irwin Gillespie 'On the Redistribution of Income in Canada' *Canadian Tax Journal* 24 (July-August 1976) 419–50 and *The Redistribution of Income in Canada* (Toronto: Gage 1980); and see David A. Dodge 'Impact of Tax, Transfer and Expenditure Policies of Government on the Distribution of Personal Income in Canada' *The Review of Income and Wealth* series 21 (March 1975) 1–52. These studies show that the impact of contemporary governmental expenditures is progressive overall, and consequently the net incidence of tax plus expenditure effects shows a clear shift in income to lower income classes as a result of total governmental fiscal activities. Of course these progressive expenditure effects would be much reduced in the period 1867 to 1939 when public expenditures on education, health, and social welfare were relatively much less important than they are now.

25 G. Bruce Doern *Science and Politics in Canada* (Montreal: McGill-Queen's University Press 1972) 45

26 The most recent reorganization, the 1976 Government Organization (Scientific Activities) Act, altered the administration of federal grants for scientific and technological research in the university sector by setting up the Natural Sciences and Engineering Research Council to promote and assist university research in the sciences, excluding the health sciences, and limiting the NRC to running its scientific research establishment and industrial research and development support programs.

27 The Alberta government set up a research council in co-operation with the University of Alberta in 1921; Ontario's Research Foundation was established in 1928; the British Columbia Research Council was formed as a non-profit joint enterprise in 1944; and Saskatchewan established its research council at the University of Saskatchewan in 1947. The other provincial agencies are the New Brunswick Research and Productivity Council, the Quebec Centre for Industrial Research, the Nova Scotia Research Foundation, and the Manitoba Research Council.

28 A.E. Safarian *The Canadian Economy in the Great Depression* (Toronto: University of Toronto Press 1959) 145

29 The 'new political economy' or the 'new economics' was the phrase applied to

economic management based on Keynesian principles when it achieved general acceptance by policy-makers in the United States in the early 1960s. For an account of this policy development see Walter Heller *New Dimensions of Political Economy* (New York: Norton 1967) chapter 2; see also Arthur M. Okun *The Political Economy of Prosperity* (New York: Norton 1970).

30 Department of Reconstruction *Employment and Income with Special Reference to the Initial Period of Reconstruction, 1945* (Ottawa: King's Printer 1946) 23

31 W.A. Mackintosh 'The White Paper on Employment and Income in Its 1945 Setting' in Canadian Trade Committee *Canadian Economic Policy since the War* (Montreal: Private Planning Association 1965) 21

32 *Employment and Income* 11, 21

33 A good short account of post-war fiscal policy is provided by J.C. Strick *Canadian Public Finance* 2d ed. (Toronto: Holt, Rinehart and Winston 1978) chapter 7.

34 Economic Council of Canada *First Annual Review: Economic Goals to 1970* (Ottawa: Queen's Printer 1964) chapters 3, 6

35 For an account of this effort see David Wolfe 'The State and Economic Policy in Canada, 1968–75' in *The Canadian State: Political Economy and Political Power* edited by Leo Panitch (Toronto: University of Toronto Press 1977) 277–81.

36 The Supreme Court's decision on the Anti-Inflation Act is analysed by Peter Russell in 'The Anti-Inflation Case: The Anatomy of a Constitutional Decision' *Canadian Public Administration* 20 (Winter 1977) 632–5. Under provisions of the act, guidelines for wage and salary increases were 10 per cent in the first year of the program, 8 per cent in the second year, and 6 per cent in the third year. If an occupational group had experienced a low rate of increases in the past, an additional 2 per cent was possible; if the past experience was one of high increases, the guidelines could be reduced by 2 per cent. No individual annual increases were permitted to exceed $2,400 and increases up to $600 were exempted from the guidelines. Profits, more difficult to control, were restricted to the firm's average profits per unit in the period preceding controls; and price increases were to be approved only for increases in costs. An excellent analysis of both the decision to adopt controls and the decision-making behaviour of the Anti-Inflation Board is provided by Alan M. Maslove and Gene Swimmer in *Wage Controls in Canada, 1975–1978* (Montreal: Institute for Research on Public Policy 1980).

37 Eugene Swimmer 'Six and Five' in *How Ottawa Spends 1984: The New Agenda* edited by Alam M. Maslove (Toronto: Methuen 1984) 243–60

38 C.B. Macpherson *Democracy in Alberta: Social Credit and the Party System* 2d ed. (Toronto: University of Toronto Press 1962) 23

CHAPTER 3

1 Kenneth Bryden *Old Age Pensions and Policy-Making in Canada* (Montreal: McGill-Queen's University Press 1974) 21

2 Harry M. Cassidy *Public Health and Welfare Reorganization in Canada: The Post-war Problems in the Canadian Provinces* (Toronto: Ryerson Press 1945) 412

3 Richard B. Splane *Social Welfare in Ontario, 1791–1893: A Study of Public Welfare Administration* (Toronto: University of Toronto Press 1965) 69

4 Ibid. 69–75, 79–80

5 Ibid. 84–8

6 Bryden *Old Age Pensions and Policy-Making in Canada* 23

7 Splane, *Social Welfare in Ontario 1791–1893* xiii–iv, 273–7

8 A.E. Grauer *Public Assistance and Social Insurance: A Study Prepared for the Royal Commission on Dominion-Provincial Relations* (Ottawa: King's Printer 1939) 45

9 'The early programs were often only available to widows who were "fit" mothers. In addition to these conditions as to the character or competence of the mother, residence and need, citizenship, asset limits, and age of dependent children restricted eligibility. Maximum benefit levels were always specified and there was apparent discretion to pay less.' See Interprovincial Task Force on the Administration of Social Security *The Income Security System in Canada* (Ottawa: Canadian Intergovernmental Conference Secretariat 1980) 13.

10 For a discussion of poverty-line incomes during this period, see Terry Copp *The Anatomy of Poverty* (Toronto: McClelland and Stewart 1974) 30–43.

11 Bryden *Old Age Pensions and Policy-Making in Canada* 8

12 T.H. Marshall *Social Policy* (London: Hutchinson 1965) 48

13 Ibid. 49

14 Copp *The Anatomy of Poverty* 125

15 Nova Scotia, 1915; British Columbia, 1916; Alberta and New Brunswick, 1918; Manitoba, 1920, Saskatchewan, 1929; Quebec, 1931

16 Andrew F. Johnson 'A Minister as an Agent of Policy Change: The Case of Unemployment Insurance in the Seventies' *Canadian Public Administration* 24 (Winter 1981) 630

17 Kathleen Herman 'The Emerging Welfare State: Changing Perspectives in Canadian Welfare Policies and Programs, 1867–1960' in *Social Space: Canadian Perspectives* edited by D.I. Davies and Kathleen Herman (Toronto: New Press 1971) 131–2

18 Asa Briggs 'The Welfare State in Historical Perspective' *Archives Européenes de Sociologies* 2 (1961) 228

19 Richard Titmuss *Commitment to Welfare* (London: George Allen and Unwin 1968) 133
20 Of Leonard Marsh's report Kenneth Bryden says, 'The report was not in the main stream of government policy-making, but it was a well-researched and reasoned study which propounded in specifically Canadian terms the rising doctrine of overarching social security.' See Bryden *Old Age Pensions and Policy-Making in Canada* 110.
21 In 1975 the federal government proposed a new Social Services Act to replace the provisions covering welfare services in the Canada Assistance Plan. After two years of negotiations with the provincial governments, objections by Quebec and two other provinces in the summer of 1977 caused the federal government to drop its proposal. In September 1977 the federal government announced a new proposal to assist the financing of social services by unconditional grants to the provinces, and legislation was introduced in May 1978 to convert the federal CAP contribution for social services to block funding. In August, however, Prime Minister Trudeau announced a major program of expenditure restraint; shortly afterwards the proposal to provide block funding was abandoned. For an analysis of the place of social services in the social security review from 1973 to 1978 see Rick Van Loon 'Reforming Welfare in Canada' *Public Policy* 27 (Fall 1979) 488–92.
22 Bryden *Old Age Pensions and Policy-Making in Canada* 75–8
23 Leonard Marsh *Report on Social Security for Canada* (Ottawa: King's Printer 1943) chapter 13
24 Bryden *Old Age Pensions and Policy-Making in Canada* 144
25 My account of the evolution of health insurance is based mainly on Canada, Royal Commission on Health Services *Report* vol. 1 (Ottawa: Queen's Printer 1964) 381–422. For an excellent recent history see Malcolm G. Taylor *Health Insurance and Canadian Public Policy* (Montreal: McGill-Queen's University Press 1979).
26 Malcolm C. Brown 'The Implications of Established Program Finance for National Health Insurance' *Canadian Public Policy* 6 (Summer 1980) 530
27 Under the Federal–Provincial Fiscal Arrangements and Established Program Financing Act, 1977, the federal government's 50 per cent cost-sharing of provincial hospital and medical insurance schemes was converted from a conditional to an unconditional grant. The amount of the federal transfer no longer is tied to provincial spending on hospital and medical care. Conversely, the provinces now can spend the transferred funds on activities other than health. In his study Brown concluded that in six provinces there was discernible change in public spending on health as a result of the introduction of Established Program Financing. In three provinces (Manitoba, Saskatchewan, and British Columbia) he found a positive correlation, but there was no particular reason to assume this

reflected a causal relationship. Only in the case of Alberta did budgetary policy appear to have been intentionally altered. See ibid. 528–30.

28 Marshall *Social Policy* 66

29 The 1973 amendments also permitted provinces to vary the scale of benefits. Quebec now varies family allowances by age of child and number of children in the family, and it adds a provincial supplement to the federal payment. Alberta also varies monthly allowances by age of child. Subsequently the principle of universality was affected by the introduction of the federal child tax credit. Beginning with the 1978 tax year, families became eligible for a basic $200 tax credit (or benefit for those with no taxable income) for each dependent child under eighteen with the credit diminishing by five cents for each dollar of family income over $18,000. Significantly, the child tax credit was financed mainly by reducing family allowance payments from an average $25.68 to $20 a month, thus putting the 1979 allowance back to what it was in 1973. By 1983 the full child tax credit had been increased to $343 for those with taxable incomes below $26,330, and the family allowance was $28.52 a month for each child under the age of eighteen.

30 Bryden *Old Age Pensions and Policy-Making in Canada* 119–23

31 John Kenneth Galbraith *The Affluent Society* (Boston: Houghton Mifflin 1958) 332–3

32 Michael Harrington *The Other America: Poverty in the United States* (Baltimore: Penguin 1963) 155

33 Economic Council of Canada *Fifth Annual Review: The Challenge of Growth and Change* (Ottawa: Queen's Printer 1968) 103

34 Using the 1969 pattern of family expenditures as the base, statistics for 1982 indicate a national poverty rate of 12 per cent, with one out of every ten families and three out of every ten single individuals living below the poverty line. Using 1978 family expenditures as the base, the poverty rate in 1982 was 16 per cent, 13 per cent among families and 37 per cent among unattached individuals. See Statistics Canada *Income Distributions by Size in Canada 1982* (Ottawa: Minister of Supply and Services 1984) table 85.

35 Special Senate Committee on Poverty *Report: Poverty in Canada* (Ottawa: Queen's Printer 1971) 169

36 An excellent recent analysis of proposals for a guaranteed annual income in Canada appears in David P. Ross *The Working Poor* (Toronto: James Lorimer 1981) part 3.

37 A.W. Johnson 'Canada's Social Security Review 1973–75: The Central Issues' *Canadian Public Policy* 1 (Autumn 1975) 466

38 In August 1977 the federal government withdrew its offer for the support and supplementation programs, saying that only two provinces (Manitoba and Sas-

katchewan) had given a clear commitment to implement the proposals. Three provincial programs that provide income supplementation for the working poor should be noted: Saskatchewan's Family Income Plan (1974), the Quebec Work Income Supplement Program (1979), and the Manitoba Child Related Income Support Program (1981). On these provincial initiatives see Ross *The Working Poor* 50–4.

39 Johnson 'Canada's Social Security Review 1973–75' 466

CHAPTER 4

1 According to Adam Smith, 'It is not from the benevolence of the butcher, the brewer, or the baker, that we expect our dinner, but from their regard to their own interest. We address ourselves, not to their humanity but to their self-love, and never talk to them of our own necessities but of their advantages.' See Adam Smith *The Wealth of Nations* (New York: Random House 1937) 14.

2 Vincent Bladen *From Adam Smith to Maynard Keynes: The Heritage of Political Economy* (Toronto: University of Toronto Press 1974) 245

3 Charles E. Lindblom *Politics and Markets* (New York: Basic Books 1977) 45

4 Theodore H. Lowi *The Politics of Disorder* (New York: Norton 1971) 21–3

5 Bliss concludes that 'Canadian anti-combines legislation during these years was insignificant and ineffectual; it did not reflect a serious desire by legislators to resist economic consolidation or restore the forces of the free market.' See Michael Bliss 'Another Anti-trust Tradition: Canadian Anti-combines Policy, 1889–1910' in *Enterprise and National Development* edited by Glenn Porter and Robert Cuff (Toronto: Hakkert 1973) 39.

6 W.T. Stanbury *Business Interests and the Reform of Canadian Competition Policy* (Toronto: Methuen 1977) 47, 49, 53

7 The report of the Royal Commission on Corporate Concentration issued in May 1978 endorsed the competition board as a means for civil review of anti-combines practices and barriers to entry, but it argued that the plan to review mergers should be dropped or at least applied only to a limited number of big mergers. A month before Parliament was dissolved in 1979, the minister of consumer and corporate affairs announced that a third version of the merger amendments would be introduced. No policy was forthcoming before the election, however; nor did the minority Conservative government do anything to bring in a new policy. After the re-election of a Liberal government in June 1980, a bill covering merger amendments was said to be high on the agenda, but it was not tabled in the House of Commons until April 1984. The amendments included a more precise definition of what constitutes an illegal merger or illegal anti-competitive behaviour by dominant firms, the transfer from criminal to civil

courts of mergers and offences arising from abuse of dominant position (which should lower the burden of proof and make it easier to win a conviction, and the introduction of court orders to restore competition – for example, by un-scrambling an offending merger or by selling off certain assets – which will replace the traditional criminal fine. The bill did not pass before the session ended in June 1984, and it remains to be seen whether the Conservative government elected in September 1984 will adopt its provisions. Apparently, however, government officials, business leaders, and consumer advocates agree that there is not much possibility of a better compromise. See Giles Gherson 'Competition Law: End in Sight to Years of Stalemate' *The Financial Post* 21 April 1984, 9.

8 Stanbury *Business Interests and the Reform of Canadian Competition Policy* 56
9 Stuart Jamieson 'The Third Wave Reconsidered – Labour Unrest and Industrial Conflict in Canada, 1960–1975' (Vancouver: University of British Columbia: Department of Economics 1977) 1–3
10 Ibid. 36. See also Stuart Jamieson *Times of Trouble: Labour Unrest and Industrial Conflict in Canada, 1900–66* (Ottawa: Information Canada 1971) 471–2.
11 The brief history below is based mainly on H.D. Woods *Labour Policy in Canada* 2d ed. (Toronto: Macmillan 1973) 19–99.
12 Michael Bliss *A Living Profit* (Toronto: McClelland and Stewart 1974) 74, 87
13 Jamieson 'The Third Wave Reconsidered' 36
14 See Helen Jones Dawson 'An Interest Group: The Canadian Federation of Agriculture' *Canadian Public Administration* 3 (June 1960) 134.
15 A useful brief account of the emergence of marketing boards is provided by W.H. Drummond 'The Role of Agricultural Marketing Boards in Canadian Food Marketing' in Royal Commission on Price Spreads of Food Products *Report* (Ottawa: Queen's Printer 1960) vol. 3, 36–42, 47–9; reprinted in *The Canadian Economy: Selected Readings* edited by John J. Deutsch, Burton S. Kierstead, Kari Levitt, and Robert M. Will (Toronto: Macmillan 1965) 246–56.
16 Since August 1974 producers have had the option of selling feed grains for domestic consumption to the board or on the open market. The board remains the sole buyer and seller of feed grains for export.
17 Grace Skogstad 'The Farm Products Marketing Agencies Act: A Case Study of Agricultural Policy' *Canadian Public Policy* 6 (Winter 1980) 99
18 Drummond 'The Role of Agricultural Marketing Boards in Canadian Food Marketing' 47–9
19 Economic Council of Canada *Reforming Regulation* (Ottawa: Minister of Supply and Services 1981) 65
20 Michael J. Trebilcock, Leonard Waverman, and J. Robert S. Prichard 'Markets for Regulation: Implications for Performance Standards and Institutional De-

sign' in Ontario Economic Council *Issues and Alternatives 1978: Government Regulation* (Toronto: Ontario Economic Council 1978) 16–28

21 My account of the evolution of the board is based primarily on Arthur R. Wright 'An Examination of the Board of Transport Commissioners for Canada as a Regulatory Tribunal' *Canadian Public Administration* 6 (December 1963) 349–85.

22 House of Commons *Debates* 9 January 1967, 11572. Cited by Hudson N. Janisch 'The Canadian Transport Commission' in *The Regulatory Process in Canada* edited by G. Bruce Doern (Toronto: Macmillan 1978) 168.

23 For a study of the CTC's opposition to Part III of the National Transportation Act see Richard W. Schultz *Federalism, Bureaucracy, and Public Policy: The Politics of Highway Transport Regulation* (Montreal: McGill-Queen's University Press 1980).

24 Janisch 'The Canadian Transport Commission' 174

25 Cited by E.A. Weir, *The Struggle for National Broadcasting in Canada* (Toronto: McClelland and Stewart 1965) 133

26 Frank W. Peers *The Politics of Canadian Broadcasting: 1920–1951* (Toronto: University of Toronto Press 1969) 283–4

27 Royal Commission on National Development in the Arts, Letters and Sciences *Report* (Ottawa: King's Printer 1951) 18

28 Ibid. 28

29 The six regional stations were located in Montreal, Toronto, Ottawa, Vancouver, Halifax, and Winnipeg.

30 Arthur Siegel *Politics and the Media in Canada* (Toronto: McGraw-Hill Ryerson 1983) 173, 176

31 John Meisel 'Political Culture and the Politics of Culture' *Canadian Journal of Political Science* 7 (December 1974) 607

32 Siegel *Politics and the Media in Canada* 173

33 Ibid. 182

34 Royal Commission on Canada's Economic Prospects *Final Report* (Ottawa: Queen's Printer 1958) 390

35 See the polls summarized in Ronald Manzer *Canada: A Socio-political Report* (Toronto: McGraw-Hill Ryerson 1974) 170–1.

36 See, for example, Kari Levitt *Silent Surrender: The Multinational Corporation in Canada* (Toronto: Macmillan 1970); John Fayerweather *Foreign Investment in Canada: Prospects for a National Policy* (White Plains: International Arts and Sciences Press 1973); and A.E. Safarian 'Issues Raised by Foreign Direct Investment in Canada' in *Issues in Canadian Economics* edited by L.H. Officer and L.B. Smith (Toronto: McGraw-Hill Ryerson 1974) 80–93.

37 Task force on the Structure of Canadian Industry *Foreign Ownership and the*

Structure of Canadian Industry (Ottawa: Queen's Printer 1968); *Direct Investment in Canada* (Ottawa: Information Canada 1972)

38 In areas that affect Canada's cultural heritage or national identity, all foreign investment continues to be subject to review by Investment Canada. Otherwise, the new agency is not empowered to review direct takeovers involving assets of less than $5 million, indirect acquisitions of Canadian business having assets of less than $50 million, or foreign investment in new businesses. For foreign investment proposals still subject to review, the criterion for approval is a 'net benefit' to Canada rather than a 'significant benefit,' and the final decision is made by the minister of regional industrial expansion rather than by the entire cabinet. Under the new legislation Investment Canada also is charged with aggressively promoting investment opportunities and facilitating joint ventures between foreign and domestic firms. See Thomas Walkom 'Foreign Investors Welcome as Tories Lowering Barriers' *The Globe and Mail* 8 December 1984, and Miles Gherson and Fred Harrison 'Mulroney's Investment Message to U.S. Like "Fresh Air"' *The Financial Post* 15 December 1984.

39 The three types of environmental impacts are described in Barry Commoner *The Closing Circle: Nature, Man, and Technology* (New York: Knopf 1972) 126–7.

40 For an account of the early conservation movement see Thomas L. Burton *Natural Resource Policy in Canada: Issues and Perspectives* (Toronto: McClelland and Stewart 1972) 28–34.

41 H.V. Nelles *The Politics of Development* (Toronto: Macmillan 1974) 212, 214

42 Burton *Natural Resource Policy in Canada* 39

43 Michael Whittington 'Environmental Policy' in *Issues in Canadian Public Policy* edited by G. Bruce Doern and V. Seymour Wilson (Toronto: Macmillan 1974) 219–20

44 Ibid. 211–17

45 Reg Lang 'Environmental Impact Assessment: Reform or Rhetoric?' in *Ecology Versus Politics in Canada* edited by William Leiss (Toronto: University of Toronto Press 1979) 233. The brief account of environmental impact assessment that follows is based mainly on Lang's excellent essay.

46 Ibid. 241

47 *The Toronto Star* 18 July 1981, B4

48 Science Council of Canada *Canada as a Conserver Society: Resource Uncertainties and the Need for New Technologies* report no. 27 (Ottawa: Minister of Supply and Services 1977) 91

49 Ibid. 72

50 Economic Council of Canada *Responsible Regulation* (Ottawa: Minister of Supply and Services 1979) 124

51 Gil Reschenthaler, Bill Stanbury, and Fred Thompson 'Whatever Happened to Deregulation?' *Policy Options* (May/June 1982) 37. They note that 'studies have been conducted for the Law Reform Commission, the Institute for Research on Public Policy, the Ontario Economic Council, and, early in the 1970s, by the Canadian Consumer Council. Official inquiries include the Ontario Professional Organizations Committee and Commission on Freedom of Information and Individual Privacy; the ''Regulation Reference'' of the Economic Council of Canada, the Parliamentary Task Force on Regulatory Reform (the Peterson Committee); and the Lambert Commission.'

52 Ibid. 37. In May 1984 the minister of transport directed the CTC to deregulate the Canadian airline industry by ending the distinctions between national, regional, and local airlines and allowing them to seek approval to fly anywhere (except northern routes) in Canada. Airlines also should be allowed to discount fares as much as they wish without intervention by the CTC.

53 Michael J. Trebilcock 'The Consumer Interest and Regulatory Reform' in Doern *The Regulatory Process in Canada* 95

54 Gilles Paquet, 'The Regulatory Process and Economic Performance' ibid. 49–50

CHAPTER 5

1 The liberal assumption of the prevalence of individual conflict as opposed to group conflict has a serious limitation. The emergence of conflict between large social groups that have opposing values or interests can undermine the rule of law in two ways. First, the legitimacy of the law is eroded when dominant social groups use it to impose their values and interests to the detriment of the values and interests of subordinate groups. Second, it is much more difficult to use physical force to control the dissent of relatively large social groups than to control the deviance of isolated individuals. Accordingly, when serious group oppositions emerge, the continued legitimacy of the social order depends on extending or supplementing the rule of law by recognizing and somehow accommodating the opposing group values and interests.

2 See A.V. Dicey *Introduction to the Law of the Constitution* 10th ed. (London: Macmillan 1961) part 2, chapters 4, 10, and 14.

3 Kenneth McNaught 'Political Trials and the Canadian Political Tradition' in *Courts and Trials: A Multidisciplinary Approach* edited by Martin L. Friedland (Toronto and Buffalo: University of Toronto Press 1975) 138, 142

4 For a clear statement of the pluralist position see Richard Quinney, *The Social Reality of Crime* (Boston: Little, Brown 1970), especially chapters 1–3.

5 A.J. MacLeod 'Criminal Legislation' in *Crime and Its Treatment in Canada* edited by W.J. McGrath (Toronto: Macmillan 1965) 93

6 John Stuart Mill 'Considerations on Representative Government' in *On Liberty, Representative Government, the Subjection of Women: Three Essays* (London: Oxford University Press 1912, 1960) 187, 198

7 James Fitzjames Stephen *A History of the Criminal Law of England* vol. 2 (New York: Burt Franklin 1883) 77. Accordingly, although representative assemblies had existed in the colonies since 1758 in Nova Scotia, the British government's acceptance of responsible government in Nova Scotia, New Brunswick, and the Province of Canada in 1848 was undoubtedly a necessary and timely step in gaining acceptance for retributive or repudiative justice as a main principle of social order. Responsible government was granted to Prince Edward Island in 1851, to Newfoundland in 1855, to British Columbia and Manitoba in 1870, and to Alberta and Saskatchewan in 1905. See R. MacGregor Dawson and Norman Ward *The Government of Canada* 4th ed. (Toronto: University of Toronto Press 1963) 19.

8 Cesare Beccaria *On Crimes and Punishments* (Indianapolis: Bobbs-Merrill 1963), especially chapters 2, 12, 15, and 23. Beccaria contended that punishments administered in the eighteenth century, being more severe than was necessary to deter, accordingly were unjust and should have been reformed.

9 Nigel Walker *Crime and Punishment in Britain* (Edinburgh: Edinburgh University Press 1965) 136

10 Jeremy Bentham 'An Introduction to the Principles of Morals and Legislation' in Jeremy Bentham and J.S. Mill *The Utilitarians* (Garden City: Dolphin 1961) chapter 14

11 See W.R. Jackett 'Foundations of Canadian Law in History and Theory' in *Contemporary Problems of Public Law in Canada* edited by Otto Lang (Toronto: University of Toronto Press 1968).

12 John K. Elliot 'Crime and Punishment in Early Upper Canada' *Ontario Historical Society's Papers and Records* 27 (1931) 335–40

13 J. Douglas Borthwick *History of Montreal Prison* (Montreal 1886) 269

14 The Northwest Mounted Police, formed in 1873 to police the western plains, was reorganized into a national police force, the Royal Canadian Mounted Police, in 1920. The first provincial police force was established in Quebec in 1870; its main responsibilities for some years were escorting prisoners and keeping order in provincial courts. A Manitoba police force was created in 1870 when Manitoba joined Confederation; and the British Columbia police force, set up at the time of union between Vancouver Island and British Columbia in 1866, became the third provincial police force when British Columbia entered Confederation. Saskatchewan and Alberta formed provincial police forces in 1917 when the Royal Northwest Mounted Police withdrew from its contracts, in

force since 1905, because of wartime manpower shortages. In 1928 Saskatchewan renewed its contract with the RCMP, which absorbed the members of the
provincial police. Alberta and Manitoba followed in 1932. New Brunswick
(from 1927), Nova Scotia (from 1928), and Prince Edward Island (from 1930)
operated provincial police forces only briefly before they were absorbed by the
RCMP in 1932. The British Columbia provincial police force and the Newfoundland Rangers established in 1935 were replaced by the RCMP in 1950. See William
and Nora Kelly *Policing in Canada* (Toronto: Macmillan 1976) 15–24. On the
Ontario Provincial Police see Allan K. McDougall 'Policing in Ontario: The
Occupational Dimension to Provincial-Municipal Relations' PH D thesis, University of Toronto 1971.

15 Canadian Committee on Corrections *Towards Unity: Criminal Justice and
Corrections* (Ottawa: Information Canada 1969) 16
16 Stephen *A History of the Criminal Law of England* vol. 2 80–1
17 Paul Weiler 'The Reform of Punishment' in Law Reform Commission of Canada
Studies on Sentencing (Ottawa: Information Canada 1974) 159
18 John Stuart Mill 'Utilitarianism' in *The English Philosophers from Bacon to Mill*
edited by Edwin A. Burtt (New York: Modern Library 1939) 945
19 Peter B. Waite *The Confederation Debates in the Province of Canada/1865*
(Toronto: McClelland and Stewart 1963) 46
20 For a useful analysis of the original Criminal Code, see George H. Crouse 'A
Critique of Canadian Criminal Legislation' *Canadian Bar Review* 12
(November-December 1934) 545–78, 601–33.
21 For a description of the early years at Kingston Penitentiary, see J. Alex
Edmison 'Some Aspects of Nineteenth-Century Canadian Prisons' in *Crime
and Its Treatment in Canada* 285–93.
22 Eschel M. Rhoodie *Penal Systems of the Commonwealth* (Pretoria: Academica
1967), 73–4. The permanent additions to the penal system after 1880 were
Saskatchewan Penitentiary (1911), Collins Bay Penitentiary (1930), and the
Women's Prison at Kingston (1934).
23 Royal Commission to Investigate the Penal System *Report* (Ottawa: King's
Printer 1938) 22–4, 104, 116, 126
24 Ibid. 17; C.W. Topping, *Canadian Penal Institutions* (Toronto: Ryerson 1929)
62–3
25 Royal Commission to Investigate the Penal System *Report* 100
26 Sharon L. Sutherland 'The Ministry of the Solicitor General: Correctional
Service of Canada' in *Spending Tax Dollars: Federal Expenditures 1980–1981*
edited by G. Bruce Doern (Ottawa: Carleton University School of Public
Administration 1980) 177, 180–1
27 For a discussion of after-care services, see A.M. Kirkpatrick 'After Care and
the Prisoners' Aid Societies' in *Crime and Its Treatment in Canada* 384–409.

28 From 1945 to 1958 paroles granted by the Remission Service varied from 800 to 1,500 a year. In its first year of operations the National Parole Board granted 2,038 paroles or 42 per cent of its applications; over the next five years it continued to grant 1,800 to 2,500 paroles a year with approval rates of 30 to 40 per cent. After 1965 paroles granted and rates of approval both increased until 1970–1 when the board approved 5,259 paroles, or 65 per cent of those who applied. Paroles granted by the board were reduced to 4,714 (58 per cent approval) in 1971–2 and 3,376 (45 per cent approval) in 1972–3. Since then the board has granted 2,500–3,000 paroles a year, representing rates of approval ranging from 35 to 45 per cent.

29 House of Commons, Standing Committee on Justice and Legal Affairs, Subcommittee on the Penitentiary Sytem in Canada *Report to Parliament* (Ottawa: Minister of Supply and Services 1977) 15

30 Committee to Inquire into the Principles and Procedures Followed in the Remission Service of the Department of Justice in Canada *Report* (Ottawa: Queen's Printer 1956) 41–7

31 John Fornataro 'Canadian Prisons Today' in *Crime and Its Treatment in Canada* 307–21

32 Mann says, 'In 1961 Guelph Reformatory, 14 years after the instituting of the Department of Reform Institutions, was basically a punitive authoritarian prison in which reformation of character was very largely in the direction of anti-social and criminal attitudes. Owing to the role of the inmate sub-culture, it might have been more justly labled a deformatory.' See W.E. Mann *Society behind Bars: A Sociological Scrutiny of Guelph Reformatory* (Toronto: Social Science Publishers 1967) 139.

33 See, for example, D.F. Cousineau and J.E. Veevers 'Incarceration as a Response to Crime: The Utilization of Canadian Prisons' *Canadian Journal of Criminology and Corrections* 14 (June 1972) 10–31; or Kenneth A. Carlson 'Some Characteristics of Recidivists in an Ontario Institution for Adult Male First-Incarcerates' *Canadian Journal of Criminology and Corrections* 15 (October 1973) 397–411.

34 Fornataro 'Canadian Prisons Today' 322; emphasis in original

35 Alan Mewett, 'The Criminal Law 1867–1967,' *Canadian Bar Review* 45 (December 1967) 735, 740

36 Weiler, 'The Reform of Punishment' 161

37 John Hogarth *Sentencing as a Human Process* (Toronto: University of Toronto Press 1971) 41; Stuart K. Jaffary *Sentencing of Adults in Canada* (Toronto: University of Toronto Press 1963) 51–4

38 Hogarth *Sentencing as a Human Process* 135

39 William Johnson 'Controlling the Violent Offender' *The Globe and Mail* 8 January 1983, 10

40 Canadian Committee on Corrections *Towards Unity* 15
41 George Herbert Mead 'The Psychology of Punitive Justice' *American Journal of Sociology* 23 (March 1918) 592; cited by Weiler, 'The Reform of Punishment' 161
42 Canadian Committee on Corrections *Towards Unity* 188
43 Restitution is punishment that requires some payment or action by an offender in order to make good the damage done to his victim. The purpose of restitution is to compensate, as far as possible, the victim's financial, physical or psychological loss. The form of restitution may be a monetary payment, a work order, or an apology. See Law Reform Commission of Canada *Restitution and Compensation/Fines* working papers 5 and 6 (Ottawa: Information Canada 1974) 8.
44 Stephen Schafer *Compensation and Restitution to Victims of Crime* 2d ed. (Montclair: Patterson Smith 1970) 11
45 Law Reform Commission *Restitution and Compensation/Fines* 8
46 Schafer *Compensation and Restitution to Victims of Crime* 117–19
47 Law Reform Commission *Restitution and Compensation/Fines* 14
48 Ibid. 6. Perhaps the far-reaching policy implications of the restitution approach can be seen best in the commission's working paper on diversion. There the commission's philosophy of accepting conflict as an aspect of social living, of reducing the impact of the criminal law, and of substituting reconciliation of the offender and his victim for an adversary trial between the offender and the state leads to a series of proposals to deal with more conflicts in the community outside the criminal-justice system, to increase the role of the police in diverting and mediating conflicts, to deal with more cases at the pre-trial level by settlement of mediation procedures, and to make greater use of alternatives to imprisonment including restitution. See Law Reform Commission of Canada *Diversion* working paper 7 (Ottawa: Information Canada 1975).
49 Subcommittee on the Penitentiary System *Report to Parliament* 2
50 Ibid. 16
51 Ibid. 38
52 Ibid. 37; emphasis in original
53 Ibid. 38–39

CHAPTER 6

1 The influence of industrialization on education and the campaigns for more science and technical subjects in curricula are discussed in Robert M. Stamp 'Education and the Social Milieu: The English-Canadian Scene from the 1870s to 1914' in *Canadian Education: A History* edited by J. Donald Wilson, R.M. Stamp, and Louis-Philippe Audet (Scarborough: Prentice-Hall 1970) 292–7.

2 Quoted in William Johnson 'The Religion of Independence in Quebec' *The Globe and Mail* 10 February 1977, 7. Leger's statement is applied specifically to Quebec as an argument for its political independence, but as a general statement of the aims of individual and cultural development it expresses equally well the educational aspirations of English-speaking ethical liberals.

3 Legislation establishing common schools had been passed early in the century in New Brunswick (1802), Nova Scotia (1808), and Upper Canada (1816); but those were schools for the children of the lower classes, the 'common' people, rather than democratic institutions for popular education.

4 Alison Prentice *The School Promoters: Education and Social Class in Mid-Nineteenth Century Upper Canada* (Toronto: McClelland and Stewart 1977) 182–3

5 Ibid. 40–1, 47, 52, 132

6 Ibid. 131

7 C.E. Phillips *The Development of Education in Canada* (Toronto: Gage 1957) 486–7. Evidence from one recent study suggests that important differences exist between English-Canadian and French-Canadian national education in the content of their history courses. Marcel Trudel and Geneviève Jain found that English and French textbooks advanced different interpretations of history, different assessments of historical figures, and different values. In their educational objectives, for example, the French-language histories aimed at inculcating a moral education; the English-language books used history to give future citizens a political and social education. The divergence between English and French textbooks was particularly striking in their treatment of post-Confederation history. 'Here the two groups do not even seem to be talking about the same country! The English-speaking authors do their best to give an overall history of Canada, while the French authors take less and less interest in regions other than Quebec. If the latter still talk about the Maritimes it is because of the Acadians; if they talk about the West it is mostly about the role played by French Canadians there; in short, they hardly talk about anything but the history of Quebec and its expansion beyond its borders.' See Marcel Trudel and Geneviève Jain *Canadian History Textbooks: A Comparative Study* Study no. 5 of the Royal Commission on Bilingualism and Biculturalism (Ottawa: Queen's Printer 1970) 124. The conclusion reached by Trudel and Jain is based on their study of textbooks published during the 1950s and early 1960s. It seems likely that similar differences between French and English textbooks existed in earlier periods. A committee to study history textbooks set up by the Canada and Newfoundland Education Association during the Second World War found that 'another characteristic of Canadian history texts – and the one which has been of particular concern to this Committee – is the difference in content

between texts in the English and French languages. Generally speaking, French-language texts tend to pass quickly over the history of the English provinces, while English-language books do not have sufficient attention to events or persons important in French Canadian history. In some of the English-language texts, the history of the French before and after the conquest is too briefly treated; the exploits of Madeleine de Verchères, Dollard, d'Iberville, the early French explorers, the battles of Barillon, Ste-Foye, Chateauguay, the political struggles of the French-Canadians, and their role in the making of Confederation, are skimmed over or even omitted. No text mentions the rights of the French language under the Constitution, and the school question is hardly touched upon in any of them. Likewise French-language texts give little space to the Hudson's Bay Company, the English explorers, the Loyalists, the economic development of the country, and the history of provinces other than Quebec. Needless to say, the relations of Canada with Britain receive a much different treatment in the two series of texts. A foreigner would have an altogether different view of Canadian history according to whether he read a school textbook in the French language or in the English language.' See Canada and Newfoundland Education Association 'Report of the Committee for the Study of Canadian History Textbooks' *Canadian Education* 1 (October 1945) 9–10.

8 *Lord Durham's Report on the Affairs of British North America* edited by C.P. Lucas (Oxford: Clarendon Press 1912) vol. 2, 288; vol. 3, 288

9 Andrè Siegfried *The Race Question in Canada* edited by Frank H. Underhill (Toronto: McClelland and Stewart 1966) 59

10 Historically, the first principle of educational policy in Canada was denominationalism. According to the denominational principle, the essence of education is religious instruction in Christian doctrine. Among the three major social institutions that guide learning – family, church, and state – the denominational principle makes the church the ultimate authority in determining what values are to be cultivated. The family is accepted as an essential partner of the church in conveying religious instruction to young people, but the parents' obligation for the spiritual development of their children is clearly understood to be subordinate to the accepted beliefs of the religious community to which they belong. The state tends to be relegated to filling a promotional and protective role, providing financial support for the educational activities of the church, and enforcing as necessary the authority of the church to control religious instruction.

11 Charles Phillips has commented, 'An amazing aspect of the separate school controversy in Canada West was the complete assurance with which Protestant non-conformists maintained that the religious exercises and the reading of the

Bible were entirely undenominational. Had it not been for this zealous lack of perception, successful legislation might have been drafted early in the 1840's to establish two-denominational schools in Canada East and neutral common schools in Canada West. There would then have been no separate schools in Ontario or the middle west, and no mention in the British North America Act of educational rights of religious minorities, except in Quebec.' See Phillips *The Development of Education in Canada* 311.

12 Royal Commission on Bilingualism *Report, Volume 2: Education* (Ottawa: Queen's Printer 1968) 34. The report quotes C.-J. Magnon *L'Instruction publique dans la province de Québec* on the situation in 1932: 'School boards decide the main language of instruction in each school by engaging either English-speaking or French-speaking teachers. Where English-speaking Catholics are in the majority, they run their own schools. Neither the government nor the department of Public Instruction intervenes in matters of language, except to maintain the rights of the minority, whether Anglophone or Francophone.'

13 Phillips *The Development of Education in Canada* 340

14 Royal Commission on Bilingualism and Biculturalism *Report, Volume 2: Education* 48

15 Regulation 17 empowered the chief inspector to approve the use of French beyond the first form (grades one and two) if pupils did not understand English. French also could be taught as a subject of study beyond those grades if it had been offered previously, but it could not be taught for more than one hour a day without the permission of the chief inspector.

16 The dispute over regulation 17 is well described in C.B. Sissons *Church and State in Canadian Education* (Toronto: Ryerson Press 1959) 86–91. An opinion expressed at a Toronto by-election rally in 1916 by the cabinet minister responsible for administering regulation 17 serves to illustrate the intensity of British-Canadian hostility to bilingual education: 'This bilingual question is the greatest of the issues before us. It entirely overshadows nickel and booze and every other question. It touches the vitals of our province and our Dominion. If it is not dealt with the whole national fabric will be destroyed. The government I represent upholds British traditions, British institutions and one flag and one language for this Dominion. Unless something is done to meet this French-speaking invasion, this national outrage, this Dominion will be stricken to its foundation as this war has not stricken it.' See Peter Oliver *G. Howard Ferguson: Ontario Tory* (Toronto: University of Toronto Press 1977) 78.

17 Compulsory attendance was set at a full school year for children aged eight to fourteen in Ontario in 1889 and raised to include those up to sixteen in 1921. British Columbia established its requirement at six months for children aged seven to twelve in 1876 and gradually extended it to a full school year for children aged seven to fourteen, first in municipal districts in 1912 and in all

school districts after 1921. By 1921 Saskatchewan and Manitoba also provided for a full school year for children aged seven to fourteen, and Alberta had compulsory attendance covering those aged seven to fifteen. In the Maritime provinces, the law was less stringent. Prince Edward Island required twenty or thirty weeks for children aged seven to thirteen, Nova Scotia covered children aged seven to twelve at the option of local boards, and New Brunswick provided for eighty days of schooling for children aged seven to twelve. Neither Quebec nor Newfoundland had compulsory schooling laws until 1942.

18 School boards in cities and towns were appointed jointly by municipal councils and the provincial cabinet until fairly recently in New Brunswick (1967) and Prince Edward Island (1972). In Nova Scotia trustees are appointed, except in the cases of the now relatively unimportant boards of rural and village sections.

19 School grants from central governments to local districts based on weighted population, fixed unit, and variable percentage are described by Charles S. Benson *The Economics of Public Education* 2d ed. (Boston: Houghton Mifflin Company 1968) 146–51.

20 In New Brunswick and Prince Edward Island the provincial government collects taxes, builds schools, employs teachers, and makes decisions on programs. Local school boards have only limited taxing and decision-making powers to provide programs over and above those provided by the province. In Newfoundland virtually all funds needed by the school boards come from provincial governmental operating grants to the boards and construction grants to the churches. The boards do make limited use of poll and/or property taxes. See David Siegel 'Provincial-Municipal Relations in Canada: An Overview' *Canadian Public Administration* 23 (Summer 1980), 296–7.

21 Provincial Committee on Aims and Objectives in the Schools of Ontario *Living and Learning* (Toronto: Ontario Department of Education 1968) 55

22 Ibid. 21

23 Robert S. Patterson reports that 1,097 of the 3,852 foreign students registered at Columbia Teachers College from 1928 to 1938 came from Canada. He adds, 'The majority of the leading Canadian educational reformers of the period had some educational experience in centres such as Columbia, Chicago, and Stanford. Canadian periodicals frequently drew from American sources to describe new developments in education.' See R.S. Patterson 'Society and Education during the Wars and Their Interlude: 1914–1945' in *Canadian Education: A History* 373. W.G. Fleming has noted that 'many of the ideas and some of the wording' of the 1937 program of studies for grades one to six in Ontario were taken from the Hadow Reports published in Britain between 1927 and 1934. See W.G. Fleming *Ontario's Educative Society, Volume III: Schools, Pupils, and Teachers* (Toronto: University of Toronto Press 1971) 123.

24 Alberta Department of Education *Program of Studies for the Intermediate*

School: Grades VII, VIII, and IX (1935) 36, cited by Patterson 'Society and Education during the Wars' 376

25 Fleming *Ontario's Educative Society* 9
26 Hilda Neatby *So Little for the Mind* (Toronto: Clarke, Irwin 1953)
27 New Brunswick Department of Education *The Organization of Instruction for New Brunswick Schools* 1972 revision 3
28 Quebec Ministry of Education *Review of Educational Policies in Canada: Quebec* (Toronto: Council of Ministers of Education 1975) 84; emphasis in original
29 British Columbia Department of Education *The Public School System: Directions for Change* (Victoria 1974) 1, 4
30 Ministers of Education for the Provinces of New Brunswick, Newfoundland, Nova Scotia, and Prince Edward Island *Review of Educational Policies in Canada: Atlantic Region* (Toronto: Council of Ministers of Education 1975) 20
31 Ministers of Education for the Provinces of British Columbia, Alberta, Saskatchewan, and Manitoba *Review of Educational Policies in Canada: Western Region* (Toronto: Council of Ministers of Education 1975) 37
32 Ibid. 39
33 *Review of Educational Policies in Canada: Quebec* 86
34 *Review of Educational Policies in Canada: Atlantic Region* 25
35 *Review of Educational Policies in Canada: Quebec* 88–90
36 John Stuart Mill 'On Liberty' in *The English Philosophers from Bacon to Mill* edited by Edwin A. Burtt (New York: Modern Library 1939) 1033–4
37 The most important attempt to expand the domain of denominational schooling during the 1960s was a vigorous campaign by the Roman Catholic minority in Ontario to extend public support for its separate schools from grade ten, where it had been settled in 1908, to grade thirteen. The campaign ended in failure in 1971 when the Conservative government, opposed to extending public support, decisively won re-election over the Liberal and the New Democratic parties, which had supported the Roman Catholic position. In June 1984, however, Premier Davis announced that public funding for Roman Catholic secondary schools would be implemented for one additional grade each year beginning in September 1985 so that full support would be achieved by 1988. The most important attempt to reduce significantly the formal position of denominational schooling was a recommendation advanced in 1966 by the Royal Commission on Education in Quebec that non-sectarian, secular school boards be set up and empowered to provide Catholic, Protestant, or neutral schools depending on local parental demand. In June 1982 the Quebec Minister of Education tabled a white paper that would abolish Catholic and Protestant school boards in the province. Outside Montreal regional councils would administer the schools of

both languages and both denominations in their districts. Each school would be governed by an administrative council of parents, teachers, and (at the secondary level) students. The council would determine whether its school would be Catholic, Protestant, multi-faith or neutral in its orientation; it would have the power to choose textbooks, set budgets, and hire and evaluate staff. On Montreal Island denominational boards would be replaced by eight French and five English-language boards. In June 1984 the minister withdrew bill 40, which would have implemented these reforms, and replaced it in November with a modified bill. Under the new bill schools are still divided by language rather than by religion, and within school boards each school is able to decide whether it is Catholic, Protestant, or non-denominational. The number of boards is reduced from 250 to about 150, but there is less decentralization of power from the boards to the school councils.

38 My description of provincial grants to private schools is based mainly on J. Donald Wilson 'Religion and Education: the Other Side of Pluralism' in *Canadian Education in the 1980s* edited by J. Donald Wilson (Calgary: Detselig 1981) 97–113.

39 Royal Commission on Bilingualism and Biculturalism *Report, Volume 1: The Official Languages* (Ottawa: Queen's Printer 1967) 121, 123. See also the commission's discussion of education in volume 2 of their report.

40 William Johnson 'Creating a Nation of Tongues' *The Globe and Mail* 26 June 1982, 10. My description of heritage-language programs is based primarily on this article.

41 Ibid.

CHAPTER 7

1 Donald V. Smiley *The Canadian Charter of Rights and Freedoms, 1981* (Toronto: Ontario Economic Council 1981) 1

2 In addition to the widely used categories of political, legal and egalitarian rights, claims for protection of individual rights may be made with respect to economic and social rights and minority language rights. See, for example, the federal government's proposal in Department of Justice *A Canadian Charter of Human Rights* (Ottawa: Queen's Printer 1968) 15–27. Its classification of Canadian rights policies into five categories was drawn from a scheme suggested by Bora Laskin 'An Inquiry into the Diefenbaker Bill of Rights' *Canadian Bar Review* 37 (1959) 77–134. Another important category of rights in Canada is aboriginal rights. Primarily for reasons of space, the description and interpretation of human rights policies in Canada in this chapter has been limited to the three general categories of political, legal, and egalitarian rights.

3 The argument in this paragraph is based on points made by Donald Smiley. See Smiley *The Canadian Charter of Rights and Freedoms, 1981* 1–6.

4 Ibid. 5–6

5 Robert A. Dahl and Charles E. Lindblom *Politics, Economics and Welfare* (New York: Harper and Row 1953) 283

6 C.B. Macpherson *The Life and Times of Liberal Democracy* (Toronto: Oxford University Press 1977) 79. Macpherson adds that the only adequately descriptive term for this model is pluralist élitist equilibrium. 'It is pluralist in that it starts from the assumption that the society which a modern democratic political system must fit is a plural society, that is, a society consisting of individuals each of whom is pulled in many directions by his many interests, now in company with one group of his fellows, now with another. It is elitist in that it assigns the main role in the political process to self-chosen groups of leaders. It is an equilibrium model in that it presents the democratic process as a system which maintains an equilibrium between the demand and supply of political goods' (77).

7 Robert H. Dahl *Polyarchy: Participation and Opposition* (New Haven: Yale University Press 1971) 3

8 My summary of the development of political rights in Canada restates my previous account in *Canada: A Socio-political Report* (Toronto: McGraw-Hill Ryerson 1974) 270–80.

9 S.D. Clark *Movements of Political Protest in Canada 1640–1840* (Toronto: University of Toronto Press 1959) 42, 44

10 My description of press censorship is based primarily on W.H. Kesterton *A History of Journalism in Canada* (Toronto: McClelland and Stewart 1967).

11 Clark *Movements of Political Protest in Canada* 488

12 My description of restraints on suffrage is based on John Garner *The Franchise and Politics in British North America 1755–1867* (Toronto: University of Toronto Press 1969); Norman Ward *The Canadian House of Commons: Representation* (Toronto: University of Toronto Press 1960) 211–39; Terence H. Qualter *The Election Process in Canada* (Toronto: McGraw-Hill 1970); and Royal Commission on the Status of Women in Canada *Report* (Ottawa: Information Canada 1970).

13 Escott Reid 'The Rise of National Parties in Canada' in *Party Politics in Canada* edited by Hugh G. Thorburn (Toronto: Prentice-Hall 1963) 14

14 R. MacGregor Dawson and Norman Ward *The Government of Canada* 5th ed. (Toronto: University of Toronto Press 1970) 312

15 Ward *The Canadian House of Commons* 226–7

16 For a complete list see William Rodney *Soldiers of the International* (Toronto: University of Toronto Press 1968) 18 note

17 D.A. Schmeiser *Civil Liberties in Canada* (London: Oxford University Press 1964) 218

18 See *Leading Constitutional Decisions* edited by Peter Russell (Toronto: McClelland and Stewart 1965) 204–15.

19 Walter S. Tarnopolsky *The Canadian Bill of Rights* 2d ed. (Toronto: McClelland and Stewart 1975), 37, 181

20 Governmental censorship of the press during the two world wars was accepted in Canada as a patriotic necessity. Censorship was particularly strict during the First World War. One paper and a press were seized for infractions; 151 newspapers were denied use of the mails and possession of copies of them was made illegal; and in 1918 it was made a crime to import, publish, post, or possess a publication in an enemy language. About fifteen Communist weeklies were suppressed in the early months of the Second World War before the Soviet Union became an ally, but otherwise there were only a few convictions for minor security violations, which resulted in small fines but did not interrupt publishing schedules.

21 Russell *Leading Constitutional Decisions* 166–75

22 Ibid. 174

23 One feature of suffrage legislation after 1920 was the slowness of Quebec to accept reforms being adopted in other jurisdictions. The property qualification, which had been removed from the provincial franchise in Nova Scotia in 1920, lasted in Quebec until 1936; and women in Quebec were not accorded voting rights on equal terms with men until 1940.

24 Smiley *The Canadian Charter of Rights and Freedoms, 1981*, 9

25 Donald V. Smiley *Canada in Question: Federalism in the Seventies* 2d ed. (Toronto: McGraw-Hill Ryerson 1976) 40–2

26 Task Force on Canadian Unity *A Future Together: Observations and Recommendations* (Ottawa: Minister of Supply and Services 1979) 108

27 Peter Russell 'The Effect of a Charter of Rights on the Policy-Making Role of Canadian Courts' *Canadian Public Administration* 25 (Spring 1982) 27

28 This argument concerning the dominance of an ethical liberal conception of human rights is strengthened when due account is given to section 27 of the Charter: 'This Charter shall be interpreted in a manner consistent with the preservation and enhancement of the multicultural heritage of Canadians.'

29 In this discussion of legal rights in Canada I shall limit my considerations to individual rights in criminal cases.

30 Russell 'The Effect of a Charter of Rights' 21

31 The Charter of Rights and Freedoms provides protection against involuntary exile in section 6(1), which guarantees that 'Every citizen of Canada has the right to enter, remain in and leave Canada.'

32 Theodore F.T. Plucknett *A Concise History of the Common Law* 5th ed. (London: Butterworths 1956) 25
33 Tarnopolsky *The Canadian Bill of Rights* 222–3
34 Albert S. Abel 'The Bill of Rights in the United States: What Has It Accomplished' *Canadian Bar Review* 37 (1959) 154–5
35 In 1868 the Fifteenth Amendment added the words 'nor shall any State deprive any person of life, liberty, or property, without due process of law.' By making reference to cruel and unusual treatment, and not simply punishments, the Canadian charter goes significantly beyond the provisions of the English and American bills of rights and makes section 13 potentially applicable to many situations arising outside criminal cases. The first test of the section in the courts, for example, involved a severely retarded six-year-old boy whose parents objected to a life-saving operation. Child-welfare officials argued for the boy's right to life; his parents argued for his right to die peacefully and be spared cruel treatment. The trial court found for the parents, but the British Columbia Supreme Court gave overriding weight to the boy's right to life.
36 See Stanley Aron Cohen *Due Process of Law: The Canadian System of Criminal Justice* (Toronto: Carswell 1977) 11–12; and Tarnopolsky *The Canadian Bill of Rights* 230–3.
37 Cohen *Due Process of Law* 12
38 In *Curr v The Queen* Mr. Justice Laskin referred to the violation of pre-trial due process in a case considered by the American Supreme Court, which held that a suspect's right to due process had been violated by police forcing an emetic on him in order to obtain the morphine capsules he had swallowed. See Tarnopolsky *The Canadian Bill of Rights* 232–3.
39 Ibid. 228
40 The addition in the Charter of Rights and Freedoms over the 1960 and 1968 provisions is the arrested person's right to be informed of the right to counsel.
41 See *Statutes, Treaties and Documents of the Canadian Constitution 1713–1929* 2d ed., edited by W.P.M. Kennedy (Toronto: Oxford University Press 1930) 156.
42 Hilda M. Neatby *The Administration of Justice under the Quebec Act* (Minneapolis: University of Minnesota Press 1937) 308–9. Neatby's description of a typical trial is based on the records of the Court of King's Bench sitting at Kingston in 1789.
43 This paragraph on the establishment of judicial independence in Canada is based on Bora Laskin *The British Tradition in Canadian Law* (London: Stevens 1969) 35–41.
44 Tarnopolsky *The Canadian Bill of Rights* 256
45 Alan W. Mewett 'The Criminal Law, 1867–1967' *Canadian Bar Review* 45 (1967) 734

46 Jeff Sallot 'Judges Reject Liberal Views in Charter Cases' *The Globe and Mail* 7 January 1983, 8

47 Tarnopolsky *The Canadian Bill of Rights* 66

48 Quoted ibid. 70–1

49 Gordon Fairweather 'The New Human Rights Act: What It Gives Us' *Perception* 1 (January/February 1978) 11

50 See Schmeiser *Civil Liberties in Canada* 257–61.

51 Tarnopolsky *The Canadian Bill of Rights* 72

52 Schmeiser *Civil Liberties in Canada* 263

53 Ian A. Hunter *Human Rights Legislation in Canada: Its Origin, Development and Interpretation* research paper prepared for the Code Review Committee of the Ontario Human Rights Commission (August 1976) 4; quoted in Ontario Human Rights Commission *Life Together: A Report on Human Rights in Ontario* (Toronto: Queen's Printer 1977) 15. See also Ian Hunter 'The Origin, Development and Interpretation of Human Rights Legislation' in *The Practice of Freedom* edited by R. St J. Macdonald and John P. Humphrey (Toronto: Butterworths 1979) 79.

54 Tarnopolsky *The Canadian Bill of Rights* 68

55 In its 1970 report the Royal Commission on the Status of Women in Canada observed that only a few complaints had been made under provincial equal pay laws and none under the equivalent federal law. The commission concluded that the laws were 'virtually inoperable' largely because of an unreasonable standard of proof that jobs are 'the same' or 'identical.' The commission recommended the standard of 'equal pay for work of equal value' and this criterion was adopted in the Canadian Human Rights Act. See Royal Commission on the Status of Women in Canada *Report* 67–77.

56 Tarnopolsky *The Canadian Bill of Rights* 295–308

57 Ibid. 160

58 Department of Justice *A Canadian Charter of Human Rights* 25–6

59 Section 15(2) does provide an exemption for 'any law, program or activity that has as its object the amelioration of condition of disadvantaged individuals or groups including those that are disadvantaged because of race, national or ethnic origin, colour, religion, sex, age or mental or physical handicap.'

60 Smiley *The Canadian Charter of Rights and Freedoms, 1981* 16–17

61 Russell 'The Effect of a Charter of Rights' 24–5

62 Smiley *The Canadian Charter of Rights and Freedoms, 1981* 16

63 Clifford Orwin and Thomas Pangle 'The Philosophical Foundation of Human Rights' in *Human Rights in Our Time: Essays in Memory of Victor Baras* edited by Marc F. Plattner (Boulder: Westview 1984) 2

64 Ibid. 3

65 Ibid. 18

CHAPTER 8

1 Space limitations prohibit a detailed study of post-war cultural policy in Canada, but its development is an excellent example of the increased attention being given to individual development. 'I do not believe it is yet realized what an important thing has happened,' said Lord Keynes, commenting on the creation of the British Arts Council in 1945. 'State patronage of the arts has crept in ... At last the public exchequer has recognized the support and encouragement of the civilizing arts of life as part of their duty.' Quoted in Royal Commission on National Development in the Arts, Letters and Sciences *Report* (Ottawa: King's Printer 1951) 374–5. Perhaps the first clear articulation of the federal government's responsibility to nurture Canadian cultural development appeared in the 1929 report of the Royal Commission on Broadcasting. The arguments for national public broadcasting were taken up by the Royal Commission on National Development in the Arts, Letters and Sciences (the Massey Commission) as the rationale for a comprehensive cultural policy that included significant financial support for Canadian arts and scholarship and a rationalization of federal support for national and regional cultural institutions. The model of the British Arts Council, for example, was advocated for Canada by the Massey Commission, and was realized when the Canada Council was set up in 1957. The Massey Commission gave 'culture' a fairly narrow meaning, and rejected the concept of a national ministry of culture, citing the potential problems arising from state control of the arts. The federal government (through the department of the secretary of state) and most provincial governments, however, did set up departmental administrations to co-ordinate their cultural policy-making. Cultural policy development also was broadened to cover popular culture, sports, and recreation. As in education, individual access to cultural institutions and activities became a guiding principle of policy. According to one observer, 'While postwar affluence made the Canada Council possible, this larger cultural revolution that began in the 60s is a more pervasive and, in many ways, more definite reflection of the recognized needs and aspirations of a whole range of Canadian society. It has been motivated by an altered sense of federal and provincial goals, the expansion of political theory to embrace culture, however awkwardly, and the call for government at all levels to develop a "quality of life" in the phrase of the politicians. Culture has become, with education, a major social commodity.' See Dale McConathy 'The Canadian Cultural Revolution: An Appraisal of the Politics and Economics of Art' *Arts Canada* 32 (Autumn 1975) 74.

2 The traditional socio-economic features of French Quebec were recorded in an 1860 monograph, which described a typical North Shore parish: 'a self-

sufficient economy; isolation from the influence of cities or commerce; aversion to post-elementary education as something that corrupted and unsettled accepted norms; tenacious family ties that had the family farm as a physical and symbolic point; a strong Catholic faith that supported the local curé with tithes and endowed him with considerable authority over local affairs.' Cited in Dale Posgate and Kenneth McRoberts *Quebec: Social Change in Political Crisis* (Toronto: McClelland and Stewart 1976) 21. Even as French Quebec became an urban and industrial society, these traditional ideals were strenuously defended.

3 Lloyd D. Musolf *Public Ownership and Accountability: The Canadian Experience* (Cambridge, Mass.: Harvard University Press 1959) 23

Bibliographical Notes

The classic modern interpretations of Canadian public philosophy and political culture are advanced by Kenneth McRae in 'The Structure of Canadian History' in *The Founding of New Societies* edited by Louis Hartz (New York: Harcourt, Brace and World 1964) and by Gad Horowitz in 'Conservatism, Liberalism and Socialism in Canada: An Interpretation' *Canadian Journal of Economics and Political Science* 32 (May 1966) 143–71. Horowitz has replied to criticisms of his interpretation in 'Notes on "Conservatism, Liberalism and Socialism in Canada"' *Canadian Journal of Political Science* 11 (June 1978) 383–99. A recent treatment of Canadian political culture that includes a good discussion of various approaches to studying political culture is provided by David Bell and Lorne Tepperman in *The Roots of Disunity: A Look at Canadian Political Culture* (Toronto: McClelland and Stewart 1979). In *Political Parties and Ideologies in Canada* 2d ed. (Toronto: McGraw-Hill Ryerson 1983) William Christian and Colin Campbell trace the evolution of conservative, liberal, and socialist ideologies in the national political parties with particular reference to the ideas and values of party leaders.

In studies of Canadian political ideology Quebec merits special attention. Denis Monière makes a comprehensive analysis of the evolution of political ideas, their socio-economic origins, and the nature and extent of their influence on Quebec society and politics in *Ideologies in Quebec: The Historical Development* (Toronto: University of Toronto Press 1981). This book won the governor-general's award for non-fiction in French in 1978. Another useful analysis of the changing political values of French-speaking Quebec can be found in Léon Dion *Quebec: The Unfinished Revolution* (Montreal: McGill-Queen's University Press 1976), which examines conservative, liberal, social democratic, and socialist expressions of Quebec nationalism.

The classic history of Canadian economic development is *Canadian Economic History* (Toronto: Macmillan 1956) by W.T. Easterbrook and Hugh G.J. Aitken, which traces Canadian economic development from its European background through its beginnings in the staple trades to the emergence of the wheat economy and the rise of industrialism. Easterbrook and Aitken give special attention to the role of transportation, the strategy of Canadian economic development in the crucial formative period from 1849 to the National Policy of 1878, and the role of financial institutions and labour organizations in Canadian development. A more recent but less comprehensive treatment of Canadian economic history can be found in Richard Pomfret *The Economic Development of Canada* (Toronto: Methuen 1981). *Approaches to Canadian Economic History* (Toronto: McClelland and Stewart 1967), edited by W.T. Easterbrook and Melville H. Watkins, is an excellent collection of essays and excerpts from books by such eminent Canadian economic historians as V.C. Fowke, A.R.M.Lower, H.A. Innis, and W.A.Mackintosh. Of particular interest to students of Canadian public philosophy, Easterbrook and Watkins reprint the seminal essay by Hugh G.J. Aitken 'Defensive Expansionism: The State and Economic Growth in Canada,' originally published in *The State and Economic Growth* edited by Hugh G.J. Aitken (New York: Social Science Research Council 1959). *The Canadian State: Political Economy and Political Power* edited by Leo Panitch (Toronto: University of Toronto Press 1977) is a collection of original essays written from a Marxist perspective which analyse the role and nature of a Canadian state that reflects and sustains an advanced capitalist economy.

Dealing with particular aspects of Canadian economic development, R.T. Naylor, in *The History of Canadian Business 1867–1914* (Toronto: James Lorimer 1975), has produced a detailed account of Canadian developmental strategy as one of 'industrialization by invitation.' He argues that the transition from a mercantile agrarian economy to an industrialized economy was made by relying on British and American capital, with ultimately unfavourable consequences for Canadian economic independence. David Wolfe skilfully presents the history of stabilization policy in 'The Rise and Demise of the Keynesian Era in Canada: Economic Policy 1930–1982' in *Modern Canada 1930–1980's* edited by Michael S. Cross and Gregory S. Kealey (Toronto: McClelland and Stewart 1984), the fifth volume in their excellent series Readings in Canadian Social History. In *Public Money in the Private Sector: Industrial Assistance Policy and*

Canadian Federalism (Kingston: Queen's University Institute of Inter-governmental Relations 1982), Allan Tupper describes a variety of federal and provincial industrial subsidies and grants, state purchasing policies, and government financial services that are used to assist industrial development. He focuses in particular on the influence of federalism on policy-making and the causes and consequences of intergovernmental rivalry in industrial-assistance policy-making. In *Canadian Public Policy: Ideas, Structure, Process* (Toronto: Methuen 1983), G. Bruce Doern and Richard Phidd are mainly concerned with the basic elements of making policy, but their work includes chapters on post-war federal policies for industry, energy, and the labour market which provide very useful overviews of these three fields of economic policy. Two outstanding studies of provincial policies for economic development are *The Politics of Development: Forests, Mines and Hydro-electric Power in Ontario, 1849–1941* (Toronto: Macmillan 1974) by H.V. Nelles and *Prairie Capitalism: Power and Influence in the New West* (Toronto: McClelland and Stewart 1979) by John Richards and Larry Pratt, who study the development of the oil, natural gas, and potash industries of Alberta and Saskatchewan.

A good brief introduction to the problem of poverty and the development of income-security programs in Canada which includes an exposition and appraisal of guaranteed income programs is found in David P. Ross *The Working Poor: Wage Earners and the Failure of Income Security Policies* (Toronto: James Lorimer 1981). Dennis Guest gives a more detailed history of Canadian federal and provincial policies for maintaining the continuity and adequacy of incomes against universal risks to income interruption in *The Emergence of Social Security in Canada* (Vancouver: University of British Columbia Press 1980). For a masterly study of the nineteenth-century origins of Canadian income-security policies see Richard B. Splane *Social Welfare in Ontario 1791–1893: A Study of Public Welfare Administration* (Toronto: University of Toronto Press 1965). Unemployment as the central problem of social policy between the wars is analysed by James B. Struthers in *No Fault of Their Own: Unemployment and the Canadian Welfare State 1914–1941* (Toronto: University of Toronto Press 1983). His study of Canada's greatest economic crisis is a convincing illustration of the contradiction between advocating social reform and defending capitalist markets that lies at the core of liberal public philosophy. In *The Welfare State and Canadian Federalism* (Montreal: McGill-Queen's University Press 1982) Keith G. Banting examines from a comparative perspective the impact of political institutions on the post-war development of the Canadian income security system. He concludes that the evolution of federalism in Canada has had important consequences for both the scope of income security programs and their redistributive effects. Kenneth Bryden *Old Age Pensions and Policy-Making in Canada* (Montreal: McGill-Queen's University Press 1974) and Malcolm G. Taylor *Health Insurance and Canadian Public Policy: The Seven Decisions that Created the Canadian Health Insurance System* (Montreal: McGill-Queen's University Press 1978) are excellent case studies of the development of particular income security policies.

Perhaps the best general introduction to regulatory policy in Canada is found in Christopher Green *Canadian Industrial Organization and Policy* (Toronto: McGraw-Hill Ryerson 1980), which includes chapters on public policy toward business in Canada, competition policy, and economic regulation of public utilities with special reference to transport, communications, and energy. *The Regulatory Process in Canada* edited by G. Bruce Doern (Toronto: Macmillan 1978) includes several general essays on the regulatory process as well as specific studies of three regulatory agencies (the Canadian Transport Commission, the National Energy Board, and the Atomic Energy Control Board) and two regulated industries (national air transportation and telephone service in Nova Scotia). Based on responses to a series of questionnaires, C. Lloyd Brown-John, in *Canadian Regulatory Agencies* (Toronto: Butterworths 1981), provides an overview of the place of regulated agencies in the Canadian political system and a good introduction to the regulatory policy process; presents profiles of the regulators, regulated, and intervenors and concludes with an analysis of the politics of public hearings. Two studies by the Economic Council of Canada, *Responsible Regulation* (Ottawa: Minister of Supply and Services 1979) and *Reforming Regulation* Ottawa: Minister of Supply and Services 1981), analyse the nature and extent of economic regulation in Canada and offer sensible suggestions for the reform of regulatory policy-making.

Criminal Justice in Canada: An Introductory Text (Toronto: Butterworths 1980) by Curt T. Griffiths, John F. Klein, and Simon N. Verdun-Jones gives an overview of police organization and powers, the criminal-court system, sentencing policies, and correctional institutions and the alternatives of probation and parole. These topics are also covered in *Crime and Its Treatment in Canada* 2d ed. (Toronto: Macmillan 1976), an excellent collection of original essays edited by W.T. McGrath.

Although studies of the economics and politics of Canadian education are beginning to be published, the best approach to understanding educational policies in Canada still lies through historical studies. The classic interpretation is Charles E. Phillips *The Development of Education in*

Canada (Toronto: Gage 1957). A more recent textbook edited by J. Donald Wilson, Robert M. Stamp, and Louis-Philippe Audet, *Canadian Education: A History* (Scarborough: Prentice-Hall 1970), is well focused on the evolution of governmental policies toward education and is more structured in depicting the historical phases of educational development. Unfortunately, it is now somewhat dated, and recent collections such as *Canadian Education in the 1980s* edited by J. Donald Wilson (Calgary: Detselig 1981) have not succeeded in providing a comprehensive or systematic treatment of the changes that occurred in Canadian education during the 1970s. Several provincial histories of education are available, including recent and useful studies by Robert M. Stamp, *The Schools of Ontario 1876–1976* (Toronto: University of Toronto Press 1982), and Roger Magnuson, *A Brief History of Quebec Education: From New France to Parti Québécois* (Montreal: Harvest House 1980).

On the development of human rights in Canada, the best analysis is Walter Tarnopolsky's in *The Canadian Bill of Rights* 2d ed. (Toronto: McClelland and Stewart 1975). Tarnopolsky's focus is the Canadian Bill of Rights, but his study takes a broad view and includes an analysis of the public problem of human rights in Canada, references to federal and provincial legislation, and interpretation of court decisions affecting political, economic, legal, and egalitarian rights in Canada. Also useful is the collection of essays edited by R. St. J. Macdonald and John P. Humphrey, *The Practice of Freedom: Canadian Essays on Human Rights and Fundamental Freedoms* (Toronto: Butterworths 1979). This volume includes, for example, an outstanding essay by Ian A. Hunter on the origins, development, and interpretation of human rights legislation in Canada. J. Patrick Boyer *Political Rights: The Legal Framework of Elections in Canada* (Toronto: Butterworths 1981) focuses on ten basic political rights or freedoms that are vital to Canadian federal and provincial elections – for example, the right to elect governments periodically, the right to free speech, the right to freedom of assembly, and the freedom to form a political party; Boyer considers the nature, source, restrictions, and particular issues concerning each right. In *Fragile Freedoms: Human Rights and Dissent in Canada* (Toronto: Clarke, Irwin 1981) Thomas R. Berger uses specific cases of minorities and dissenters, such as the Acadians, the Métis, Japanese-Canadians, Jehovah's Witnesses, and Nishga Indians, to show the changing extent of rights and the limits on dissent.

With the proclamation of the Charter of Rights and Freedoms in April 1982, Canadian public policy on human rights entered a new stage. Two volumes of essays that begin the process of analysing and evaluating the new Canadian constitution are *And No One Cheered: Federalism, Democracy and the Constitution Act* (Toronto: Methuen 1983) edited by Keith Banting and Richard Simeon and *Canada and the New Constitution: The Unfinished Agenda* (2 vols.) edited by Stanley M. Beck and Ivan Bernier (Montreal: Institute for Research on Public Policy 1983). Of particular interest are two essays by Walter Tarnopolsky, 'The Constitution and Human Rights' in Banting and Simeon, and 'Human Rights and Constitutional Options for Canada' in Beck and Bernier, volume I.

Index

The [...] a a
variety o[...] ral,
and so[...] But
there i[...] s of
how Canad[...] mic
development, relieve po[...] ool
systems, and protect human rights.

Manzer identifies three stages in Canadi[...] oad
changes in the priorities of policy-maki[...] nial
regimes social order was considered [...] the
primary means of achieving it[...] nportant
contribution to economic develo[...] limited to modest
grants for volunteer efforts.

In the nineteenth century, these principles were altered, first in a system of criminal justice based on retribution, and later in a strategy of economic development based on capital accumulation. Industrialization and urbanization created new kinds of poverty and new pressures on markets, but policies for income redistribution and market regulation remained weak until the 1930s.

From the economic misery of the depression and the political idealism of the second world war grew a much broader conception of the role of the state in satisfying individual needs. State intervention was extended in economic policy and social welfare; educational systems were reformed; human rights policies were expanded.

Manzer concludes that Canadian principles of policy-making have been drawn overwhelmingly from the tenets of liberalism. Conservative and socialist ideologies have had some influence, but the predominant pattern has been the joint heritage of American and British liberal traditions. In identifying the evolution of that pattern, he is able to show the challenge for Canada's future political development.

RONALD MANZER is a professor at Scarborough College and in the Department of Political Science at the University of Toronto.